The Interpretation of Object-Oriented Programming Languages

Springer
London
Berlin
Heidelberg
New York
Barcelona
Hong Kong
Milan
Paris
Singapore
Tokyo

Iain Craig

The Interpretation of Object-Oriented Programming Languages

Second Edition

 Springer

Iain Craig, MA, PhD

British Library Cataloguing in Publication Data
Craig, Iain D.
 The interpretation of object-oriented programming
 languages. – 2nd ed.
 1. Object-oriented programming (Computer science)
 2. Programming languages (Electronic computers)
 I. Title
 005.1'17
ISBN 1852335475

Library of Congress Cataloging-in-Publication Data
Craig, I.
 The interpretation of object-oriented programming languages / Iain D. Craig.. -- 2nd ed..
  p. cm.
 Includes bibliographical references and index.
 ISBN 1-85233-547-5 (alk. paper)
  1. Object-oriented programming (Computer science) I. Title.
 QA76.64 .C73 2001
 005.1'17—dc21

                                                     2001040621

ISBN 1-85233-547-5 2nd edition Springer-Verlag London Berlin Heidelberg
ISBN 1-85233-159-3 1st edition Springer-Verlag London Berlin Heidelberg
A member of BertelsmannSpringer Science+Business Media GmbH
http://www.springer.co.uk

© Springer-Verlag London Limited 2002
Printed in Great Britain

First published 2000
Second edition 2002

04-25-02

Typesetting: camera-ready by author
Printed and bound at the Athenæum Press Ltd., Gateshead, Tyne and Wear
34/3830-543210 Printed on acid-free paper SPIN 10847137

For Adam

Preface to the Second Edition

I was extremely surprised to learn that this book was so well received; I was even more surprised when a second edition was proposed. I had realised that there was a need for a book such as this but had not thought that the need was as great; I really wrote the book for myself, in order better to organise my thoughts on object-oriented languages and better to understand them.

For the second edition, I have found and corrected mistakes and have added a completely new chapter on the C# language. The chapter on mixed-paradigm languages has been relegated to an appendix, and a new appendix on the BeCecil language has been added.

C# is extremely popular. Given its apparent role as the major competitor to Java, it was clear that a chapter was necessary in which a comparison could be made. That chapter concentrates on the language and not on the runtime and support system. C# contributes some new features to the C++ derivatives. The language has rough edges (as Java does still). It will be interesting to watch its development and to see whether it becomes accepted more widely.

The appendix on BeCecil is added so that the coverage of Cecil can be a little more comprehensive. When writing the first edition, I was unable to obtain copies of the Cecil definition, which turned out to be a much larger (and more fascinating) document than I had thought. Given the time allocated to me for the production of the second edition, it was impossible to include more on Cecil—a complete chapter seemed necessary. The existence of BeCecil, a core language, seemed perfect for my needs. Cecil and BeCecil are of interest because they rationalise much of object-oriented programming languages. I believe that we need more of this and that Cecil points the way towards the future.

The mixed-paradigm languages chapter was relegated to an appendix because there appears to be little work in the field.

My major disappointment since writing the first edition is that databases and prototype-based languages have still failed to converge. The reason for this is, probably, that prototype-based languages are still a highly specialist area and the languages that do exist are still research prototypes. There is an ample literature in the AI area on the combination of prototype-like structures with long-term storage upon which to base proposals. Perhaps this is either too obscure or acts to deter research. Perhaps there is work out there that I have not seen.

Acknowledgements. I would first like to thank Beverley Ford, Rebecca Mowat and all at Springer for their help in producing this and the first edition. They left me alone to get on with it, and answered questions quickly and accurately. My brother Adam drew the figures and made a variety of suggestions; for the second edition, his comments on what to include and what to exclude were extremely helpful. Margaret deserves special thanks for her moral support and encouragement, even though she is far away. I would also like to thank my good friend Walter Connor for his encouragement and for the great kindness he has shown towards me. Finally, and this seems unjustly neglected, I would like to thank those who have bought the book, for, without them, this edition would not have come about. I hope the book is still of use and will stimulate people to think about programming languages and the way in which we program.

Iain Craig
Merrion
Dublin
June 2001

Preface

Object-oriented languages are probably the most important development in computing for many years. They allow us to describe and to model the physical as well as more abstract worlds. They allow us to provide the computational entities we describe with a dynamics that is encapsulated, thus leading to a more distributed notion of state, a notion which, *inter alia*, makes programming and analysis somewhat more tractable.

Unfortunately, if one wants to understand the concepts that are currently employed in object-oriented languages, one must refer to the proceedings of conferences such as *OOPSLA* or *ECOOP*. These proceedings might be hard to obtain or obscure; in any case, without a background in the area, the reader will almost certainly encounter concepts which will send them back to the literature.

The aim of this book is to provide, in one place, an interpretation of the primary concepts in object-oriented programming languages. In some cases, for example, multiple inheritance, there is no single interpretation that is accepted by all; in such cases, the different approaches are explained. An attempt has been made to be as comprehensive as possible, but certain concepts have been omitted for the reason that they are not often encountered or they have fallen from grace. The concept of the instantiable module appears to be one example of this.

This having been said, it was, at all times, considered to be important to cover as many languages as possible in order to give as great a coverage as possible. Thus, the reader will find references to many languages that have been derived from LISP (it must be remembered that a considerable amount of research into object orientation was done in the LISP and AI communities before it became fashionable or appropriate to software engineering in general).

One area in which more work is required is in prototype-based langauges; I believe that they are an extremely important development and that they will assume considerable importance as time progresses. However, there have only been a very few large-scale attempts at producing prototype-based languages and the area is still a relatively immature one. The relationships between prototype-based languages and databases have yet to be explored (and one might find some interesting advances), as has reflection.

My own research area of computational reflection is also included in this book. I have, though, been extremely careful only to include material that is directly relevant to the rest of the book and not to be speculative in what I have included. There is, contrary to the view of some, a great deal more work required in the area of computational reflection and its implications for computing in general are insufficiently clear. The chapter on reflection is, therefore, less wide-ranging and less "aggressive" than I would have liked. Having read the chapter, the interested reader should try to read the implementation chapters in Goldberg and Robson's excellent book on Smalltalk-80 (the so-called "Blue Book"). The book is, sadly, out of print, but many libraries still carry copies; it is an exciting book and, for those interested in reflection, amply repays the effort required to obtain it.

Finally, I have included a chapter on a so-called 'mixed paradigm' language, one combining functional and object-oriented concepts. Mixed paradigm languages combine the best features of different ways of construing programming and computation. It is possible that research into mixed paradigm languages will present us with new concepts and approaches to the programming process. The combination I have adopted in this book appears to hold out the promise that program transformation can be performed in various ways; in particular, it suggests that, if we include reflective capabilities in such a language, we can engage in *meta-programming* in various ways, one of which is program transformation. Given the general policy on speculation, these issues are not considered further.

Acknowledgements. I would like to thank Günter Blaschek for his review of the manuscript; his comments have helped considerably. Next, I would like to thank my brother Adam for drawing the figures, for reading the manuscript and for suggesting ways in which the text could be made easier to read. My wife, as ever, has supported me constantly throughout the writing of the manuscript and has often acted as a sounding board when I have been unsure as to how I should phrase things (and has always urged me to continue when things looked bad); for this, I thank her. Rebecca (Moore) Mowat of Springer deserves special thanks for her calm attitude to the writing and completion of the manuscript during a period in which I had to pay considerable attention to other matters.

Iain Craig
Merrion
Dublin
December 1999

Contents

1. Introduction

1.1 Introduction

Object-oriented programming has opened a great many perspectives on the concept of software and has been hailed as part of the solution to the so-called "software crisis". It has given the possibility that software components can be constructed and reused with considerably more credibility. There are now many case studies in which the reuse of object-oriented components has been made and analysed. Object-oriented programming relates the programming activity to that of modelling or simulation; objects are identified by a correspondence with the objects found in the application area of the program and are used to model those domain operations. Object-oriented programming also opens the prospect of more flexible software that is able to respond dynamically to the needs of the application at runtime.

It is very easy to think that object-oriented programming can be performed in only one way. The prevalence of C++ and Java suggests that they are the *only* way to approach the problem of what an object-oriented programming language should look like. There are many approaches to this way of programming and C++ and Java exemplify just one of these different approaches. Indeed, the way in which the concept of the *object* is interpreted differs between approaches and between languages.

The two main approaches found in object-oriented programming langauges are, respectively, *class-based* and *prototype-based* languages. Class-based languages are exemplified by Smalltalk [40], C++ [92, 91] and Java [58]. This approach is based upon the identification of common properties of objects and their description in terms of a definitional structure called a *class*. The objects manipulated by class-based programs are the result of *instantiating* classes. In class-based programming, instances exist at runtime while classes typically do not. Even in an interpreted language, instances are the entities that are manipulated by programs; classes serve to define instances.

With the second approach, the *prototype-based* approach, matters are different. According to the prototype-based approach, objects are created by means of a copy operation (called *cloning*) which is applied to a *prototype*. Prototypes define stereotypical objects. A clone of a prototype replicates the structure of that prototype. Prototypes can be copied and modified to produce new prototypes that can then be cloned to form new objects.

The prototype-based approach is less common than the class-based one, although, as will be seen, it has a great deal to offer. There are other approaches, but they are somewhat rare in their use. For example, instantiable modules can be called objects. An instantiable module is a module (as found in Modula-2 [99]) which can be instantiated to produce multiple, independent objects or entities (normally modules are declared and used—there is usually only one instance of a module).

A significant problem with object-oriented programming is that it is very difficult to find an account of the interpretation of the various constructs and an explanation of the various concepts employed in such languages. The vast majority of books on object-oriented programming or languages concentrate on a single paradigm, typically the class-based one. If one is interested in prototype-based langauges or in multiple inheritance, for example, it is necessary to engage in extensive bibliographic searches.

The aim of this book is to present a comprehensive account of the primary approaches to object-oriented programming languages and their concepts. It describes the interpretation of the constructs commonly found in object-oriented languages; it presents an account of the semantics in English. In order to be as comprehensive as possible, the book deals with class-based languages (such as Smalltalk, Java and C++) as well as prototype-based ones (such as SELF and Omega). In addition, instantiable module languages are considered where appropriate.

Because the class-based approach to languages is the most common, it receives the greatest emphasis. Prototype-based languages are less common and they are given their own chapter, a chapter which attempts to be as comprehensive as possible within a small but growing field.

Many issues interact in the semantics of object-oriented programming languages. Types, messages, inheritance and dispatch methods are just four general issues, each of which can be considered in much more detail and which interact in complex ways in a full programming language. It is hoped that all important issues are considered in adequate detail below. Along the way, other issues relating to object-based languages are raised and discussed.

1.2 Essential Properties of Objects

Object-oriented languages are defined by a small set of properties. The extent to which a particular language satisfies these properties defines how much of an object-oriented language it is, as will be discussed below in section 1.4. The properties which will shortly be listed are, with the exception of the last, uncontroversial and all languages which are properly said to be "object-oriented" exhibit these essential properties.

An object is an independent entity which can be treated in isolation of all other objects. It can be passed into and returned from procedures, can be assigned to variables and stored in data structures like lists and arrays (i.e., is a *first-class* construct). Each object has an identity which is distinct from all others. Given any pair of objects, it is always possible to determine whether they are the same or different. Objects are composed of data and operations; the operations associated with an object typically act upon the data which it contains. Objects represent *logically distinct* entities in a computation.

Objects also exhibit some more general properties:

- encapsulation;
- inheritance;
- polymorphism; and
- dynamic method binding.

We will briefly outline each of these properties. The reader is warned that a more comprehensive and detailed account of each of these properties is given at various points in the rest of this book. Indeed, inheritance and polymorphism are so important (and so complex in their implications) that they are represented by chapters in their own right. The above properties are also closely related and have mutually interacting implications; for this reason, they will be the subject of repeated discussion below, each time in a slightly different context and drawing out slightly different implications.

The property of *encapsulation* is the property of information hiding. Encapsulation typically refers to the hiding of data and of the implementation of an object. Data and code, when encapsulated, are hidden from external view. When an external observer views an encapsulated object, only the exterior interface is visible; the internal details are invisible and cannot be accessed. Thus, data which is encapsulated cannot directly be manipulated and, in particular, cannot be directly updated. Objects in object-oriented programming languages contain a local state which is encapsulated; they also have data associated with them that defines what they are. The implementation of an object should, ideally, be hidden from view.

Objects tend to be defined in terms of other objects. When a new object—or kind of object—is defined, it is defined in terms of those properties that make it special. Because objects are frequently defined in terms of other objects, a mechanism is present so that the properties of those objects upon which a new one depends can be transferred to the new object from the old one. This mechanism is called *inheritance*.

According to one interpretation of the object-oriented concept, objects are defined by descriptions; a description can be used many times to create individual objects. The description is expressed in terms of the properties of the objects which can be created by its application. The way in which inheritance works for this kind of language is that descriptions are constructed on the basis of other descriptions. When a new description D_n is created on the basis of an old one, D_o, the properties that were defined in D_o become automatically available to D_n. It is in this sense that it is said that D_n *inherits from* D_o. Thus, any object created using D_n will automatically have the properties defined in D_o. It should be noted that D_o can generate objects of its own; they will have the properties defined by D_o and by inheritance from the descriptions used to define D_o. Objects produced using D_o do *not* have any properties defined in D_n. The reason for this is that D_o is an *ancestor* of D_n; inheritance works by obtaining properties from ancestors.

Inheritance enables programmers to re-use the definitions of previously defined structures. This clearly reduces the amount of work required in producing programs.

Next, we turn to *polymorphism*. The word "polymorphism" literally means "having many forms". In programming languages, polymorphism is most often taken to be that property of procedures by which they can accept and/or return values of more than one type. For example, a procedure which takes a single argument is said to be polymorphic if it can accept actual parameters of more than one type. If P is such a procedure and τ_1 and τ_2 are two types, P is polymorphic if and only if P can be called with an argument of type τ_1:

$$P(x : \tau_1)$$

and can also be called with an argument of type τ_2:

$$P(x : \tau_2)$$

Similarly, given a function f and two return types, ρ_1 and ρ_2, f is polymorphic if and only if f can be called with an argument of type τ_1, returning a value of type ρ_1:

$$f : \tau_1 \rightarrow \rho_1$$

and can also be called with an actual parameter of type τ_2, returning a value of type ρ_2:

$$f : \tau_2 \rightarrow \rho_2$$

Polymorphism is extended to assignment to variables in the following way. Let v be a variable and let o_1 be of type τ_1 and o_2 be of type τ_2. Then assignment to v is polymorphic if and only if the following assignments are both well-typed:

$$v := o_1$$

$$v := o_2$$

Polymorphism is pervasive in object-oriented languages. Given the inheritance relation outlined above, if there are two objects, o_1 and o_2 such that o_1 inherits from (is defined in terms of) o_2, then o_2 can replace o_1 and the program remains well-typed. This implies, in particular, that:

- o_2 can be assigned to a variable that can be assigned to o_1;
- o_2 can be an actual parameter bound to a formal parameter that can also be bound to o_1;
- o_2 can be returned by a function that can also return o_1.

If objects are considered to be types, the direct correspondence can be seen.

Polymorphism has some profound implications for programming languages. In object-oriented languages, polymorphism interacts strongly with inheritance, as has just been indicated. Sometimes polymorphism arises because it is necessary to redefine an operation so that it is particularized to a particular object or set of objects. We will spend considerable time below on polymorphism.

Finally, there is *dynamic binding*. Dynamic binding means that the operation that is executed when objects are requested to perform an operation is the operation associated with the object itself and not with one of its ancestors. In some languages (C++ is one), when an object is assigned to a variable, passed as a parameter, returned as a result, referenced by a pointer, the operation that is performed need not be the one defined for the object that is *actually* assigned, passed, returned, pointed to, etc., but the operation associated with one of the object's ancestors.

This comes about because of the following. In C++, if one kind of object, o_1, is defined in terms of another, o_2, the two object kinds are identified with types. If o_2 is the ancestor of o_1, then it is considered to be a *supertype* of o_1. Because an object of a type can always be assigned to a variable whose type is a supertype of that type, it is possible to assign o_1 to the same variables as o_2. C++ considers only the static type of the variables (the pointers, parameters, return types, etc.). If a variable is declared to be of a supertype, when a subtype is assigned to that variable, only those operations associated with the supertype can be performed. There is a way of making C++ perform dynamic binding, but the scheme described in this paragraph is the default (it is called *static* binding).

Dynamic binding is another property that has profound implications for object-oriented languages. At a practical level, it means that the operations that are performed are always those associated with the object asked to perform them (unless it must inherit the operation). At a more theoretical level, dynamic binding interacts with inheritance and with the type structure of a language.

1.3 Objects and Messages

In Smalltalk, the active components, the methods associated with classes (the operations), were activated by means of messages. Message passing is a central concept in object-oriented programming languages. When one object wants to activate a method in another object, it sends the other object a message. The message specifies which method is to be executed and provides the parameters required to activate the method.

When a message is sent from one object to another, the receiver examines the method specification. This specification, called the *selector*, is used to look up the appropriate method in a *method table*. Each object has a method table which associates selectors with methods. When the appropriate method has been determined, its code is executed and a result might be returned to the sender of the message.

The use of selectors provides a level of indirection between messages and the code (or *method body*) which implements them. It also provides a mechanism for determining which methods are provided by which objects. If a selector is not present as a key in the method table of the receiving object, the object can *inherit* the method from one of its parent objects. This means that a request is made to the object's superclass to return the appropriate method; should the method not be located there, the superclass of the superclass is consulted. This process continues until either the method is located and returned for execution, or there are no more classes and an error is signalled.

Selectors separate the names by which methods are known from the code which implements them. Thus, a method might be known by more than one name (selector) in a program; as long as the selectors mentioned in messages map to the correct code so that the correct behaviour is elicited from the system.

The Smalltalk implementation of message passing, like those in SELF [25], Omega [11] and the language proposed by Malenfant *et al.* [66], are based upon actually passing messages between objects. These languages are all sequential (SELF is implemented as threads, but the treatment described here is general) and messages do not need to be enqueued. Instead, a message is directly passed to the receiver object. The receiver object then picks up the message (as a pointer, typically) and executes. Because of the synchronization constraint inherent in sequential languages, this direct message handling technique becomes possible; were the languages to support asynchronous interactions, some form of queueing would be required.

In many languages, message passing is replaced by procedure call. In object-oriented languages using procedure calls, methods are implemented as procedures. Because messages are directly handled, the selector can be replaced by the name of the method in the receiver and the parameters supplied in the message are replaced by procedure parameters. Instead of indexing a method table, the procedure call approach, in its simplest form, involves the direct execution of the method named by the selector; the parameters which are to be passed to the method are typically passed on the runtime stack as parameters to the procedure implementing the method. The procedure call can be seen as an optimization of the message technique; the runtime stack is used instead of creating a new message in the heap and then filling the various slots of the message. The interpretation of message passing as procedure call removes the indirection of the selector-based message passing technique and method tables can be compiled down into a simpler form.

1.4 Pure and Impure Languages

A distinction is often made between so-called *pure* and *impure* object-oriented languages. Pure object-oriented languages contain only constructs that directly relate to object orientation. Every procedure must be written as a method and associated with an object. Programs in pure languages are always expressed in terms of object-oriented constructs. Impure languages (which are sometimes called *hybrid* languages), on the other hand, are typically composed of an object-oriented component and a procedural one. Impure languages allow the programmer to write object-oriented programs or procedural ones.

Smalltalk [40], Java [58], Eiffel [67] and Sather [76, 77] are examples of pure object-oriented languages. C++ [92, 91], CLOS [82] and Ada [9] are examples of impure languages.

Impure languages are very often designed by taking a procedural programming language and adding a set of constructs that support object-oriented programming. This was the case, for example, in the transition from the 1983 Ada standard [13] to the Ada95 [9] version. In addition to general modifications to the language, object-oriented extensions were added so that Ada95 became an impure language. C++ is another example of such an embedding (its history is described in [90]). Essentially, it was felt that the C language was in need of modification and improvement, so object-oriented features were added, as were features intended to increase the type safety of C and features for the representation of constants. The language grew in popularity and the object-oriented features were increased and/or improved. For example, single inheritance in the first version became multiple inheritance in the second; *protected* class components were similarly introduced, as was the distinction between *public, protected* and *private* superclasses. Object-oriented exceptions were introduced at the same time. Other languages have been enriched with object-oriented extensions including Pascal and COBOL.

The trend towards object-orientation has also been reflected in the development of languages like Oberon [72]. There is an object-oriented component in Oberon, but it does not look much like that in C++ or Smalltalk. Oberon relies upon a module system to provide modularity and concepts such as abstract classes and object-specific methods are also lacking; Oberon employs special handler procedures and record inclusion in its object-oriented component.

A similarly unusual language is represented by JavaScript [38], a language for programming World-Wide Web browsers. JavaScript is an interpreted relative of C but includes a form of prototype mechanism. Prototype objects can be defined and copied in JavaScript; a variety of operations can also be performed on the objects which it supports. The objects supported by JavaScript are, however, really just associative tables, a fact which does not reduce the utility of the language.

Pure object-oriented languages, however, are typically designed from scratch or on designs for other object-oriented languages. Smalltalk was partially based upon Simula67 [36], but introduced many new features. Beta [54] is also based on Simula67, but clearly displays the wppisdom of many years' exposure to object-oriented programming. Sather [76, 77] is based upon Eiffel [67], a language which was designed from scratch to be an effective and reliable tool for software engineering.

Given the fact that there are languages which emphasize procedural aspects more than object-oriented ones and that there are languages at the opposite end of the object-orientation spectrum, as well as those in the middle of the two extremes, it seems fairer to think of object-orientation as being a continuous property. Typically, object-orientation is thought of as being an all or nothing property. Inspection of the literature shows that this black or white view is inappropriate. It is far better, when comparing the claims for object orientation made of two languages, to consider the *degree* to which they are object oriented. Smalltalk and Java, at the one end, exhibit a high degree of object orientation, while Oberon, at the other, exhibits a relatively low degree.

As we move from one end of the object-orientation spectrum to the other, properties of the languages will change. For example, in impure languages, procedure call tends to replace message passing; inheritance might be replaced by some other concept and encapsulation might be supported by some other mechanism (e.g., packages in Ada). At the other end, the properties of object-oriented languages that are taken as being definitional are present in clearer forms.

1.5 Mixed-Paradigm Languages

It is possible, although currently very rare, for the object-oriented component to be embedded into a functional, logic or constraint-based context. Languages which are based upon such a mixture are often called *mixed-paradigm* languages.

At the end of this book, we show how functional and object-oriented programming can be made to coexist and explore some of the benefits of such a coexistence. Our discussion of this so-called *mixed-paradigm* language will start with an impure version and then we consider a purer version; the two will be compared.

1.6 Organization of this Book

Chapters 2 to 7 are concerned with the class-based paradigm. This paradigm is the one most frequently encountered in everyday programming. Languages such as Smalltalk, C++, Java and Ada are based upon the concepts of class and instance.

Chapter 2 introduces the basics of class-based programming. The primary concepts – encapsulation, inheritance, polymorphism and dynamic binding – are all introduced. The concepts of class and instance are presented, explained and related to the concept of the type. This connection is often to be found in languages of this kind, notably C++, Java, Ada, CLOS and Dylan. The discussion of the concept of instance includes consideration of what instances are and what they contain. As part of this, the concept of the method is also introduced. The idea that slots can have different levels of visibility is also introduced and discussed, as are the alternative ways in which slots can be accessed. Class and instances variables are also considered.

In Chapter 2, the concept of inheritance in the form of single, linear, or simple, inheritance is also considered and some of the implications are drawn. The simpler form of inheritance is the best starting point for discussing inheritance; inheritance can be viewed in many ways and it interacts with other concepts, sometimes in a very subtle fashion. Next, the concept of the abstract class is introduced. Its use is summarized and is related to inheritance. Iterators and part objects complete the chapter.

Next, in Chapter 3, an alternative, though rarer, but still important approach is discussed. This alternative is the prototype-based approach as exemplified by the SELF, Omega and Kevo languages. In these languages, the concepts of copying and modifying objects are employed. This typically leads to languages and systems that support exploratory programming and persistent storage, and to languages that lack strong type disciplines. However, the Omega language shows extremely well that strong types can easily co-exist with prototypes. Unfortunately, at the time of writing, prototype-based languages have not received the attention that class-based ones have. Delegation is introduced and explained. The Actor family of languages is also presented briefly.

Inheritance is the topic covered in Chapter 4. The chapter begins with the single inheritance concept introduced in Chapter 2 and examines its limitations. The relationship between inheritance and subtyping is discussed; this is a natural topic, given the frequent interpretation of classes as types. Code sharing and interface inheritance are considered, followed by consideration of how to invoke methods defined in classes higher in the inheritance structure. The controversial topic of multiple inheritance is then introduced, motivated and explained. A number of popular interpretations of multiple inheritance are considered:

- graph inheritance;
- tree inheritance;
- linearized inheritance;
- mixin inheritance.

The interactions between multiple inheritance and object component access is considered in detail. Some alternatives to multiple inheritance are examined. Inheritance is then contrasted with delegation and aggregation, the primary competing approaches to inheritance.

Chapter 5 deals with methods. Methods implement the operations associated with objects. In the class-based approach, they are usually defined as part of the definition of classes. The relationship between objects and methods is considered first, and then the role of constructor functions. The concept of higher-order functions and their relationship to methods is next considered; many languages, in particular the so-called "pure" languages like Eiffel and Java, do not permit higher-order functions, but permit other techniques. In the section on higher-order methods, I consider those techniques and discuss the flexible approach based on blocks adopted in Smalltalk and SELF; this approach simplifies the definition of the language because many control structures can be implemented directly as blocks. Next, the interaction between methods and inheritance is considered again, and the method-combining structures in FLAVORS and CLOS are explained. Static and dynamic method binding constitute the next topic. Dynamic method binding is often considered the binding strategy most appropriate to object-oriented programming. The differences between the two binding techniques are discussed, as are their implications. The implementations of dynamic binding used in Smalltalk and in C++ are discussed.

There follow two chapters on the concept of type as it relates to class-based languages. The first is concerned with matters such as the overloading and redefinition of methods. Inheritance, particularly in connection with the classes-as-types interpretation, interacts with typing; in particular, it implies the operation called *downcasting* which we discuss in some detail. Next, the problem of determining the type of an object. Some authors, for example Stroustrup [90], argue that runtime type tagging is to be avoided, in which case the user must either abandon hope or introduce their own scheme for tagging. I argue that runtime type determination mechanisms that do not require the introduction of type functions and predicates are to be preferred.

It is frequently stated that *polymorphism* is a central property of any object-oriented programming language. Overloading, downcasting and redefinition are characteristics of object-oriented polymorphism. These issues are next considered, as is the concept of a generic object. The concept of the root class is introduced and discussed as a way of introducing a simple and powerful form of polymorphism. The concept of *variance*, often considered to be one of the more complex and obscure in object-oriented programming languages, is discussed and, I hope, demystified.

The second chapter on types is concerned with a ragbag of issues, including:

- types and implementations;
- classes and type operations.

As part of the discussion, the idea that a class can have multiple implementations is explored in a little detail.

In the penultimate chapter, Chapter 8, reflection is introduced. Reflection is the process whereby a program can engage in computation about itself. This leads to programs which are able to alter their structure at runtime and which can be extended by user-defined constructs. In order to do this, it is often necessary to introduce a root class and then to provide it with a class; this leads to an infinite regression which must be handled—how to handle it is considered in some detail. Interestingly, in prototype-based languages, this infinite regression does not occur. Extension of languages by user-defined constructs are considered to be on the same level as those defined in the original language and can, themselves, be used as the basis for further extension. I give many examples of such modifications, introducing the concept of the meta-object protocol or MOP, as we do. Reflection is a research topic of considerable promise. The intention, here, is to introduce the area to the reader in the hope that they will see its enormous power. Most of the discussion in the chapter is concerned with class-based languages, but we also consider how simple forms of reflection can be included in prototype-based languages.

The last chapter, Chapter 9, is a description of C#, a new language developed by Microsoft. The form of this chapter is slightly different because those features of the language that relate to object orientation are described and compared with features in C++ and Java, the languages that it most closely resembles. C# introduces some new concepts into object-oriented languages and refines some others. The object of the chapter is to show how the new language has developed from older concepts, a task made easier because C#'s design is fairly conservative.

Appendix A contains a brief description of some of the features of BeCecil, a language defined as a core upon which extensions can be defined. BeCecil, as its name suggests, is related to Cecil, and both languages are based on the concepts of prototypes and multi-methods. BeCecil is included because it is the product of reductionist thinking.

Finally, the so-called *mixed-paradigm* languages are discussed in Appendix B. The idea which motivates these languages is that they should combine the best aspects of the component paradigms. For a variety of reasons, I focus on a language composed of objects and functions; in particular, one based on functional and class-based programming. In order to do this, I first outline the primary concepts of functional programming. I present an outline design of a class-based component and then briefly consider how the functional component must be adjusted in order to cope with the object-based component.

At this stage, it is necessary to emphasize that the language defined in Appendix B is *not* to be considered definitive or even practical. The point of the exercise is merely to show how one *might* approach the problem and how the various design choices impact upon each other.

2. Class Fundamentals

2.1 Introduction

The first object-oriented programming languages, Simula67 [36] and Smalltalk [40], were based on the concepts of class and instance. The majority of the object-oriented languages now in use are based upon these two concepts. Indeed, we can correctly refer to these languages as promoting *class-based* programming, a style of program construction based upon the idea that the programmer first defines a collection of classes and instantiates those classes when required. Classes represent the primary concepts employed in the program and instances represent particular exemplars of those concepts. The concept of the class is very similar to that of the abstract data type, and the two are frequently identified; when constructing a class-based program, the programmer identifies complex (abstract) data types and uses them to structure the program. The identification of classes with types implies that class-based languages have extensible type systems or, when dynamically typed like Smalltalk or Lisp, possess extensible structuring methods.

Many, if not the majority of object-oriented languages now in use are based upon the class concept. This chapter will discuss the concepts of class and instance and will explain how they are related. In addition, it will address the issue of *inheritance*, a relationship between classes, which gives this style of programming its considerable power. As will be seen, inheritance is a somewhat controversial issue, and I will adopt the simplest interpretation in order to provide the reader with sufficient background to continue with the remainder of the book. The aim of this chapter is to introduce the reader to many of the major concepts of object-oriented languages and so, in addition to the class/instance difference, other issues of importance will be considered, in particular:

- the correspondence between classes and abstract data types;
- information hiding (encapsulation);
- the internal structure of classes;
- restricting what is visible to descendent classes.

Many of the concepts discussed at a relatively superficial level in this chapter will be considered in greater detail in subsequent chapters.

Object-oriented programming languages, or, more correctly, class-based languages are claimed to have the following exceptional properties:

- encapsulation;
- inheritance;
- polymorphism and
- dynamic binding.

The class, in class-based programming, is the key to these claims. The concept of the class is that of a device which collects together data and procedural elements into an entity which presents a well-defined interface to its users. As such, it hides the details of its implementation. This is *encapsulation*. In fact, because classes can be said to act as templates, they can be instantiated to create objects (the objects in this kind of programming are the instances of classes, not classes themselves); the internal structure of objects is invisible to the computational processes which manipulate them. An interface for the class is defined; the interface makes visible, or exposes, part of the class's structure.

If encapsulation were the entire story, classes would not be very interesting because they would be little more than instantiable modules. What makes them more than modules is the *inheritance* relation which holds between classes. Inheritance makes families out of individual classes. When one class inherits from another, they share some of their internal structure. If class C inherits from class S, C is said to be a *subclass* of S, while S is said to be the *superclass* of C. In such a case, the data and operations defined for S will be accessible to C. This means that there is a kind of code sharing between the sub- and superclass. A superclass can have more than one subclass. Each subclass inherits components from the superclass. Inheritance allows a class to be extended by the addition of new internal elements, some of which will be made visible to users as its interface.

Next, there is *polymorphism*. This term means literally "many formed" and refers to the property of object-oriented languages that they permit routines to have more than one type of assignment. In languages like Pascal, it is required that a routine be associated with a unique set of input specifications; if the routine is a function, there must be a unique return type associated with it. A polymorphic routine can be associated with many input and output specifications. Class-based programming makes this possible by attaching procedural elements, called methods, to class definitions and allows methods with the same name to be present in different classes. This is a technical subject which is dealt with in more detail in Chapter 5, below.

Finally, there is *dynamic binding*. This is an approach to the invocation of the operations defined in a class. Dynamic binding basically means that the operation that is actually called is the one associated with the object *itself* and not with the type of the variable or pointer which refers to it. In essence, dynamic binding means that the operation the programmer expects to be performed is the one that is *actually* performed. Thus, when an object of one kind is passed into a procedure, the parameter to which it is bound might not reflect the full set of properties of the object that is being passed. Within the procedure, an operation might be called. This operation will be common to both the declared kind of object and the actual one. However, there might be differences between the formal and the actual parameter in terms of the details of the operation that is to be called. If the operation associated with the formal parameter is called, anomalous behaviour might be exhibited by the procedure. It is also counter-intuitive for an object to perform an operation that is not associated with it. Dynamic dispatch can only be completely understood when inheritance and polymorphism have been comprehended.

The next section (Section 2.2) introduces the concept of the class. The class as a form of template, a form of structure and a form of type definition are all introduced. Classes are also related to abstract data types. Next, the concept of the instance is presented (Section 2.3). Instances in class-based programming are the objects with which programs actually deal; they do not manipulate classes, but, instead, the instances of classes. The components of objects (instances), their slots and methods are defined and motivated (Section 2.4); the ways in which they can be accessed are then discussed (Section 2.5). If slots and methods can be accessed, they must be visible. However, not all slots and not all methods should be visible to everyone—this would violate the assumptions about encapsulation made about classes—so we discuss how visibility and accessibility can be controlled (Section 2.6). The process of instance creation is discussed in Section 2.7. Following on from this consideration of instances, inheritance is discussed in Section 2.8. The form of inheritance which is discussed is the simple form, often called *single* inheritance for it imposes the constraint that each class is permitted only to have one superclass. Section 2.9 introduces the concepts of abstract classes and methods. Iterators (a high-level method for writing loops that does not violate encapsulation) are the subject of Section 2.10. Part objects, an issue raised by the Beta language [54], is the subject of Section 2.11.

2.2 Classes

In this section, we will consider the concept of the class. The class is central to class-based programming languages and serves as a mechanism for defining sets of objects, together with operations to manipulate them. Objects are instances of a concept; a class defines a concept of some kind. For example, a class can represent a linked list, a window on a display, a file, a page of text or a piece of furniture. Classes act as encapsulating mechanisms that are instantiated to create instances; this is the way in which classes resemble templates. Classes collect the definition of data and operations. The data definition states what the data elements local to an instance will be (some languages allow more than this to be specified, but we leave such issues until later); the operation definitions specify the operations that can be performed on the data elements defined for the class. The operations also define (part of) an interface for manipulating the entities the class represents. A consequence of viewing classes as templates is that the process of instantiation implies the sharing of code among the instances of a class.

It is essential first to define classes so that they can be instantiated. In class-based programming, it is usual to manipulate the results of class instantiation, not classes themselves. Although the approach we take in this section is based upon the relationship between classes and types, the reader should keep in mind the idea that a class is a kind of template.

In class-based programming, the concept of the class is associated with a number of different, but not always competing, interpretations. The term "class" can variously be interpreted as:

- a set of objects;
- a program structure or module;
- a factory-like entity which creates objects; and
- a data type.

The first interpretation associates the term "class" with a collection of related entities. The entities have properties or behaviours in common and can be regarded as being of the same class. Thus, a class defines properties or operations (or both) that are common to a collection of objects. The class is a construct that defines collections of objects in terms of the properties they must have. The objects thus described are manipulated by programs and exist at runtime only.

The second interpretation considers a class to be a kind of module. Modules encapsulate types, data (variables) and operations (procedures and functions); data defined within a module can remain invisible outside the module and an explicit operation must be performed for parts of the module's internals to be made visible to the outside world. Modules are usually defined and included within a program; modules import and export other modules. An imported module provides data types, variables and routines to the importing module; an exporting module provides types, variables and routines to modules which import it. In some languages, modules are defined and included in a program; in others, they can be instantiated (Ada packages are an example of instantiable modules). If a module can be instantiated, many copies of the module exist at runtime within a single program.

Classes are similar to modules in that they export some entities (often operations) and they can be made to import others. Modules hide their internal details and so do classes; in both cases, for a component to be made visible to the outside world, an explicit operation must be performed. This view of the class considers it to be an instantiable module and considers objects to be instances of the same modular object. Just as every instance of an instantiable module has a similar structure, so too do the instances of a class.

The third interpretation is the factory object concept. This is an interesting interpretation because it emphasizes the dynamic nature of object-oriented languages. Here, the class is seen as a device that can create objects. The objects created by a class all have the same properties and can perform the same operations. The definition of the class contains a description of what the objects produced by the class will look like and how they will behave. When an object of a particular kind is required in a program, the relevant factory is used to produce it. Different factories produce different objects.

The factory object concept is quite interesting because it opens the way to describing objects in a parametric fashion. That is, the factory object can allow the creation process to accept parameters when it creates a new object. The parameters define the details of the object that is produced; this leads to a more flexible view of how objects are created and what they are. The other interpretations of the term "class" all imply that objects will have the same structure and behaviour; the factory interpretation implies that objects produced by the same class (or falling within the same class) can have slightly different specifications. Factory objects are used fairly extensively in the Java library.

Finally, the concept of the class is often identified with the concept of an abstract, or encapsulated type [60]. Classes in many languages, for example C++, Java, Ada and Dylan, are considered to be types. Languages treating classes as types allow the programmer to declare variables with a type that is a class; in some languages, and in some contexts, such variable declarations, when executed, cause the class to be instantiated (see Section 2.3 below).

Thus, in one of these languages, given a class, C, and a variable, v, the following is legal:

$$v : C$$

This declares the variable, v, to be of type C. In the particular case of a class-based language that identifies types and classes, this declaration states that variable v has *type* C. We consider languages permitting such declarations because they are frequently encountered.

If a variable can be declared to be of a class type (a type which is defined by a class), what is a class?

A class defines a collection (a set in practical terms) of entities with the same internal structure and which behave in the same way; in addition, a class defines an external appearance (interface) for the objects that fall within the class. The class defines what is common to the elements of the collection. The objects are all composed of the same data elements and have the same behaviour. We can equally think of a class as defining a set of properties and a set of operations. Given these definitions, similarities between classes and *abstract data types* can be seen.

An *abstract data type* is sometimes called an *encapsulated* data type because the details of its implementation are hidden from the user. Similarly, once a class has been defined, its external interface is all that should be used in determining the properties of the class. The external interface of a class is almost always represented by a collection of operations over that class and some of its properties. The external interface tells the user of the visible properties of the class and what operations are defined over it. The internal details of a class can consist of properties and operations, but they are not required for the user to be able to understand what the class represents and how it can be treated. The process of hiding the internal details (the implementation details) of a class is called *encapsulation*.

We could, for example, define a complex number type. We can define it in terms of two variables of floating point type. These numeric variables represent the real and the imaginary components of the number. In addition, we would define operations over complex numbers to represent such things as addition, multiplication, and so on. We might also want to include two operations, one to convert the representation to polar co-ordinates and one to convert from polar co-ordinates. Naturally, the latter will be the identity if we opt to represent complex numbers as pairs of reals; if we had chosen to represent them as a radius and an angle, the conversion operation to polar co-ordinates would be the identity. That we would include both conversion operations is an important point, the reason for which is that we want to hide the way in which we choose to represent complex numbers. In a similar fashion, we could represent a stack type as an encapsulated or abstract data type (or as a class). When building a stack type, we must provide operations to push and pop elements, test whether the stack is empty and so on. We have to decide how we want to represent the structure to hold the stack's elements. We can decide to represent this as a (singly) linked list or as a vector. If we know that the stack will have a maximum number of elements, we might choose the vector representation; if we have no such knowledge, the list is probably safer. Once the representation decision has been made, we can then define the details of the operations we have defined for our type. We also need to add one other operation to the set of operations that we have defined for the class: we need to define an operation for creating stacks for us (this is called a *constructor* function).

In both cases, we do not want the user to know how we represented complex numbers or stacks. The internal details do not matter to them. As long as the class behaves in the correct ways, and as long as we can construct an object of the appropriate type, the details of how it works internally should be of no interest to us. (Consider, for example, how floating point numbers are represented. In some cases, the IEEE standard is adopted, in others it is not. As far as the user is concerned, as long as the operations over floating point numbers work as expected, their internal representation is of no relevance.)

We have described exactly what it is to be a class in a class-based language that considers classes to be types. The internal details of a class are hidden from the user (principle of encapsulation) and an interface, typically expressed in terms of a constructor and a set of operations is available for use. The constructor and operations defined by the class constitute most of the information available to the user in order to determine what a class represents and how it should operate (they need this information in order to use the class).

The process of definition of a class amounts to the identification of a new concept having a particular behaviour. For example, if we defined a highway simulation, we would want a class (type) to represent an automobile. This is because automobiles represent an important class of road user. Equally, we might want a class to represent trucks of various kinds as well as buses. We would define classes for these kinds of vehicle because the vehicle types are important and distinct concepts in such a simulation. Now, each of these classes have properties and behaviours in common and they have properties that differ from each other. For example, most vehicles have an engine size, and each vehicle has a current speed property; however, automobiles tend to carry fewer than four passengers while buses can carry fifty or sixty and trucks (depending upon the behaviour of the driver!) tend only to carry a driver. Engine size, current speed, number of passengers, and number of wheels, are all properties of the vehicle class. An operation could be defined to compute the vehicle's current position on the road for any one of these classes (in fact, we would define it in a parent class and define the other classes in terms of that parent—this involves inheritance, a process which we will describe below in Section 2.8). Not all of the details of each type of vehicle would be available for inspection; we might want to encode the make of the vehicle as an integer or we could have some complex structure to represent the destination or the cargo that it carries).

In the automobile simulation, we define different kinds of class to define the different types of vehicle. Each class represents properties of the thing it represents and it also represents operations that can be performed on that object. An operation to set the vehicle's speed might be one such operation; another operation would return the licence plate number, while another would return the year of manufacture. The properties and operations defined for each class are appropriate for the object the class is intended to represent. As we saw in the case of complex numbers, classes can denote conceptual entities as well as physical ones.

In order to construct a realistic simulation of a highway, we would want lots of instances of the automobile class. This is extremely important.

2.3 Instances

When we declare an integer variable in a program, we are creating a variable to contain an instance of the type integer. There can be many integer variables in a program, each with a different name and each containing a different instance of the integer type. What these variables have in common is that they hold instances of that type.

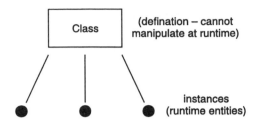

Fig. 2.1. *A class and its instances.*

We noted in the last section that if we wanted to build a highway simulation, we would need to define classes for each of the kinds of vehicle we wanted to include, and, most importantly, we would need to define lots of instances of the classes that represent vehicles. The instances of the classes are similar to the integer values we described in the previous paragraph. Just as we manipulate instances of the integer type, we manipulate, at runtime, instances of classes. A class itself serves as the definition for a collection of instances, but it cannot usually be manipulated at runtime. In class-based programming languages like Java and Eiffel, it is the instances of classes that are manipulated at runtime. Thus, in the highway simulation, instances of the various automobile classes must be created in order to run the program.

In class-based programming, the term "object" properly refers to the instances of classes. However, because so much effort is expended in defining the classes in the first place, the term "object" is often used (incorrectly) to refer to class definitions. A class is a definition of what is common to all of its instances. The instances of a class are objects which have an identity and a lifetime within the execution of the program. Because of the way classes are defined, instances almost always have variables and constants defined within them that allow different values to be stored at runtime. Thus, two instances can differ in the values that are stored within them. It is also very common for the variables and constants to be accessed and updated at runtime.

The update of variables is how the state of an object-oriented program is affected at runtime. The state of an object-oriented program at runtime is organized in terms of the instances, each instance encapsulating part of the state. The state represented by one instance is usually distinct from that represented by another (there are exceptions, but they tend to be rare), so the global (program) state can be thought of as being distributed among the various instances of the classes used by the program.

Instances of classes can be bound to variables and, in some languages, they can be pointed to. Instances of classes are passed as arguments to procedures and are returned as results from procedures. It is worth emphasizing that *instances* can be bound, pointed to and passed in and out of procedures. *Instances* are, because of this, *first-class* citizens. Classes serve only as definitions; it is not possible to bind a class to a variable, nor is it possible to point to a class or pass one to a procedure.

Above, when we considered abstract data types, we stated that the operations defined over that type are considered part of the abstract type's definition, and that, in an identical fashion, operations (called "methods") are defined in classes. Methods are used to manipulate the internal state of instances and to perform transformations, as well as doing the usual things that procedural entities do. Methods are applied to instances and methods return instances as results. Methods *do not* operate on classes because classes are not, in class-based programming, first-class citizens.

The creation and manipulation of instances forms the dynamic structure of a class-based object-oriented programming language. The static structure is determined by the definitions of classes and the relationships which obtain between class definitions (inheritance and part-of relations play a particularly significant role in defining static structure).

With these basic distinctions out of the way, we can move to a more detailed examination of the concepts of class-based programming languages.

2.4 Slots and Methods

The definition of a class contains the definition of slots. Some slots hold data, while others refer to pieces of procedural code that implement the operations defined for the class. The slots that are defined by the class (and their types), determine what the class's instances will represent. The operations that are defined also serve to define the class. For the reason that classes and instances encapsulate data and operations, it is necessary for the operations to be part of the definition of the class.

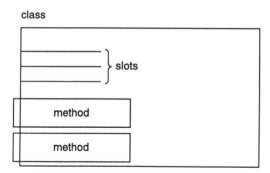

Fig. 2.2. *Slots and methods.*

Data slots hold the data that is local to the instances of a class. The instances are, in the class-based approach, the objects that are handled at runtime; space is actually allocated for slots in instances, not in classes. The data in their slots is part of the way in which they represent things. Sometimes the values in data slots can be changed by programs, while some slots are constants. If we defined a class to represent a stack, for example, instances of the class would each contain a slot holding the implementation of the stack (either a vector or a linked list) and might hold a slot pointing to the top of the stack. This data is hidden inside the instances of the stack class, but is made available to the operations defined over the stack class (*push, pop, top, empty?*, etc.).

Although most object-oriented languages, and almost all class-based languages, consider methods to be separate from the slots in an instance, we will continue to speak as if methods were held in special slots. In class-based languages, methods are defined as part of the class. Instances have access to the methods that are defined in their class because of the definitional mechanism. What is really the case is that methods are shared between instances. However, it is natural to think of methods as being part of instances, so we will strictly abuse the terminology in the way stated above. We will, therefore, refer to "method slots" and "date slots", where the former refers to slots (notionally) holding methods, and the latter refers to slots holding data and references to instances of classes.

It is important for the reader to remember that instances are the objects that are really manipulated at runtime. Therefore, when we talk of accessing a class's slots (as we do in the next section), we are, in fact, talking about accessing the slots present in an instance of that class. When we talk of a slot in a class being constant or variable, we will be referring to the runtime operations that are defined in the class for that slot.

2.5 Slot Access

Slots containing methods are usually considered to be read-only. It only makes real sense to call a method or to pass it as a parameter; it does not usually make much sense, in an object-oriented language, to re-define a method at runtime. One reason for this is that inheritance (see below, Section 2.8) allows methods to be re-defined in a structured and controlled fashion. Matters are completely different when data slots are considered.

Data slots can represent variable or constant information. That is, a slot can be read-only or read-write. Clearly, if a slot is intended to be read-only, it makes no sense to try to update its value. Some languages allow the programmer to mark a slot as being constant; others make the distinction in other ways. One particularly important way is based upon how slots are accessed.

It seems natural to access a slot in an instance as if it were a variable. In other words, it makes some sense to allow access to data slots in a direct fashion. Thus, when we write:

$$i.s$$

to access the slot s in instance i, we are in fact writing a direct access to the slot. When we write:

$$i.s := exp$$

we are directly updating the slot s in instance i. In both cases, the internal structure of the instance is directly accessed and, perhaps, modified. We have a way to get inside an instance.

When compiled, the slot is an offset to a pointer or a fixed address in the store. When defining slots, the distinction between a constant and a variable slot can be made. In Java, for example, a slot can be marked as *final*, making it a constant; otherwise, the slot is treated like a variable; C++ allows slots to be defined as constant.

The direct approach to a slot is simple. It has faults. For example, it allows direct access to the contents of an instance, thus violating the encapsulation (visibility) barrier that a class should maintain (instances are automatically encapsulated by means of the creation process which reveals no internal details to the user). Direct access to the slots of a class reveals the names of slots (revelation of methods appears less of a problem, though, but see below).

A second approach, one adopted by CLOS and Dylan, *inter alia*, is based upon the idea that slot access should be through the intermediary of reader and writer functions. In this scheme, when a data slot is defined, additional functions are defined. If it is intended that values in the slot be readable, a *reader* function is defined. Similarly, if it is intended that it should be possible to update the slot's contents, a *writer* function is defined. In some languages, if a slot is to be readable and writable, the reader and writer functions can be combined in a single function called an *accessor* function. When defined, these functions are globally accessible (if CLOS permitted nested class definitions, the visibility of these functions would be restricted to the class in which the nested class is defined). For example:

```
slot aslot,
     reader: read_aslot,
     writer: write_aslot;
```

defines a slot which is called *aslot*. This slot has a reader function (called *read_aslot*) and a writer function (called *write_aslot*). The slot is both readable and writable. If we wanted the slot to be read-only (a constant slot), we would just define a reader function (and also equip the slot with an initial value).

If we want to read the value in the slot, we would write:

```
v := i.read_aslot()
```

and to update the slot, we would write something like:

```
i.write_aslot(v)
```

(Dylan allows the writer function to be written as $i.aslot := v$.)

The justification of the function-based approach to slot access is that it de-couples access and update from naming. If a reader function is defined for a slot, the name of the slot inside the class matters not one iota; what matters is the name given to the reader function. In the above example, it does not matter at all what we define the slot's name to be. We decided to call the slot *aslot*, but we could call it *slot1*, *Bill*, *Joe* or *dwiddle* (it is good practice for slots to have intelligible names that describe their role). Slot names must be unique within a class. The name is used internally by the class in order to allocate slots. What matters to the outside world is that the access functions are defined and have meaningful mnemonic names.

The use of access and updater functions to read and write slots separates the names visible outside a class's definition from those that are visible inside (and to subclasses). This provides valuable additional support for encapsulation in languages supporting these features.

2.6 Visibility and Accessibility

So far, we have assumed that all the slots in a class are visible to the user. In particular, we tacitly assumed that all slots were available to subclasses as part of their explicit definition. The definition of a class is its interface. One assumption about classes is that they will make visible all the most important aspects of their interface. This implies not only that their slots remain constant, but also that all of the "important" slots be visible and accessible to subclasses as well as to users (quite what "important" means must be left undefined for it relates to the *intension* of a class, not its extension).

Some early languages, Smalltalk and LOOPS, for example, as well as some more recent ones such as SELF, do not make any provision for hiding slots. All slots in these languages are on equal footing and are all equally visible. Slots containing methods, typically, must be accessible to all parts of a program and to all subclasses of the one in which they are defined for the reason that they must be called or used in the definition of other methods. When the language is not of the pure object-oriented variety, it is necessary for methods to be visible so that they can be called by procedures and functions that are not attached to any class. Given this basis, data slots are sometimes left as universally accessible. In an interpreted language like Smalltalk or LOOPS, data slots are visible because, during exploratory programming, programmers do not often know which slots to hide.

Under certain circumstances, it is not desirable to allow all slots to be visible to every program component and to the user. The restriction in visibility of slots is a natural part of interface design. It is also a natural part of good design. For example, two methods in a class might call the same operation, the common operation being another method defined in that same class. This common operation might not be used elsewhere, so there is little point in making it visible or accessible to everything. An example of such a method is one that checks the index to a dynamic array or vector; this method is needed inside the class by all methods that access the array or vector—it is not required (and probably makes no sense) outside the class. Another example, this time of a data slot, is the reference counter on an object stored in a reference-counted heap. Only the operations to reference and dereference the object need access the reference counter slot (variable), so hiding the counter in the class appears to promote a better interface.

Before continuing, I need to introduce some terminology. A class represents a program region in which definitions of slots are made. These slots are *visible* within the class itself and, should they not be restricted, they are also visible outside their defining class. I prefer to use the term scope to refer to the region of a program text in which a variable or function (procedure) can be accessed; this corresponds to the standard interpretation of the term in the λ-calculus and in block-structured languages. Given this distinction, a slot has a scope within a method defined in the same class (it is global to the method), but is visible within the definitions at the same level of the class. Outside the class, the slot can be *visible* or not; it cannot be in scope until its name is used in any independent procedure or function. A slot can be *visible* to another class.

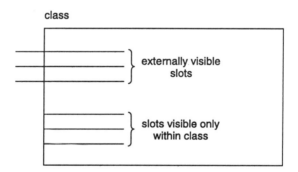

Fig. 2.3. *Slots visible and invisible outside a class.*

I prefer to use this terminology in order to separate procedural elements from classes. A class is, typically, a restricted, flat name space, whereas a procedure tends to involve nesting of declarations. Furthermore, a variable in a procedure definition is in scope (and hence visible) only within the procedure in which it is defined and within all procedures defined within that procedure (unless the variable is hidden by the definition of another variable with the same name); a global variable is in scope in all procedures defined within the global scope and in all procedures which are defined within these procedures. A scoped variable is visible only in a "downward" sense. A slot in a class, unless hidden, is visible within its defining class and within all other classes and procedures unless over-ridden by another (local) definition. In this sense, slots have a two-dimensional region within which they are accessible or visible to other entities.

class 1

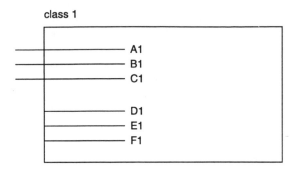

class 2

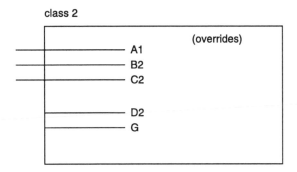

Fig. 2.4. *Public slot visibility and access.*

An obvious distinction to make is to define some slots as visible and others as hidden. CLOS adopts the approach that all slots are accessible; if programmers want to hide some, they may write code to make this distinction, the code being included at runtime in the class-processing code. The CLOS approach depends upon a Meta-Object Protocol (or MOP), an issue to which I will return in Chapter 8, below.

Even if it is decided to make some slots hidden and some visible, there are questions that must be asked. In both cases, the question arises as to who can see the slot. If a slot is visible, to whom is it visible? To all objects? If a slot is hidden, from whom is it hidden? A visible slot might be visible to everything; that is, it is exported from the class's interface and can be accessed by anything (provided it is not over-ridden). A hidden slot might be visible only to those entities within the class in which it is defined. Such a slot could not be accessed outside of its defining class, nor could it be accessed in any classes derived by specialization from that defining class.

The C++ and Java approach to visibility is one that allows a relatively fine control over the visibility of slots. They introduce distinctions between *public*, *protected* and *private* slots. It is possible to make methods private, as well as data slots. Furthermore, in C++, it is possible to have a superclass that is private (the default is a public superclass). The distinction between the three kinds of visibility are as follows.

A *public* slot (data or method) is visible to all entities within the class in which it is defined, as well as in all other classes. For C++, we must add the possibility that the slot is visible in all routines external to any class and in which the identifier of the slot has not been over-ridden by a local definition. For C++, it is also necessary to add the constraint that visibility is restricted to the file in which the slot is defined. For Java, there are no procedures or other constructs external to classes and Java classes exist in name spaces, not files; these facts have the implication that the visibility rule for Java amounts to the first sentence of this paragraph. To an approximation, a public data slot can be referenced, accessed and updated anywhere in the program; a public method slot can be referenced and called anywhere in the program.

A *private* slot (data or method) is *only* visible within the class in which it is defined. A private slot can be referenced (and called), accessed and updated (if it is a data slot) by methods local to the class in which the slot is defined; it can be stored in any container object defined in the class. Private slots are also visible in the sense of variable scope in all classes that are defined locally to the class in which the slot is defined. Private slots cannot be seen in classes that are external to the one in which they are defined. When a C++ class declares its superclass to be private, all public and protected slots of the superclass become private slots of the subclass; the default is for superclasses to be public, in which case their public slots become public slots of the subclass.

There is a third distinction made in these languages. Some slots can be declared to be *protected*. A protected slot is visible within the class in which it is defined (and in all locally defined classes) and it is visible within all subclasses (and their locally defined classes) of its defining class. It is not visible anywhere else. A protected data slot is one that can be referenced, accessed or updated within its defining class and within all of the subclasses of its defining class. A protected method slot is one that can be referenced and called within the class in which it is defined (and its locally defined classes) and within all subclasses (and their locally defined classes) of its defining class.

A completely different scheme is adopted by Eiffel. Here, a distinction is made between those classes in which particular slots can be inherited. Slots in Eiffel are called *features*; the term refers to data and to method slots. The visibility of features can be stated either in an export clause or in the definition of the feature in the defining class. An export clause takes the form of a list of feature references annotated with a visibility constraint. For example:

```
export
  {ANY} f, g;
```

```
{NONE} x;
{D} h
```

is such a feature list. Each line defines the visibility of the variables that appear to the right of the entity named between braces. With the exception of the entity named *NONE*, each entity mentioned between the braces is a class. The export list says that f and g are visible to class *ANY* and to all of its descendants. It also says that feature h is visible to class D and to all of its descendants. Therefore, f and g are visible to all classes because *ANY* is the root of all classes in Eiffel (it is a pre-defined class). The feature named x, though, is visible to no other classes; the specification of *NONE* makes the feature private to the class in which it is defined.

Eiffel also allows visibility specifications to be made on feature definitions:

```
feature {A}
    i : INTEGER
```

This states that i is visible to class A and all of its descendants.

It should be clear that there are interactions between inheritance and visibility. The standard rule applies for inheritance: unless over-ridden in a subclass, all visible definitions in the superclass are carried over into the subclass. For example (this example is taken from [67], p. 99), if we define class B as:

```
class B
    feature
        x, y: INTEGER
    feature {A}
        f, g, h: INTEGER;
end
```

and class C as:

```
class C inherit B
    export
        {D} x;
        {ANY} f;
        {NONE} g;
    end
end
```

The features of the subclass, C, have the following status. Feature y is visible to all classes. Feature h is visible to class A and all of its subclasses. In class C, these two features retain the same status they had in class B. Meanwhile, in C, x is now available to D and all of its subclasses, and f is visible in all classes, while g is now private to C. This means that the status of x, f and g has changed. It is important to remember that the status has changed with respect to C, not to B; in B, their status is as defined in that class. When we have an instance of B, the features defined in B have the status that is defined there; when we have an instance of class C, the features that are defined in that class have the status defined there. Consequently, we can access the g in instances of B from any class we care, but we cannot access the g in instances of C. If we attempt to access x from an object that is not an instance of D, we can do it without error if the x is in an instance of B, but access in an instance of C will be blocked (it will cause a compile-time error). It can be seen that Eiffel allows classes to inherit features which are public and then to make them wholly private, but on a selective basis, not, as in C++ on a per-class basis.

A second issue, related to visibility, is how a slot is allocated. There are two main choices:

- the slot is allocated in each instance of the class;
- the slot is allocated once and is shared by all instances of the class.

This distinction is made in Smalltalk, LOOPS, CLOS, C++ and Java; the slot might be hidden or public, but can be allocated in these ways. A third way is for there to be no allocation and a per-program specific mechanism is supplied by the programmer; this mechanism is called a *virtual slot* in Dylan. The Dylan virtual slot is included so that other mechanisms can provide what look like slots: a read-only slot might be implemented as an input side of a stream or pipe, for example.

The distinction made by Smalltalk, LOOPS, CLOS, C++ and Java, as well as Dylan, is between the way in which a slot is allocated, no matter what its visibility constraints are. The distinction, using Smalltalk terminology, is between *class* and *instance* variables. A class variable is instantiated once and is shared by all instances of a class. The instances are able to update the variable's value, as well as reading it. An instance variable is allocated for each instance of the class; it is not shared between instances. In C++ and Java, the default is for slots to be allocated on a per-instance basis. Hence, in these languages, instance variables are the default. If a slot is to be defined once for all instances, it must be allocated as a *static* (own) variable in these languages, such slots can be hidden or public.

Class variables require runtime storage to be allocated with each class. They also allow instances to update their values. A class variable is a common runtime variable whose scope can be restricted.

2.7 Instance Creation

A class is of little use unless it can be instantiated. Instantiation is necessary in order to produce the objects which, at runtime, are the basis of computation. Instantiation allows independent entities of a given type to be created. Slight differences can exist between instances of the same class. Two instances of a class representing the application of a binary arithmetic operator to its arguments can differ in the following ways:

- one might represent a multiplication, the other an addition;
- one might represent a multiplication of a variable by a constant, the other an addition of two variables.

If we have instances of the binary arithmetic operator application class that both represent multiplications, they can differ in the following sense:

- one might be the multiplication of two variables, the other the multiplication of a variable by a scalar constant.

Instances can differ slightly or to a considerable extent. Imagine that we are building an object-oriented program to process data about families (say for a census or for a food store). People can differ in their height, for example, by considerable amounts; preferences can vary wildly. One person's favourite food might be beef steak, while another might prefer lemon sorbet to anything else in the world. However, people all have in common a set of basic properties. A class defining People would capture these commonalities, but it would also leave room to represent the differences between people.

In a program, instances of a class all share a common structure and a common set of properties. In addition, they all share the same set of methods. By setting the values in one instance in one way, we can make it differ from all other instances of that same class: this is the essence of parameterization, an extremely important property of the concept of an instance.

One way in which instances can be created, a way in which the structure of the class is respected, is to arrange for there to be a "master object". The master object resembles a class in the sense that it defines the structure of its instances and defines the methods which apply to its instances. It defines the slots and methods that are to form the objects. When an instance of the master object is required, the master object is simply copied. The way in which the copy is performed depends upon what is required. There are two choices:

- shallow copy;
- deep copy.

Under shallow copy, the container is copied and its contents are shared; under deep copy, the container is copied and the contents are copied and assigned to the correct place in the copied master object. Since methods are usually implemented as pointers either to special method-representing or method-handling objects or to the entry point of the method code, the decision as to whether a deep or shallow copy is performed is irrelevant. I focus, therefore, on data slots.

When a master object is shallow copied, only the container structure is replicated. The contents of the container object are shared between all copies. Thus, when a change is made to the master object, say a new value is assigned to a data slot, that change will be seen by all copies of the master objects. An object can be copied so that it exactly replicates the structure and content of its master object; the object (instance) can then be updated to introduce differences. If, on the other hand, the master object is deep copied, the container *and* the contents are copied. When a change is made to the master object, the copies are unaffected and do not see the change.

The master object approach underpins object-oriented programming based on *prototypes* (see Chapter 3 for more details). It also underpins another approach to object-oriented programming, one that is far less commonly encountered. This rare approach considers objects to be, in effect, instantiable modules which present well-defined interfaces. The instantiable module approach suffers from inflexibility and is not often encountered in the mainstream. Prototype-based programming, on the other hand, is an exciting and relatively poorly explored area.

The most common approach to object-oriented programming by far is that which makes a distinction between classes and instances. The instance-producing process is called *instantiation*. There are various approaches to instantiation, depending upon the particularities of the language. Languages like C++ can instantiate objects on the runtime stack or in the heap and the language provides constructs for instantiating classes that reflects *where* they are to be created. In other languages, particularly those in the LISP and Smalltalk families, instance creation is performed by a single, unified mechanism. Whatever the decisions made about where instances are created, the instantiation mechanism works by using the class as a structural template which is used to allocate the slots and methods that are to appear in the instance. In most class-based languages, instances have an internal structure that reflects the structure of their class. Thus, the process of creating an instance remains fundamentally the same despite constraints on where instances are allocated.

In C++, given that C is a class and v a variable, a legal way to create an instance of C is:

```
C v;
```

In a procedure, the instance would be allocated on the stack. The variable v would be taken to be a variable in the ordinary way, so if $v1$ is another variable of type C, the assignment $v := v1$ is quite legal and should (in C++ there are factors that can prevent this) perform the assignment of $v1$'s instance of C to v. Note that the variable v is not a pointer to an instance; the entire instance is allocated on the stack when the block containing the declaration is entered. If we wanted a pointer to an instance of C, we would have to write:

```
C *v;
V := new C;
```

Where *new* is an instance-creating primitive which returns a pointer to a heap-allocated instance.

It is all very well to create instances of classes, but without the ability to set at least some of their slots to specific values, instantiation is a blunted tool. Thus, again in C++, we could define a stack-allocated instance of C by:

```
C v(99, ''foo'');
```

which instantiates v to be an instance of C, but, this time, two of v's slots are initialized to the integer 99 and to the string "foo". In C++, as in many other languages, it is possible to parameterize the declaration of a variable so that values can be passed into the instance to initialize some or all of its slots.

In CLOS and related languages, there is an equal control over the creation of instances, and values can be passed to instances for slot initialization. However, unlike many languages, in CLOS and other LISP-related languages (Dylan being one), the language provides an instance-creation function. This function typically takes, as its first parameter, the name of the class to be instantiated. It also takes a variable number of parameters, each one supplying a value to be used to instantiate a slot.

In CLOS and related languages, all instances are allocated in the heap, so a single instance-creating mechanism can be supplied; in languages like C++, Java and Eiffel which allow instances to be created on the local stack or in the heap, a mechanism for each storage area must be provided. Each operator must allow for the creation of parameterized instances.

2.8 Inheritance

2.8.1 Introduction

Class-based programming is powerful. It encapsulates data and procedures into units which can then be instantiated. Class-based programming is very often associated with inheritance or the ability of one class to extend another. Inheritance refers to the fact that the definition of a new class can assume— or rely upon the existence of—another definition; alternatively, inheritance makes a previously defined structure available for incoporation in a new one. Alternatively, if one class inherits from another, the inheriting class specializes a class which is more general. The definition of classes via inheritance involves the construction of definitions that are increasingly specialized. A final interpretation of the inheritance relation is that it enables subtypes to be produced given a definition of a supertype. The first definition given above, a highly pragmatic one, implies that inheritance is a method for code sharing. The second definition implies a logical relationship between classes (specialization/generalization), while the last implies a type-based account. All three of these interpretations are acceptable, but the code sharing one should not be mixed with the others.

In terms of the organization of classes, inheritance induces an organization upon them. This organization is extremely important to class-based programming and it forms the subject of this section. Here, we will tend to think in terms of specialization/generalization and sub/super types.

The reader will probably have encountered the concept of multiple inheritance. This is a complex and controversial subject. Consequently, I focus here on single inheritance, the form found in Smalltalk, Java, FLAVORS, LOOPS, Beta and Sather; in a later chapter (Chapter 4), I will consider multiple inheritance.

2.8.2 Definition of Inheritance

The term "inheritance" as used above is to be taken in the familiar sense in which property or wealth is inherited, or in which genes are inherited. It is the process by which one generation hands down something to a later generation. In object-oriented terms, it means the handing down of properties from a more general structure to a less general one. This is directly analogous to the ordinary language interpretation in which someone hands on something to someone else (usually a relative). In the case of object-oriented programming, it is the class that hands something to another class; that something is its slots. The process of inheritance is part of the definition of classes in class-based programming. One often defines one class as a *subclass* of another. Alternatively, we can say that the newly defined class (the subclass) is obtained by the process of *specialization* of its superclass: one class is specialized in order to create a subclass.

The reader should note that, by *superclass*, we mean *both* the *immediate* superclass and *all* the *ancestors* of a given class. The converse of a superclass is a *subclass*. I will also refer to the immediate superclass as the *direct* superclass (the converse being the direct subclass). The *ancestors* of a class is the set of all of its superclasses (the superclass, superclass of the superclass, etc.); sometimes I will assume that the ancestors are ordered in a natural fashion. When considering a class as a type-defining construct, I will refer to the subclass as a subtype; conversely, a subtype has a supertype which is its superclass. I will use the terms subclass and superclass when there is no confusion and will be more precise when I believe it to be necessary.

What this means is that when one class is defined as a subclass of another class, the subclass is able to treat the slots and methods of its superclass as if they belonged to it. The subclass is applicable to fewer situations than the superclass, so the concept of specialization is introduced. When we define classes depending upon each other in this way, we say that there is an *inheritance relation* between classes.

For example, imagine that we have a basic class, say *Data*, that represents any data type whatsoever, then we can define a *Stack* class to implement a push-down stack whose elements are instances of class *Data*. We might specialize *Data* so that we could represent integers, reals, double-precision reals, and so on. When we do this, we produce specializations of class *Data*. Now consider the *Stack* class itself. We might find that double-precision floating point numbers are of particular importance to some application, and we want to have the *Stack* hold them. We could stick with using *Data*, but the more specific type *DoubleFloat* is more suited to the current application; we could then construct a new version of *Stack* but which now only holds instances of *DoubleFloat* (we would do this by changing the types of the methods so that they input and output *DoubleFloats* and we would change the element type for the stack structures so that it was *DoubleFloat*). Inside the new stack class, we use the operations defined for *Stack*, but wrap specializing code for them.

Another example of specialization is the construction of labelled nodes for a program that manipulates graphs. Initially, it makes sense to define a class to represent the nodes in the graph. A node class might define such things as its degree and pointers to each of the nodes to which it could be connected. It might have operations to link and unlink to other nodes and, perhaps, print some information about itself. Next, we come to the labelled node. This can be represented by an instance of the node class, but with an extra slot to hold the label. To do this, we would define a new class, say *LabelledNode*, which was identical to the node class, but differs in its inclusion of the label. The operations defined for the basic node class would be inherited by *LabelledNode*, as would the pointers to connected nodes. The *LabelledNode* class would add its own slot for the label and methods to set the label and to print it on the screen. The original node class serves as the basis for all other kinds of node one would like to include in a graph; for example, rather than labelling nodes, one might want to colour them in order to find partitions, so a *ColouredNode* class could be defined as a subclass or specialization of the basic node class. The *ColouredNode* class would inherit the same operations and slots as would *LabelledNode*; it would differ in the presence of a slot to represent the node's current colour and methods to set, retrieve and display the node's colour.

The inheritance relation graphically is shown graphically in the following figure.

In the figure, it can be seen that there are two classes, C_1 and C_2. The upper class, C_1 is the superclass of class C_2; C_2 is, therefore, the subclass of C_1. In other words, C_2 is a specialization of C_1. Class C_1 has slots s_{11} and s_{12}, as well as methods m_{11}, m_{12} and m_{13}. Class C_2 has slots s_{21}, s_{22} and s_{23}, as well as methods m_{21} and m_{22}. The slots defined in each class are local to it. Equally, the methods are local to the class in which they are defined. However, C_1 and C_2 are related by means of inheritance. This means that C2 was defined as a specialization of C_1 and on the assumption that C_2 would inherit from C_1.

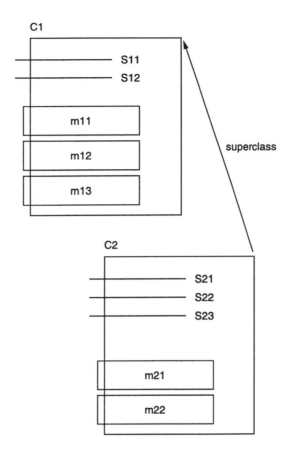

Fig. 2.5. *The inheritance relation.*

Class C_2 inherits slots s_{11} and s_{12}, as well as methods m_{11}, m_{12} and m_{13}. What inheritance means is that the slots and methods are treated as if they were defined locally to C_2. When an instance of C_2 is created, it will look as if it has slots s_{11}, s_{12}, s_{21}, s_{22} and s_{23}, and methods m_{11}, m_{12}, m_{13}, m_{21} and m_{22}. An instance of C_1 will look, therefore, as shown in Figure 2.6.

It looks just as in the previous figure. An instance of C_2 will look, thanks to inheritance, as shown in Figure 2.7.

Inheritance allows the programmer to rely upon what is already provided by a class and to extend (specialize) it to fit the more constrained circumstances of their implementation. Inheritance relates classes in a variety of ways. If we consider a class to be a definition, derivation of subclasses implies the formation of definitions that are more restrictive and, hence, applicable to fewer situations.

Assume an inheritance structure like that in Figure 2.5.

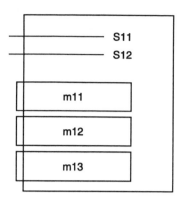

Fig. 2.6. C_1's slots.

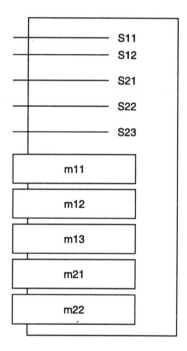

Fig. 2.7. C_2's slots.

The topmost class is the root of the inheritance graph. Each leaf node is a class that is a subclass of the root. Each leaf is related to the root by the subclass or specialization relationship; leaf classes apply to fewer cases than does the root. Alternatively, the root is a more general concept. The general concept class at the root of the tree provides operations and data that is common to all of the leaf nodes. The leaf nodes inherit these common slots

Branching Tree

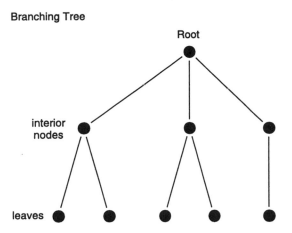

Fig. 2.8. *A tree and its root.*

and methods in order to represent their concept. (This can also be considered as *code sharing*.) Thus, whenever we encounter an instance of one of these leaf classes, it will behave as if it contained the slots of the root class and will exhibit behaviours as if it had the root class's methods defined for it. In addition, it will behave in such a way that an observer can confirm that it contains those slots and methods defined locally for it.

The organization of classes into trees is referred to as an inheritance tree or inheritance graph.

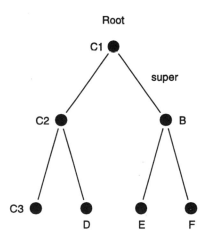

Fig. 2.9. *An inheritance graph (tree).*

When viewed from a class, it can only "see" a linear sequence of classes which stretches between it and the root class; this sequence has endpoints and is linearly ordered, so is a chain. We refer to the sequence of classes between a given class and its root class as its *inheritance chain* (sometimes this is called, colloquially, the *superchain*).

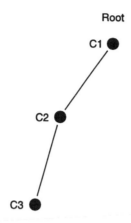

Fig. 2.10. *An inheritance chain.*

At present, we are only considering single or simple inheritance. Under single inheritance, every class has at most one superclass. Since the inheritance relation is transitive, a given class inherits from all of the classes in its inheritance chain. Furthermore, since inheritance is *transitive*, if C_1 is a subclass of C_2 and C_2 is a subclass of C_3, C_1 is also a subclass of C_3.

It is also worth introducing a little more terminology which will be of value throughout discussions of inheritance. Let us assume we have a class C. This class has subclasses C_{11} and C_{12}. Let us assume that C_{11} has subclasses C_{21}, C_{22} and C_{23}, and that C_{22} has subclass C_{31}. For ease of visualization, this is depicted in Figure 2.11 (see next page).

We say that C_{11} and C_{12} are direct subclasses of C. We also say that C_{21}, C_{22}, C_{23} and C_{31} are indirect subclasses of C. C_{21} is a direct subclass of C_{11} but an indirect subclass of C. Similarly, when considering instances of a class, we say that the instances of C are direct instances of it, but an instance of C_{11} or an instance of C_{21} is an indirect instance of C.

2.9 Abstract Classes

It is not always desirable to create instances of a class. Sometimes, it is better to create a class but forbid its instantiation. Such a class is referred to as being *abstract*, while classes for which it makes sense to create instances

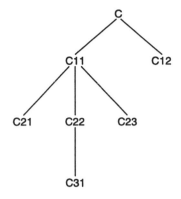

Fig. 2.11. *The inheritance tree rooted at C.*

are referred to as being *concrete*. Abstract classes serve as place-holders in the inheritance chain. (We will see, when we consider multiple inheritance that abstract classes and their near-relative, *mixins*, play an important part in class derivation.)

Abstract classes are defined to occupy a location in an inheritance chain. That is, an abstract class can refine its superclass and can have subclasses. It is worth noting that the restriction on instances has no bearing on whether a class is permitted to have subclasses. Some languages permit the explicit definition of classes which cannot be specialized; for example, the *String* class in *Java.lang* cannot be specialized and is marked as a *final* class. It would make no sense for an abstract class to be marked as *final* in a Java program.

Abstract classes very often occur at a branch-point in an inheritance hierarchy. Branch points occur when a class has many subclasses. This means that the whole inheritance graph is a rooted, acyclic graph, or *tree* (for each class, its inheritance graph is a chain, hence our terminology). At the branch-point, it might be necessary to define some data or method slots that will be inherited by its subclasses.

For example, in an abstract syntax tree, we might want to define a class to represent expressions. This class would be an abstract one because we do not normally instantiate expressions directly. Instead, we define other expression classes such as constant, variable, unary operator application, binary operator application, and so on. In a compiler or interpreter, we might want to annotate each expression with its type (or expected type). We might also want to label the expressions in some way, perhaps as some kind of colouring algorithm relating to register use. The expression type and labelling should be defined in the expression type and inherited by the subtypes (constant, variable, etc.). However, it makes no sense to instantiate the class representing all expressions; it *does* make sense for it to be abstract. The inheritance graph for expressions looks like the following:

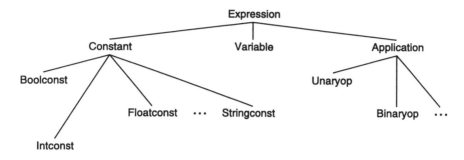

Fig. 2.12. *The inheritance graph for expressions.*

It makes sense for constants to be instantiated, for variables to be instantiated, and for the various operator application classes to be instantiated. However, it makes no sense to instantiate something which just represents a type and a label: it corresponds to nothing in a programming language (or, at least, the language being defined, we assume).

If we were to define a collection of classes that represent various foodstuffs, we might want to define a class called *FoodStuff*. This class would be the root of the inheritance tree containing the definitions of classes for different kinds of food (cheese, milk, etc.). A property that all purchased foods have is that they have a price. It might make sense to define the *FoodStuff* class with a slot called *price*. However, just as we do not normally encounter expressions, we do not normally encounter foodstuffs in the abstract. The *FoodStuff* class is intended to represent the general class of foods, not a particular food. It should, therefore, be defined as an abstract class.

An abstract class can also be defined because one or more of its operations cannot be specified for that class. This again indicates that the class will be the root of a tree of class definitions. For example, if we want to define a collection of classes to represent logical constants, logic variables, functors (functional terms) and relations as part of a unification pattern matcher, we need to define a class called *Term* to stand as the root class for constants, variables and functors. The inheritance tree is as follows.

The *Term* class is the root of the tree. There are branches for all the main subtypes of *Term*: *Const*, *Var*, *FunTerm*. It will be seen that *Const* has subclasses: *IntConst*, *SymConst*, and *RealConst*. These subclasses represent integer, symbolic and real constants. The *Const* class serves only to root these individual constant types, so it is an abstract class like *Term*.

It can also be seen that there is a subclass, *SignedFunTerm*, of *FunTerm*; this is intended to represent functors that are assigned a truth-value. This is the representation for predicates and relations in this package.

The *Term* class declares that there is a method called *unify*. The unify method performs the pattern-matching action on subterms (it is a so-called two-way matching). In other words, the unify method must be defined for

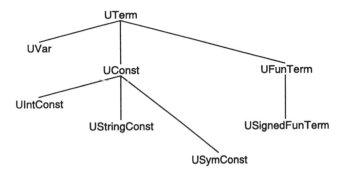

Fig. 2.13. *Types representing unifiable terms.*

each of the subclasses (*Const*, *Var*, *FunTerm* and *SignedFunTerm*). It is not possible to define unification for *Terms*, but it is possible to define it for the various subclasses, so each subclass should provide an appropriate implementation of the *unify* method. The *Term* method contains no implementation for *unify*, just its declaration. A subclass that does not provide such a definition will be, itself, an abstract class. For this reason, the *Const* class can provide no definition for *unify* and it is, therefore, an abstract class. The subclasses of *Const*, *IntConst*, *SymConst* and *RealConst* each provide an implementation of *unify*, so they are concrete classes. The *Var* class contains a definition of *unify*, so, like *FunTerm* and *SignedFunTerm*, which also define their own versions of the method, it is a concrete class.

   Some languages, Java and Dylan, for example, allow abstract classes to be explicitly marked. In Java, the *Term* class is defined as:

```
public abstract class Term{
   public abstract Bindings unify(Term  t, Bindings bdgs);
} // end class
```

The annotation *abstract* appears in the line which introduces the name of the class (and its superclass, were this relevant). The class definition contains the signature of a method called *unify* which has particular inputs and outputs (they do not concern us here). The method is marked as being abstract and has no implementation. What is meant is that the implementation(s) come later in the definitions of subclasses of this; the implementations are defined on a per-class basis and will differ because of the different structures in the subclasses. Java insists that, whenever a method is marked *abstract* so, too, is the class in which it is defined.

   In Dylan, a similar marking scheme is employed. Eiffel similarly imposes a distinction between concrete and abstract classes by means of the *deferred* annotation which means that the implementation of a feature (slot) is deferred until a later class. As in Java and Dylan, an entire class can be marked as deferred, or one or more of its features can bear such a marking.

C++ provides a mechanism, but is somewhat clumsier. In C++, the programmer can define a method as being virtual void. This means that the method is a virtual method, but its implementation is deferred to the class' subclasses. An example of the syntax here is:

```
virtual int add1(int y) = 0
```

The "= 0" annotation is the part stating that the definition has been deferred (this is the "void" part of "virtual void"). Whenever the C++ compiler sees a class with at least one virtual void method, it treats creation of instances of that class as an error. There is no class annotation for an abstract class.

It should be noted that an abstract class can still have a constructor. The constructor can be called in the normal way by constructors of the abstract class's subclasses. However, it is not permitted for the abstract class's constructor to be called directly.

2.10 Iterators

Encapsulation is the process of hiding inessential details from consumers or users. In object-oriented programming, it is often necessary to define classes which hold instances of other classes—these classes are called *container* classes. Example container classes are:

- vector;
- array;
- singly linked list;
- FIFO queue;
- LIFO stack;
- set;
- binary tree;
- random access file;

and so on. These container classes all have the common property that they are data structures that hold (contain) data.

In conventional procedural programming, if data is held in an array, it is standard to write a loop of some description to perform search or update operations. If the array is represented by a container class, a mechanism must be provided to access the elements of the array so that the encapsulation provided by its class is not violated. Similarly, if it is necessary to find an element in a list and that list is represented by a class, there must be some way to access the elements of the list without violating the encapsulation provided by the list class. If the encapsulation provided by these classes were violated, there would be *no* point in using classes at all. Encapsulation allows the programmer to treat something like an instance of a container class as a single entity. If encapsulation is violated, the contents become visible and there is

little point in pretending that they constitute a single entity (for the reason
that more than one entity can be seen and, presumably, be manipulated).

The solution is to employ *iterators*. An iterator is an entity that gives
access to the contents of a container object without violating encapsulation
constraints. Access to the contents is granted on a one-at-a-time basis in order. The order can be storage order (as in lists and queues), or some arbitrary
order (as in array indices) or according to some ordering relation (as in an
ordered binary tree). The iterator is a construct which provides an interface
that, when called, yields either the next element in the container or some
value denoting the fact that there are no more elements to examine.

Programming with iterators is a high-level, abstract approach to iteration
in programs. Iterators hide the details of access to and update of the elements
of a container class.

The simplest and safest iterators are those which permit read-only access
to the contents of an instance of a container class. In this case, when called,
the iterator yields a reference to the next element in the container instance.
The reference allows the client code to read the data represented by the
element; if the element is a complex object, it might be updated by client
code. However, the element cannot be replaced in its containing object. Thus,
if the container is an array and the iterator yields the third element in the
array, the client code cannot update the array so that a new third element is
stored there. An iterator of this kind is *not* permitted to update the container,
even though the *element* that has been extracted might be updated.

The following code fragment shows how an iterator might appear in code:

```
cont_iter := new cont_iterator();
x := cont_iter.next();
while x /= NONE do
     ...
     s(x);
     ...
     x := cont_iter.next();
end;
```

In this example, cont_iter is the name of the iterator. It is created on
the first line by instantiation of the cont_iterator class, an iterator class
defined to iterate over some container class, cont. Successive elements from
the container are assigned to x. The loop terminates when x is bound to
some empty value (here, NONE). In the middle of the loop, there is s(x) an
operation on x, the current element from the container. The next element of
the container is obtained at the bottom of the loop.

It is possible to define iterators which can update the container in various
ways. Updates to container classes include insertion, deletion and replacement
of elements. Iterators which permit this kind of destructive operation are
called *robust iterators*. The problem with robust iterators is that they must
preserve the overall structure of the container class as well as any constraints

that the container imposes on its data. Robust iterators are relatively hard to implement because they risk exposing the internal structure of the container class.

There are many ways to implement iterators, among which the following are often encountered:

- classes;
- blocks;
- functions;
- cursors.

Here, the first three approaches are considered.

The first approach, one based on classes, is employed in C++. An iterator is usually defined as an independent class that can be instantiated separately from the container class to which it refers. The iterator class must define a method that produces successive elements of the container upon which it operates. The problem of encapsulation needs to be solved because, as an independent class, the iterator can only gain access to the container class's public components.

The answer in C++ is to introduce the concept of the *friend*. If one class, F, is annotated as being the *friend* of another class, C, class F is permitted to access and update the private and protected components of C as well as C's public components. Once a class is marked as a friend of another class, it can directly perform access and updates; encapsulation is violated, but, it is argued, only on a limited basis.

If an iterator is to be written for an array class in C++, the iterator is marked as a *friend* class of the array. The iterator will contain a private integer slot to hold the index of the next element in the array to be returned. A method is defined in the iterator which will yield the next element in the array; the method returns NULL if the index runs off the end of the array. This can be written as:

```
class array_iter{
public:
  array_iter(aclass aclss){
    array_len = aclss.size;
    next_element = 0;
  }

  T *next(){ // method yielding elements of array
    T *elem = NULL;
    if (next_element < array_len)
      elem = &aclass.elements[next_element++];
    return elem;
  } // end next
```

```
private:
  int next_element;
  int array_len;
};
```

In the example, **aclass** is the class representing the array over which iteration is to be performed. The constructor of **array_iter**, the iterator class, takes a (reference to) the array class and extracts its size and stores it in the private local variable **array_len** (this is done to ensure faster access). The index into the array, **next_element**, is initialized to zero.

The **next** method is the one that returns successive elements of the array. The type of the elements in the array is assumed to be T and the **next** method deals with pointers to the elements, not the elements themselves. The method tests to see if it has gone off the end of the array. If there have been more calls to **next** than there are elements in the array, NULL is returned; otherwise, a pointer to the next element in the array is returned and the index is incremented ready for the next call.

The friend mechanism is highly dangerous. It requires considerable control in order to avoid exposing the details of classes. Control over code must be exercised and maintained, particularly on large projects where some programmers might require a set of classes to be friends to some others and where other programmers do not want such exposure. The friend mechanism is, in any case, an open invitation to disaster.

An alternative would be to define the iterator class as a nested class which is then exported. However, this poses problems for it either exposes some of the internal structure of the container or it requires a method to instantiate it and then call the iterator's element-yielding method. It might also prove to be difficult to have more than one iterator active in the same container class at the same time.

The block method is available in languages like Smalltalk which permit the definition of first-class block expressions (see Chapter 5, Section 5.4.3). In the block approach, the iterator is defined as a block inside the container class over which iteration is to be performed. The variables local to the block are used to retain local state information (e.g., indices into arrays or pointers into lists) in a fashion identical to that in the above class-based example. Because the block is defined in the local context of the class, it can access private state information. Because a block is able to retain information over a period of time (blocks are closures), once defined, it can function outside the class in which it is defined and can be invoked more than once, retaining its state information between invocations.

Functions in most programming languages are not treated as first-class entities. Thus, they are not implemented as closures. In order to employ a C routine as an iterator, it is necessary to store information between invocations; the most natural approach is to use *static* variables to hold this information. In languages without *static* or *own* variables, functions cannot easily be used to implement iterators. In the LISP family of languages, closures can easily be created, so function-based iterators can be defined. In languages providing higher-order functions as first-class entities, a function-based iterator can be created by a method defined in the container class.

The Sather language [76, 77] adopts an approach based on the class-based method, but which looks like the function-based one. An iterator in Sather is defined as a function (method). When compiled, iterator functions generate objects which have a public method that is called to yield the elements of the container. Sather iterators are defined as part of the definition of container classes; there is no textual separation for the iterator definition looks like another method in the container class. This approach also avoids encapsulation problems because the iterator is defined as a component of the class to which it applies. As a component of the class, it has direct access to everything in that class and in that class's ancestors.

2.11 Part Objects

The Beta language [54] employs single inheritance, so its semantics under inheritance are easily and simply defined. Beta is based upon the concept of a pattern, patterns can be created to represent operations as well as classes; this provides considerable uniformity to the structure of the language. The language is based upon the concept of the class and its instances, so much of its semantics is of a familiar kind. It also includes the virtual concept (as in Simula67) and block structure (as in Algol60 and its descendants). I will consider these aspects of the language in turn. I consider them here for, as we will see, they relate both to inheritance and the incorporation of slots in classes.

In Beta, the virtual concept is generalized somewhat and is available for any pattern entity, not just procedures (methods). Patterns in Beta are composed of attributes (slots, in other words) which can be filled with objects that instantiate other patterns (classes). A Beta attribute (slot) can be declared as being virtual. This implies that the properties of the virtual pattern are not all known and that full specification may occur at a later time. A virtual pattern is, therefore, the partial specification of a class or procedural entity. A virtual pattern can be construed as a parameter in the enclosing pattern.

A virtual pattern declaration has the form:

    V :< A

(this notation will become familiar when we consider overloading and polymorphism and is employed in languages such as Sather). Using this notation, V is declared as a virtual pattern (class or attribute) with *qualifying pattern* A. The pattern V can be bound to a subpattern (subclass) of A. While a pattern remains unbound, it has a default binding provided by its qualifying pattern. In more standard terms, $V :< A$ denotes a slot, method or class which has a type represented by A; however, the specification of the type is incomplete and can be completed by an entity which is a subclass of A.

A virtual pattern is instantiated by supplying a subclass of its qualifying pattern as a value. Syntactically, this can be done in two ways:

    V :: A1

or:

    V :: A1(# ... #)

where A1(# ... #) represents the explicit definition of a pattern (an anonymous class in more standard terms). In each case, A1 must be a subpattern (subclass) of A.

A pattern can be parameterized by more than one virtual pattern. This means that the pattern can be instantiated in a number of ways. However, instantiation is not generic in the sense that will be examined in Chapter 6 (or in the sense of Ada), but requires each parameter to be instantiated by a subpattern (subclass) of each parameter's qualifying pattern; virtual patterns may also remain uninstantiated. This provides considerable freedom of definition, all the more so when it is realized that, because patterns also extend to methods and other procedural entities, virtual patterns can be used in the definition of procedural patterns. This inevitably interacts with the inner statements which are used in the derivation of sub-operations (we will not give details but refer the reader to [54] which describes extensions to the virtual concept which avoid these problems).

The second aspect is block structure. Beta allows the inclusion of classes within classes; in Beta terms, the definition of one pattern within another. This is similar to the nested class definitions in C++ and Java. Beta also allows the explicit definition of one pattern within another. In Beta syntax, this is represented by:

    (#
    P : (# ... #)
    #)

where a pattern is delimited by the (# and #) brackets. Here, we have the definition of a pattern which contains an attribute called P which is filled by the pattern which is defined by the (# ... #) pattern. Within the pattern defined for P, all attributes in the outer pattern are visible. The attributes of the pattern defined for P are not visible in the containing class. This is block structure in the Algol sense (it is an implementation of the scope organization that some languages derived from the λ-calculus). Block structure, in this sense, was abandoned in Smalltalk.

Block structure can be employed to construct objects that obey a part-of organizing principle. A complex object with many complex components can be defined and treated as a single entity. Inner classes (or patterns) define the components of the whole. Because even explicitly defined patterns in Beta can be given what amount to superclasses, explicitly defined components can be permitted to engage in inheritance. (Similar things can be done with C++ and with Java, particularly now that Java permits nested class definitions.) Inner classes are local to the classes in which they are defined. This makes it possible to restrict the existence of an object and its description to the object in which it is defined. It further reduces the number of names in the global namespace. Nesting of classes also provides a mechanism for packaging related classes together in such a way that they can be accessed in a controlled fashion, and it also allows dependencies between them to be expressed and controlled inside a context which can control and manipulate them.

The formation of prototype objects is one case where block structure is of positive use. A prototype can be considered to be a class that describes properties that are related to those of other prototypes. It is an instance of some kind of class, but one with special properties. A prototype bears a relationship to other objects of which it is the prototype. There are entities for which it is a prototype and entities for which it is unrelated. The relation can be described in terms of the definition of a class. In an early paper on Beta [54], Madsen gives the following example as an instance of the prototype abstraction problem.

Consider a class called *FlightType* defining the properties of the descriptions of flights as specified in an airline timetable. Flight *SK273* connects Copenhagen and Los Angeles and is an example of a flight. This flight is available on Monday, Wednesday and Friday each week. Its scheduled departure time is 11.30 a.m. However, during some period of time, the scheduled departure time might be altered. Flight *SK273* should be modelled as an instance of class FlightType. On the other hand, flight *SK273* can be viewed as a prototype for the actual flights which take place between Copenhagen and Los Angeles. The real flights are characterized by attributes such as actual departure time, actual delay, actual flight duration, and so on. Therefore, *SK273* can be viewed as a class with actual flights as its instances and also *SK273* is a subclass of the *FlightType* class. Thus, we have a class which is an instance of itself (an example of Russell's paradox).

Madsen suggests in [54] that block structure can be employed to solve this problem:

```
FlightType: class
    begin
      source, destination: City;
      frequency : setOfWeekDay;
      departTime : timeOfDay; { departure time}
      flightTime: timePeriod;
      flight : class
          departuredate: date;
          actualDepartTime: timeOfDay;
```

```
          actualFlightTime: timePeriod;
          departureDelay: procedure ? end;
                  end class;
     end class;
```

This defines a class describing the properties of the flight prototypes in the timetable. The class also includes attributes of the actual instances of this flight type. It now becomes possible to define *SK273* as:

```
SK273: FlightType
      where
          source = Copenhagen,
          destination = LosAngeles,
          frequency = {Mon, Wed, Fri},
          departTime = 12.30 a.m.,
          flightTime = 11.5hrs;
```

and a particular flight can be represented by:

```
myFlight: SK273.flight
          where
          departureDate = Feb.1.99,
          actualDepartTime = 12.45p.m.,
          actualFlightTime = 11.25hrs
```

The where construct is used to bind the slots of an object (in Beta, this would be done using virtual patterns; in other languages, method calls or assignments are required).

The example works because the basic class defines a local class to represent the particulars of an actual flight. This local class is wholly local to the main class. The *FlightType* class represents properties of scheduled flights in general and includes information about a particular flight; information about the actual flight as instantiated on a particular day can remain incomplete until it is time to perform the instantiation (i.e., when the relevant information becomes available). Without block structure, we would have to resort to a number of *ad hoc* techniques to represent this information, for example the definition of additional classes that can be connected to the main class using pointers.

In a similar fashion, the tokens used in the implementation of a grammar can be defined in terms of a local class. In this case, as in the previous one, it is possible to refer to instances of local classes. This is seen in the above example where *SK273.flight* is referenced in the creation code. This entity is a class that is local to the *FlightType* class. Beta allows not only nested classes to be referenced in such a fashion, but also their attributes. This seemingly violates the principle of encapsulation, but Beta has separate mechanisms for distinguishing between implementation and interface.

When part objects (nested, or local, objects) are employed and when they are permitted to have real instances, it becomes necessary to determine where they reside. Beta provides a *loc* parameter that denotes an object that possibly contains the object whose parameter it is. In the above example, the *loc* of *SK273.flight* is *SK273*. In a more complex example, the location would, naturally, be far harder to determine. The loc parameter can be subjected to assignment in order to install a class or instance as the location of an object. The loc parameter is not, however, used to access the containing object; instead, it is used when objects of different classes must be similarly handled and when similarity among superclasses is insufficient for all of the classes. One particular and important reason for this is that the objects are parts of other class hierarchies.

Madsen and Pedersen consider the case of a pattern (class) representing an address (this is called *Address*) and the case of a pattern representing a kitchen (called, reasonably enough, *Kitchen*). They make the observation (Section 7) that the *kitchen* slot (holding an instance of *Kitchen*) represents a real world part of a real world object (a house), but the address part of something like a *Person* object represents an aspect of that object. It is an aspect because its representational role comes when we consider a person as living at some fixed abode. Another aspect of a person would be *Occupation*, and another would be *Hobbies*. We could fill an *occupation* slot with an instance of an *Occupation* pattern, say *Accountant*, and we could fill a *hobby* slot with an instance of a *Hobbies* pattern (e.g., *WaterSkiing*). These two slots will contain instances of the relevant patterns (classes).

The components of a part object can be accessed via Beta's renaming construct. In Beta, it is possible to rename any slot in a pattern. Slots that are directly contained in a pattern are referred to by their name, so if pattern P directly contains slot s, that slot is referred to simply as s. If, however, P contains a part object in a slot o and the part object contains a slot os, that slot can be made visible inside P as *o.os*. Beta allows this reference chain to be renamed or aliased with some simpler name, say *ss*. If *ss* is the alias of *o.os*, every time *ss* occurs in a component of P, it will refer to *o.os*. This mechanism adds considerable naming power to Beta, even though, strictly speaking, it violates the conventional conception of block structure in which objects in enclosing scopes are visible, but those in contained scopes are not (the position taken by Beta is similar to that in Ada where an enclosing block can refer to the components of an enclosed (necessarily named) block using a structured naming process).

This use of part objects replaces multiple inheritance in Beta, but, as the authors note, multiple inheritance can often be more powerful. However, Beta's virtual mechanisms allow it to represent some things which are difficult in languages supporting multiple inheritance. A virtual pattern is a partial specification of a pattern. If a virtual pattern is a part of another pattern, it constitutes a partial description of its container's structure (and, therefore, makes its container a partial description); a partial description can be completed or instantiated.

Virtual patterns imply the ability to specialize their components. An incomplete pattern can be seen as something that is more general than those versions of it that have details filled in. When a virtual pattern that occurs as a part of another pattern is specialized, that virtual pattern can be given access to its container's component slots. In their paper on part objects, Madsen and Pedersen give the example of a *Person* pattern which contains a name and an address. The *address* attribute (slot) is filled with a virtual pattern of type *Address*. The *Address* type (pattern) is virtual and can be extended (specialized) by the provision of a *printLabel* method which prints the name of the instance of *Person*. This requires the specialization of the component and has little to do with the *Person* pattern. Note that we still need to define a new pattern in order to specialize *Address*, just as we would if we had multiple inheritance. The example shows that we can do some things with part objects that we can do with multiple inheritance.

Equally, a water-skiing accountant can be defined using part objects. We need a *Person* pattern which has two attributes, one to hold the occupation and one to hold the hobby (or preferred sport), in exactly the way that we saw when we originally motivated multiple inheritance. The difference is that we now view these slots as defining aspects of the *Person*, just as we would define perspectives in Braspenning and Bakker's INCA (see Bakker's dissertation [8] for details).

3. Prototype and Actor Languages

3.1 Introduction

In the last chapter, I introduced some of the fundámental concepts of class-based programming languages. The task of this chapter is to introduce two competing paradigms that are closely related to each other: prototype and Actor languages. Historically, prototype languages developed out of the concepts of Actor languages, but they will be considered in the reverse order because prototype-based languages are now an area of active research while Actors tend to be somewhat (unfairly, in our view) neglected.

Both prototype and Actor languages are based upon the idea of copying entities and communication by passing messages. These differences contrast strongly with class-based programming.

3.2 Prototype Languages

Prototype-based languages are based upon the idea that objects that represent individuals can be created without refcrence to class-defining; this clearly distinguishes prototype from class-based languages. When a class has been defined, it can be instantiated to create objects which can be manipulated by other program components. Prototype languages based upon the idea that objects can be directly manipulated and can be related by various similarity relations; inheritance is a static property between descriptions that is not employed by prototype-based languages. Instead, prototype languages work by a process of copying existing entities and modifying the copies to produce new entities with similar, but not identical properties. Sets of objects can be formed on the basis of their similarity along one or more dimensions; they can be formed dynamically. In a class-based language, similarity is based upon the inheritance relation.

In this section, I present the basic concepts behind prototype languages and then explore some of their implications. I will explain the concept of *delegation*, the prototype language's replacement for inheritance and see how it affects such matters as structure sharing and strong typing. I also consider the role of slots and methods in prototype languages and how prototypes can be created.

Prototype-based languages are far rarer than class-based ones. In many respects, prototype languages are still a research area; many issues remain open, in particular how to relate class- and prototype-based concepts into a single object-oriented style. Because they are simpler than class-based languages and because they are better suited to exploratory programming, it is to be expected that prototype languages will become more common in the future.

3.2.1 The Concept of the Prototype

There are at least two ways of considering concepts. The first is to treat them as logical entities. They can be defined and we can produce or find instances of them. Examples of such a view of concepts are numbers and polygons. When we encounter a new object, this view of concepts says that we apply the definition of the concept in order to determine whether the object falls within the concept. Thus, if we are interested in triangles, we would look to see whether the object is closed and has three sides (or, equivalently, check to see whether the sum of its internal angles is 180°). The logical definition of a concept treats it as if it had discrete and definite boundaries. For example, we can easily tell whether a closed figure has three sides; we can tell whether a number is whole and has a positive value (in which case, it is a natural number). A decision about concept membership always gives a definite answer (either "yes" or "no"—there is no "maybe").

If the world were always amenable to logical definitions of the kind just described, life would be so simple! Unfortunately, logical definitions do not always work. For example, it is extremely hard to tell the difference between a shrub and a bush. There is certainly a botanical definition, but for ordinary, everyday purposes, the distinction appears less than simple. The concepts "shrub" and "bush" do not appear to have the crisp boundaries that mathematical concepts have. The world is full of examples of such concepts. Colours are difficult to define and do not have crisp boundaries; tastes are also extremely difficult to capture, as are emotions. Indeed, most naturally occurring things fall within concepts that have fuzzy boundaries (think of "travelling fast" from the viewpoint of walking, roller skating, ice skating, skiing, driving a car, and flying a plane—each is relative). For this reason, concepts that lack crisp boundaries are often called *natural kinds*.

Concepts with crisp boundaries can be defined and the definition used to determine whether objects do or do not fall within the concept. With fuzzier natural kinds, a definition must, of necessity, omit some aspects of the concept; indeed, a definition might be controversial in the sense that some would argue that it should concentrate on some aspects, while others would emphasize other aspects. For this reason, the concept of a *prototype* [74] was proposed.

A prototype is a representative example of a concept, one that is usually considered to be central to the concept or what most people would agree is the concept. Consider the concept of a dog. We all agree upon what a dog is; when we talk (literally, not metaphorically) of dogs, we have no problem in understanding what is said. However, each of us, when asked, might produce a description of the "typical" dog that differs from everyone else's in some details. In an experiment, it was found that undergraduate students in Northern California have a prototypical dog that is somewhere between an Alsatian and a wolf. Each student in the study might, as an individual, possess a prototype that is slightly different, but the "average" of the students was the combination described in the last sentence. What is important is that each individual possesses a prototype and is able to determine how close an entity is to the prototype. Thus, for the Californian students, a Labrador will be a better match than a Boxer; a Labrador is large, has a relatively pointed snout and often has short hair, while a Boxer, though large, has a very short tail, no snout to speak of, a flat face and wiry legs. However, a Boxer still has many properties in common with the prototypical Alsatian/wolf. The 'distance' between an entity and a prototype tells how close to the concept the entity is; nearer entities are more clearly recognized as falling within the concept than are distant ones.

For prototypes, similarity is a central concept in classification. For logically defined concepts, definition is used to classify. An entity which is closer to the prototype is regarded as being more intimately part of the concept than one that is distant. Distance plays no part in logically defined concepts. With prototypes, we can say that one entity is more an exemplar of a given concept than is another; with logic, all we can say is that one entity falls within the concept while another does not. Prototypes are more flexible as a classification device.

It is extremely important to note that there might not be a prototype that represents a particular concept. The concept might be represented by some "average" of all the prototypes of a particular kind. Thus, classification in prototype-based systems is based upon approximations. Concepts in such systems tend to emerge rather than be defined. This has implications for the way in which such systems are built and analyzed. In particular, the concept of an abstract object might not apply to a prototype-based system as closely as it does in a class-based one. The import of an abstract class is to define a cluster of properties which together are necessary for the definition of other concepts; abstract classes cannot be instantiated. The lack of instances suggest that abstract classes represent concepts that are, in some sense, "incomplete" in that they require their specializations for completion. Since the concept of an abstract class implies a concept that cannot be instantiated, it appears that there could be no equivalent representation in a prototype-based system. Prototypes are all instances of at least one concept (it can be argued that a prototype can instantiate more than one concept), so break the fundamental requirement for abstract classes.

The idea of basing an object-oriented programming language on the concept of the prototype is due to Lieberman [55]. Until that time, all languages had been class-based, Smalltalk and Simula67 being the most famous examples. Lieberman observed that a language could be designed that was based upon the concepts of prototypes and distance rather than classes and instances. In a prototype-based language, there is no notion of instantiation, for prototypes exist as independent entities. In a logic-based description system, there is the distinction between a class (a definition) and its instances, but in a prototype-based system, there are just prototypes.

Everything, in a prototype system, is a prototype and is, therefore, an independent concept. In such systems, the objects that are manipulated at runtime (the objects that make it an "object-oriented" approach) are the prototypes. Prototypes are related to each other in various ways. Relatedness is derived from the distance between prototypes. In such a system, it is impossible to instantiate a prototype, for the concept has no meaning. Instead, what happens is that a prototype is cloned and then modified. Initially, the clone is identical to the prototype from which it was derived, but undergoes modification of some kind; this modification differentiates the clone from its prototype.

We need to clarify what is meant by a prototype. By a prototype object, we mean a collection of slots. The slots can contain data or methods (other distinctions can be made). The order in which the slots appear in the object is of no consequence, but their presence is. Each slot has a filler; that filler can be data or can be a method. In a prototype, method-containing slots are stored in the object, not stored in a separate table as in class-based programming. The set of slots and their fillers "defines" the prototype. The distance between two prototypes is determined by the number of slots that they have in common and the contents of those slots. If we have two prototypes, P_1 and P_2, such that P_1 contains s_{11}, s_{12}, s_{13} and s_{14}, while P_2 contains s_{21}, s_{12}, s_{13}, s_{22}, s_{23}, the common slots are s_{12} and s_{13}. If we now consider another prototype, P_3 with slots s_{11}, s_{12}, s_{31}, s_{32}, s_{33}, s_{34}, its intersection with P_1 is s_{11} and s_{12}, but it has an empty intersection with P_2. We can say that P_1 and P_2 are more closely related than P_1 and P_3; P_2 and P_3 are unrelated (see Figure 3.1).

The cloning method affords considerably greater flexibility in definition than does the class mechanism. For example, if we had a prototype representing Accountants, we might find that we need to model a new accountant, one who waterskis. It would be necessary, in a class-based system, to define an entirely new class to represent this new kind of Accountant. There would be a problem with instantiation because we would need to ensure that there was only one instance of the new class, but class-based languages provide no such support. Thus, we could have hundreds of Water-skiing Accountants in the program, with only one of them representing the one we want to model (the others must be fictional). In a prototype-based system, on the other hand,

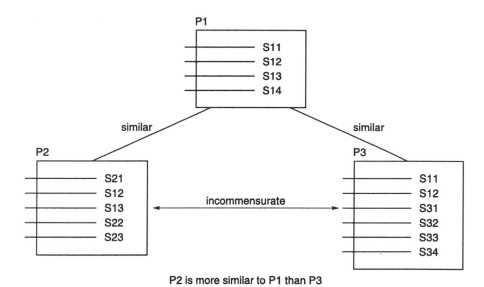

Fig. 3.1. P_2 *is more similar to* P_1 *than* P_3.

we first clone the Accountant prototype and then add a slot to represent this accountant's pastime (with filler *waterskiing*). We can, of course, clone the prototypical water-skiing accountant to produce more examples, each of which can serve as a prototype for other concepts. The different objects representing water-skiing accountants will differ in the name, so we might have one for Dave, Bill and Joe. When we clone the original prototype, we can change the fillers of its slots, so changing the name is possible. We might, then have started with Dave, a water-skiing accountant, and then discovered that Bill and Joe have a similar hobby. We can clone Dave and replace the filler of the clone's Name slot so that we name Bill and Joe.

We might also discover that Dave has two children, a boy and a girl, so we can add slots to describe this. Once these slots are defined, we have a prototype for *waterskiing accountant with two children*. This new prototype can be extended further when new objects are required or discovered. In each case, we clone the prototype that we have and add new slots and/or modify some of the existing slots. It is permitted to modify any slot in the prototype object: thus data and methods can be modified during the cloning operation. This allows the user (or a program, note) to alter prototypes as and when more information is available; it also allows the easy definition of new concepts when the need arises.

In some cases, one might want to clone a prototype a number of times, each time producing an exact copy of the prototype, and storing them in a container structure (e.g., a vector or a list). An example of such a process is the formation of a number of modules, each of which is used to store proto-

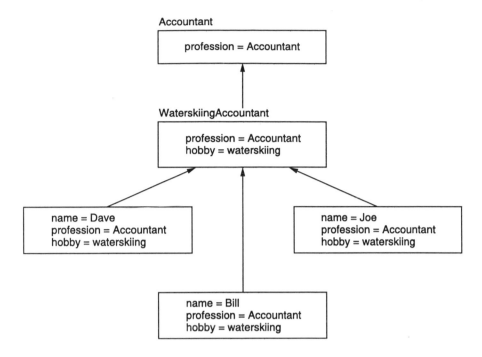

Fig. 3.2. *Prototypes and their relationships.*

types. Seemingly, each module will have an identical structure to the original prototype module. In a similar fashion, we might want to construct a number of stack prototypes by cloning an original stack object. Each stack, like each module, will be identical to the prototype (and each will be a prototype), but will have different contents. Difference of content is a valid way to distinguish between prototypes, as we saw with the examples of Dave, Bill and Joe, the water-skiing accountants. (Note that it makes the metric finer.)

Difference in the content of a prototype is employed as a way of distinguishing them. It can be used, on the other hand, as a way of classifying them. With a class-based representation, there is typically only a very few ways to classify an object. Usually, class-based systems base their classifications either on the inheritance relation or on a containment relation which relates two classes if one is used as a component of the other (cf. the part objects in Beta as well as slots in classes that are filled with instances of some class). This implies that class-based languages tend to classify objects in relatively few ways. Prototypes allow the classification of objects along multiple, simultaneous dimensions; classification is based upon similarity.

Thus, one might classify some objects in terms of their distance from some specially designated object. For example, given the accountants example above, we might select some object representing a particular accountant, one, say, who merely does his job and goes home (and has no exciting hobbies), and compare the objects representing water-skiiers, etc., with it. Accountant-representing objects are, presumably, derived from others, so we could select any of the objects used in the derivation of the accountant objects and classify with respect to them. We could select any of the properties represented by a set of prototypes and arrange them in some order; we can classify along any number of dimensions implied by the representation.

From a more systems-oriented perspective, there are other ways to classify an object if it is a prototype. For example, we can collect prototypes according to the slots they contain. If there is some slot of particular importance, it can be used to collect objects. If the author of a prototype is recorded, in a multi-programmer environment, it can be used to classify objects. The derivation of objects can also serve as a basis for collection and organization. This implies a considerable flexibility in prototypes that is seemingly lacking in class-based systems.

3.2.2 Slots and Methods

Prototypes are composed of slots. Slots, in this kind of language, are simpler than in class-based languages. Here, they are storage locations that are located in objects. Slots can be divided into two types: *data* and *method* slots. Data slots hold data items and method slots hold methods or routines. Access to slots in a prototype-based language is very often based on direct access and not on the reader/writer operations that are found in more modern class-based languages like Sather or Dylan. Methods, like data items, are directly stored in objects, so access to them is direct and based upon an object, not upon underlying tables (as is the case with the multi-methods in CLOS and virtual member functions in C++).

Data slots hold data items. Data items are just values such as integers, characters, strings and references to other objects (including the object itself). Data slots can be divided into *constant* and *mutable* slots. Constant slots are read-only, while mutable slots (sometimes called volatile slots) can be updated. When a slot is to be read, the object in which it is held is used for direct reading. In a similar fashion, when a mutable slot is to be written, the object in which it is held is first accessed and the slot is then directly updated; the update is applied to the object's structure.

Methods are stored exactly like data values. When a method is to be executed, it is extracted from the object in which the method resides. Sometimes, methods will be shared between objects, so it is to be expected that method slots will contain pointers. In [66], methods are represented by objects. This enables methods to be treated like other kinds of object (an approach to representation that was employed by Smalltalk-80 [40]) and to be allocated in a uniform fashion. Under this representation, when a method is to be invoked, its object is first accessed and the *apply* method in that object is then called to apply the method body to its arguments. It is usual for method slots to be volatile for the reason that other operations on prototypes can change (redefine) the method that is stored in the slot.

Sometimes slots are divided into *private* and *public*. A private slot is one that can only be accessed by methods and slots in the same object. A public slot is one that can be accessed by anything. Private slots are useful for hiding information that is of a partial nature (intermediate results) and can assist in ensuring modularity.

Slots are represented in a more straightforward way in prototype languages than in class-based ones. The primary reason for this is the way in which objects are created and shared.

3.2.3 Message Passing

Like Smalltalk, many prototype-based languages are based upon message passing. Messages are used to invoke methods stored in slots. Messages contain routing information, together with the parameters to be supplied to the method when it is found. The routing information consists of the name of the object to which the message is to be sent and the name of the method which is to be applied to the parameters. In fact, it is strictly incorrect to talk of the "name" of the method, for the method is indicated by an identifier called the selector.

A method selector often corresponds to the name of the slot in which the method is located in the receiving object. However, this is not necessarily the case. In Smalltalk, for instance, each class is associated with a method table that collects the class's methods into one place so that they can be located easily and quickly. The method table is indexed by the selectors declared by the class, so the table maps selectors into method objects (in Smalltalk, methods are represented by objects residing in the object memory). There is no real reason why the selector used to locate a method should be the name of the slot in which the method is stored; if that slot is ever renamed, the selector will have to be renamed as well. Typically, though, the selector is the slot name.

Messages in some languages follow the Smalltalk model and are represented by objects. This permits the interface to messages to be uniform across all message types; the interface determines the operations that can be performed on the message in order to extract the various pieces of information that it contains. Thus, the method object specifies a method which returns the name of the destination object, the selector and the various arguments. Message objects also allow the specification of a uniform method for interpreting them; objects are required to support methods for the application of method code to parameters, as well, if appropriate, as methods for obtaining methods via *delegation*.

There is no absolute reason for implementing method invocation as message passing. However, an approach based on message passing leads automatically to a more uniform interface for method invocation. Messages also allow more flexible kinds of control structure (as observed by Hewitt [47]) and also allow mechanisms such as broadcast to be implemented. Message passing also presents another opportunity for computational reflection (see Chapter 8, below).

3.2.4 Creating New Objects

In class-based languages, new objects are created by the instantiation of classes. In a classless approach such as prototype-based languages, there are no classes to instantiate. Instead, two mechanisms are usually provided:

- a mechanism for creating completely new objects, and
- a mechanism for copying existing objects.

The first mechanism is employed when there is no existing prototype upon which to base the definition of a new object. The second mechanism is the one that is most commonly used. Objects are usually constructed by cloning (or copying) existing objects and then modifying the copy.

When an object is created afresh, it is defined in terms of its slots and the values and methods that fill them. The programmer must create the object, name it (perhaps), and specify its slots. Once this has been done, the object is ready for use by the program.

More often, new objects are created from old ones using a variety of the copy-and-edit method often used to modify other kinds of document. This method is the object cloning method. When an object is cloned, a copy is made of it. The copy can then be modified in a variety of ways:

- values stored in data slots can be changed;
- constant slots can be made mutable (and vice versa);
- methods can be redefined;
- slots can be added or removed (both data and method slots can be so modified).

If the language supports them, private slots might be made public, and vice versa. Note that languages differ in the range of operations they permit on cloned objects.

Sometimes an object needs only to be copied, not modified. It is possible for many copies of a prototype to exist at the same time. Such multiple copies will be distinguished by their names (at the very least, the runtime system will employ unique names for each object).

When an object is defined by cloning and modifying another object, the modified clone is often called the *child* and the object that was cloned the *parent*. A reference to the parent object is often stored in the child.

In the original paper on prototype languages [55], it is stated that an object can be constructed from more than one prototype or parent. In such a case, each prototype will contribute some slots to the resulting object; the resulting object will also contain some methods from the objects which were composed in order to form it. In the SELF language [25], perhaps the most famous prototype language, objects tend to be constructed by cloning a single parent; I have [29] proposed a set of operations for the construction of new objects, some of which require there to be more than one parent.

As an example of the cloning process, let us consider the following derivation of the *waterskiing accountant* object we saw above. Let us assume that there is a *Person* object that serves to represent people in general. This object might contain slots to hold the name, address, sex and date of birth of the person that it represents. We might extend the *Person* object to create the Accountant object by first cloning it and then adding a *profession* slot whose value will be set to accountant. Next, we clone the *Accountant* object and add a slot to represent the person's hobbies, filling it with the value *waterskiing* (people tend to have more than one hobby, so the *hobbies* slot should probably be filled with a set of values). The value in the *hobbies* slot might be a string or symbol, or it might be a reference to another object; here, if the filler is an object pointer, the pointer will refer to an object that describes what waterskiing is about. If we desire, we can also add slots that will contain further information about accountants.

If we want to introduce a new profession, say *Dentist*, all we need do is to clone the *Accountant* object and change the *profession* slot's value to *dentist*. This will create a prototype dentist object. It will be necessary to remove all slots that are specific to accountants and to replace them with slots specific to the representation of dentists. The removal of slots leads to a change from a prototype structure to one that is more akin to a class; this process might lead to a transformation to a more rigid implementation (and relates prototypes and classes), but remains an idea for research.

3.2.5 Delegation and Shared Structure

When defining a new object, it does not always make sense to remove slots. Sometimes, it is best to add slots, making the clone more specific in an obvious way. Similarly, it does not always make sense to copy method slots. When slots that are part of the definition of an object are omitted, it is necessary to provide access to them in some way. In prototype-based languages, the operation of delegation performs this task; delegation replaces inheritance in this species of language.

Requests made to objects contain references to slots. If the slot is not present in an object, the request can be delegated to another object. Typically, requests are delegated to the parents of the object to which the request was originally made. If the immediate parent of the object does not contain the slot, the request is delegated to the parent's parent. This process continues all the way along the chain of parents. When the slot is encountered, the value which it stores is returned as the reply to the request. If the slot contains a method, the method is called and produces a value which is then returned.

If a slot with the same name as that mentioned in a request is present in the object to which the request is first sent, the value stored in that slot is returned as the result of the request (or the method it contains is evaluated to produce the result). If that slot is also present in the object's parent, the value in the parent is ignored in favour of the one stored in the object to which the request was made. This is analogous to the case with inheritance.

Delegation is an extremely powerful mechanism. Part of its power is derived from the fact that it can operate on mutable as well as constant slots. Inheritance is based upon a static (constant) relationship between classes. The relationship between classes is fixed when they are defined and cannot be changed at runtime. Delegation can operate on slots that are assignable. It is possible in some prototype-based languages to change the value of the slot being used to perform delegation, typically the parent slot. This means that the parents of an object, in a prototype-based system, can be changed at runtime, giving, thereby, access to different objects at different times. This means that requests can be interpreted in different ways at different times. This property is sometimes called *dynamic inheritance* or *computed delegation*.

Some languages require delegation to be based upon a single slot. In the SELF language [25], for example, the *parents* slot is used for delegation. In this case, the object pointed to by the *parents* slot is the next to be examined when searching for a slot. Slots can contain references to objects as well as data values such as integer or character; objects held in any slot can, in principle, be used for delegation. Some languages allow delegation to be based on the value of an arbitrary slot, while others, like SELF, require a special slot to be updated in order to achieve the equivalent result. Indeed, the value which is used for delegation can be computed by a method. This makes for a highly flexible and extremely powerful method for accessing non-local information.

It has been argued by Stein [84] that delegation is no more than inheritance and that the latter is a more powerful mechanism. When restricted to using constant slots, delegation would appear, indeed, to be a form of inheritance. However, the addition of dynamic delegation would seem to make it more powerful than inheritance. Inheritance can be simulated, at a cost, by delegation, but, in its full form, not vice versa.

The above argument works well when objects are considered as individuals. The result of cloning an object is another object. The fundamental idea of prototype languages is that a prototype is cloned in order to produce a new individual from which other prototypes can be cloned; every object, fundamentally, is considered to be an individual and to have individual properties. Individuals very often share properties. Shared properties are very easy to implement in an inheritance-based environment; a class is defined which represents the shared properties and subclasses are defined for the individuals. The need for the representation of shared structure that is akin to classes has posed a significant problem for prototype-based languages.

The prototype-based language SELF introduces the concept of a *traits* object. A traits object is employed to represent those properties (slots and methods) that are common to a set of related objects. The usual example given in the literature is of points on a two-dimensional plane. In a prototype language, points are represented by independent objects, one for each point. A *Point* object has a mutable slot for each of the x and y components of a co-ordinate. Every *Point* object has, as its parent, a *Point traits* object which represents everything that is common to all points. For example, the Point traits object will have a method for adding and subtracting points and for printing points. Modifications to the Point traits object will be automatically propagated to the individual points.

The result of adding a traits object to a prototype-based system is to introduce something akin to a class, but one which operates by delegation.

The traits approach to common structure is not the only one to be found in the literature. A notable alternative is that adopted by Taivalsaari in his Kevo language [93, 94]. Traits is very powerful, but structure and contents are the individual properties of every single object. Global changes to the structure of all objects of a particular kind are not very easy to apply when using delegation [84]; global changes of this kind are very easy to apply in class-based languages by defining an appropriate class.

The Kevo language was designed specifically to overcome this problem with delegation-based prototypes. It is based upon two fundamental mechanisms: *concatenation* and *module operations*. These two mechanisms define the structure and behaviour of objects. Paradoxically, Kevo achieves its goals by treating objects as individuals. Kevo regards shared structure as an implementation problem. The concatenation concept involves the addition of new slots to an existing set; the concept of *prefixing* in Simula later evolved into the concept of inheritance, was originally defined in terms of textual concatenation of program blocks.

Every Kevo object can be considered to be a complete set of all the properties associated with all of its parent objects. This means that Kevo objects are entirely self-contained and no parent relation is required to express inter-object derivation relationships.

Kevo objects can be constructed in the two ways described above. They can be created anew by the specification of slots and methods. Alternatively, they can be created by cloning and modification. When cloned, all properties (slots and methods) of an object are copied. Then, modifications can be made to the new object; the modifications are called *module operations*. The module operations that can be performed on an object are:

- add slot to the object;
- remove a slot from an object;
- rename a slot;
- hide a slot (i.e., make it invisible to clients; make it private to the object);
- show a slot (i.e., make it visible to clients; make it public);

- redefine a slot.

The operations listed above apply to a single object. There are variations which operate on all objects of the same kind (a clone family) or to larger groups of objects. The extended variations operate on the collections that Kevo uses in representing shared structure.

After cloning an object, it can be acted upon by one or more of the above module operations. Each of the operations changes the structure of the object; no other object is altered by the application of one of these operations.

The problem of handling shared structure is solved in Kevo by means of a dependency mechanism which records the derivation of an object. The mechanism records those objects which have been involved in the successive transformation of one object into another. This enables the system automatically to maintain clone families of objects—collections of objects that are cloned from the same source. The user has the choice of modifying one or more of the objects in a clone family, a property which distinguishes it from delegation which would require modification of all objects. By using the concept of a clone family, a single operation can be made to apply to many objects.

Similarly, module operations can be applied to larger collections of objects. The Kevo system provides an object called *Root* which divides the system into distinct subtrees that hold different kinds of object. The different kinds are maintained in a part/part-of hierarchy. For example, the *Root* object contains a reference to the *Prototypes* object which contains references to the *Object*, *Array* and *Set* objects. The user can attach their own objects to this hierarchy. Module operations can be performed on these objects and the objects derived from them; the larger group operations apply to them. As stated, the hierarchy of objects stored under *Root* is maintained by the user while the organization describing clone families is maintained by the system.

In the Omega language [11], a prototype serves as the basis for the production of clones. Clones are copies of the prototype; they are members of the same "family" of entities whose structure and behaviour is defined by their prototype. Cloning is the operation that is most commonly performed at runtime. Objects are cloned from a prototype whenever a new object of that family is needed by the computation. If the programmer needs a new object with properties that are slightly different from one of the existing prototypes, the existing prototype is copied and modified to produce a new prototype. The prototype which formed the basis of the new one remains unchanged; when a new prototype is defined in terms of an old one, the old one is copied so that it cannot be changed. That new prototype can serve as the basis for cloning. The definition of a new prototype is a separate, interactive operation which is performed by the programmer, *not* at runtime as the standard mechanism for creating objects. Should a prototype be modified by the programmer (and it can only be performed by the programmer in Omega), the changes are automatically propagated by the Omega system to all the prototypes that are defined in terms of the one that has been changed. If the programmer needs a completely new kind of operation, it can be defined as a *prototype* which can be treated like all other prototypes and, therefore, can be used as the basis for cloning at runtime.

Omega also attempts to ameliorate another problem with delegation. When an object is defined by delegation, its interface is not its own. The slots that are local to an object are part of the interface, but also the slots that are present in the object from which it was cloned. When a parent object is modified (an operation which, in an interactive environment, can occur at the same time as one of the parent object's methods is being executed), the interface can be changed to a considerable extent. Equally, two objects that start out with the same interface can be modified to such an extent that their interfaces no longer remain compatible. This implies that delegation and individual alteration of objects precludes static typing. Prototype-based languages for this reason are often associated with dynamic typing and with an exploratory programming style. Omega, using its version of inheritance and two creation methods, supports static typing of its slots.

In each case, the semantics of method application in SELF, Kevo and Omega is different from that found in class-based languages. In a class-based language, when a message is sent to an instance of a class, the required method is obtained using inheritance if necessary and applied to the message. The first argument of every method is implicitly a variable which refers to the instance to which the invoking message was sent (compilers usually insert this variable automatically). When the message is received, the method is applied to it and its first argument is bound to the receiving object. In other words, the *self* or *this* pseudo-variable that can be used in method bodies is always bound to the receiver of a call; this permits the method to access the receiver's local slots and methods.

In a prototype-based language, the method that is to be invoked is first located and is then returned to the sender of the message. The method is then applied to the sending object. The *self* or *this* pseudo-variable is bound to the sender, not the receiver. It is necessary to make some minimal assumptions about the structure of senders when defining methods for use by prototypes.

3.3 Methods in Prototype Languages

Prototype-based languages, as should now be clear, do not support inheritance. Instead, they employ delegation and cloning as alternative mechanisms. When an object is cloned, its methods will be automatically available to its progeny. This means that all the methods of a parent will be available to all of its offspring. It is possible to remove methods from prototypes, so there is the freedom to remove as well as to redefine methods.

Delegation, particularly computed delegation, allows a prototype access to a further repertoire of methods. Computed delegation allows an object to determine at runtime which methods it should invoke. These clearly indicate a more flexible mode of operation, and it must be remembered that all methods are invoked in the context of the delegating object (caller). This solves a number of problems with respect to free variables.

The SELF language, like Smalltalk, makes extensive use of block expressions. This makes it possible in SELF to make extensive use of higher-order functions. In particular, it makes possible the updating of the delegating object's slots with blocks and it makes it also possible for the delegating object (or the delegated object) to influence the behaviour of methods by supplying functional arguments. Blocks can interact with computed delegation by providing a block that determines the object to which to delegate; the algorithm can be changed by supplying a different block.

As noted when introducing prototype-based languages, methods are always executed in the context of the object that is engaging in delegation. Thus, the initiator of a request to delegate is the object which is bound to the *self* pseudo-variable, thus permitting the method to gain direct access to the delegator's local slots and ancestors. This contrasts with the case for class-based languages in which the self variable is bound to the receiver of the message or request to call a method. For class-based languages, methods can always access the local slots and inheritance structure of the object whose method is called, *not* the object which is calling the method. This difference has implications for modularity and for the way in which methods must be written. Clearly, in a class-based language, slots and inheritance structure can be made completely invisible to all other entities in a program or system. In prototype-based languages, such protection cannot be assured for methods must be able to access slots and methods in the caller; this is the opposite of what one expects from the rule of static scoping. Methods, in prototype languages, impose a structure on the objects which use them; this is a dual way to view the issue.

3.4 Actor Languages

3.4.1 Introduction

Hewitt (e.g., [47]) conceived of and developed the Actor methodology as an attempt to understand complex parallel systems. As part of this work, concepts were developed to describe concurrent computations that were fundamentally expressed in terms of message passing and simple computational entities. The Actor methodology is very powerful and can also be used to describe the semantics of many programming language constructs. Actor theory explains computation in terms of the exchange of information in the form of messages between computational entities called *actors*. The entities are caused to act when they receive messages, thus introducing the concept of causality into the description of programming structures. Work on Actor theory and on areas that developed from it has led to the introduction of concepts such as future; it also relies upon and develops concepts such as continuation.

Actors work in ways that are similar to prototype languages. The concept of delegation is central to the concept of an actor, just as it is to the concept of a prototype. In Actor languages, delegation is more general than in prototype languages because it is not restricted to the parents (if there are any) of the actor that is engaged in delegation. Even though Actors are relatively old as a research area, they still remain thought provoking. Work on Actors still continues at a number of sites world-wide.

In this section, I will first outline the fundamental concepts of the Actor methodology. As part of this, I describe concepts which are related to those discussed in the second section of this chapter. Next, I will consider some ways in which actors can be generalized. In particular, I will consider how message passing can be generalized and on how scope rules can be used to provide defaults in distributed systems.

3.4.2 Actors

In this section, I will define what an Actor is and what it does. I will also consider how actors are connected and perform complex actions. I will use the account of actors proposed by Agha [2, 1]; later, I will look at the original proposals made by Hewitt [47].

Fundamentally, an actor is a entity that can engage in computation. Each actor is known by a unique name, often called its *address*. Actors respond to *messages* which are sent to them by other actors and from sources outside an actor system. Messages are sent to a unique address; the Actor model does not permit broadcast or multicast messages. In order to send a message, an actor must know the address of the actor to which it intends to send the message. Each actor is associated with a collection of addresses of other actors (it implicitly knows its own address). The other actors are called the *acquaintances* of the actor; actors can send messages to (communicate directly with) their acquaintances. If actor A has actor B as an acquaintance, A can send messages to B, but B cannot send A messages unless A is an acquaintance of B (and it need not be); actors can receive messages from other actors of whose existence they are ignorant.

A collection of actors is shown in Figure 3.3. The figure shows directed arcs connecting the actors. The arrow on the arc shows the direction in which messages can pass between a pair of actors. If two actors can mutually communicate, there are two directed arcs connecting them. We have labelled the arcs with strings, each string denoting the symbolic identifier by which the acquaintance is known in the actor from which the arc emanates. When there is no connection between a pair of actors, there is no communication between them.

Messages contain data upon which the recipient can perform computation. They can also contain the address of an actor to which the results of the computation caused by reception of the message can be sent. The specification of an actor to whom results are to be sent is called a *continuation*. Actors specified as continuations need not be acquaintances of the actor performing the computation.

The set of acquaintances an actor possesses is not necessarily static. It is possible for an actor to add to its collection of acquaintances. Other actors can send messages containing the addresses of other actors; the receiver of these messages can extract the addresses and add them to its list of acquaintances. Thereafter, the actor can use these new names just like any other acquaintance. Similarly, an actor can discard acquaintances, for example when it receives messages saying that they have terminated.

An actor is associated with a FIFO (First In, First Out) message queue. This is where messages to an actor are held. A fundamental assumption of the Actor model is that message delivery is guaranteed. In early versions of the model, there was no assumption that messages would be delivered in the correct order; thus, if message 1 is sent before message 2, there would be no guarantee that they would arrive in that order. However, this assumption is too strict and severely restricts the range of computations that can be performed with actors; without the assumption, actors are Turing equivalent in the sense that any function computable on a Turing machine can be computed on an appropriate collection of actors.

An actor can therefore be considered to be a pair. One component of the pair is its message queue, the other is the mechanism which provides it with a behaviour. The behaviour is what is exhibited by an actor when it receives a message that it understands. We can think of the behaviour as being the methods which the actor executes when it receives a message that it understands. When an actor does not understand a message, a number of possibilities exist. First, it could signal an error. Second, it could return the message to the sender (assuming sender addresses are stored in messages). Thirdly, it can forward the message to one of its acquaintances in the hope that the acquaintance will be able to respond to it. This third option is called *delegation*.

Delegation is the response of an actor to a message to which the receiver cannot immediately respond. Having ascertained that it cannot respond itself to the message, the actor, A, forwards it to another actor, B, in the hope that the second actor is able to perform some computation on the message. Actor B performs some computation, which might include delegation, and returns a result to A. Actor A can then respond to the original message in an appropriate fashion. The delegation of a message is shown diagrammatically in Figure 3.3.

Delegation acts in a way similar to inheritance in a class-based language. Inheritance is, however, a static relation between classes and it is not possible to alter the relation at runtime. Thus, if class C is a subclass of S, it is impossible to alter its inheritance links so that C becomes a subclass of S_1.

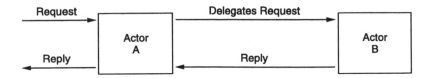

Fig. 3.3. *Delegation and reply in Actors.*

Ordinary delegation works in an equally fixed mode; it is the process of sending messages to an acquaintance in order for computation to be performed by the acquaintance. However, it is possible for an actor to perform some computation in order to determine the actor to which it should delegate a message. The computation might be based upon information contained in the current message or on information stored in the actor but not included in the list of acquaintances. In the latter case, one might see this as a form of making acquaintances explicit. By performing computation, an actor is able to extend the range of its *potential* acquaintances (after performing the computation, the result, the address of the actor to which to delegate, might be discarded—this is why we refer to them as *potential* acquaintances). Messages can explicitly contain the address of an actor to which it should be delegated; the continuation is one example of how addresses in messages can be used. When an actor receives such a message, it might examine the message and determine that it can do nothing with it; it then takes the actor address from the message and forwards the message to this other actor. The actor address contained in the message might be stored by the receiver to become a permanent acquaintance.

The behaviour of an actor is its response to a particular message. Sometimes actors are described as being purely functional in nature, while, at others, they are procedural, at least in part. A purely functional account of actors requires each actor to be side-effect free; that is, functional actors can only engage in message passing, value binding and *behavioural replacement*. Behavioural replacement occurs when a message is received by an actor. It is the operation by which an actor replaces its current behaviour and creates an actor with a new behaviour that is intended to handle the computational situation demanded by the latest message; the actor is then free to behave as it did before the message arrived. This has the implication that the actions a functional actor performs are based upon the messages that it receives because it is typical for the reception of a message to cause replacement of behaviour. When an actor replaces its behaviour, it can replace it with the same behaviour it had before; this allows an actor to respond in the same way to every message.

Let us consider the factorial actor in more detail as an example of actor programming. The actor always expects its input messages to contain a number and a continuation. The number is the value to be input to the factorial computation and the continuation says where the result is to be sent. The behaviour of the actor depends upon the message that is received and is as follows. If the message contains a continuation c and the value zero, the actor sends the value one back to c and waits for the next message. If the message contains a continuation, c, and a value, n, that is greater than zero, it creates a new actor which is an instance of the multiplication actor and sends it the value contained in the message, n, together with the continuation, c, from that message. The address of the newly created multiplication actor, m, is bound to a local variable which enables the factorial actor to send itself a message containing the multiplication actor as continuation and $n - 1$ as value. If the value of $n - 1$ is greater than zero, a new multiplication actor is created and sent $n - 1$ as its value and m as its continuation; the new multiplication actor then becomes the continuation for a message to the factorial actor.

The multiplication is defined as follows. On creation, it accepts two arguments: one denoting a numerical value and one denoting a continuation. The continuation denotes the actor to which the result of the multiplication is to be sent. The multiplication actor then waits for a message containing a value. It multiplies the value in the message with the one supplied when it was created and then sends a message to the continuation containing the product.

When computing factorial, recursion is replaced by actor creation. The value whose factorial is to be computed denotes the number of multiplication actors required to compute the result. Thus, for 3!, 3 multiplication actors are required; for 12!, there will be 12. In addition, there is an original continuation actor which is to receive the result of the factor calculation.

Some might find the above example hard to follow. When programming with actors, it is very much the case that everything that one has previously learned about programming must be forgotten in favour of a completely new way of thinking. The key to the factorial actor is that it creates an actor to perform each multiplication; each multiplication actor is supplied with the address of the actor which is to receive the result of its computation. This leads to a chain of actors, each waiting for the value output by the one before it; for actor n, the previous actor is responsible for computing the product representing $(n - 1)!$ Even though the principle might be relatively simple, it is not totally obvious; actor programming can be difficult because of the large amounts of parallelism that are possible.

Procedural actors are permitted to have an internal state, so behavioural replacement is not required. Hewitt's PLASMA [47] is an example of a more procedural account of actors, as are the ABCL languages [101]. Here, an actor is permitted to contain local read-write variables and is permitted to update these variables when required. This contrasts with functional actors whose variables are read only and have the single assignment property (they can be assigned to, or bound, only once). With a procedural actor, recursive message passing is still permitted (this is how the factorial actor worked, recall). The state of an actor now depends upon the state of its local variables, not just on the sequence of messages it has received. This has the implication that the state of an actor can be altered by assigning to its local variables; thus, when an actor sends a message to itself, the interpretation of that message can be altered by the state of the actor's local variables.

For example, a procedural factorial actor can store the result of the previous factorial in the sequence in a local variable, thus allowing the removal of the multiplication actor from the solution. However, a procedural factorial actor will be restricted to computing one factorial at a time whereas the functional one could compute many for the reason that each independent computation will have a distinct continuation. The functional actor does not store internal, intermediate state, but the procedural one does; the intermediate state held by the procedural version implies that, should a new request to compute a separate factorial arrive, the procedural actor will either have to make it wait until the current one is complete, or it must replace its behaviour so that it can handle the request. In this case, behavioural replacement will be made on the assumption that the computation of one factorial can be separated from the computation of another. Thus, when a new request comes in, the factorial actor must divide so that the current calculations become an independent process and the new calculation can be started.

The state of an actor computation is often distributed among a number of actors. This is reasonable because the Actor model is a model of naturally concurrent computation. This fact has implications for the description of a computation that is performed by a collection of actors and for the description of how the system operates. Actors work by exchanging messages; reception of a message causes the actor to change its state. The influence of one actor upon another is, therefore, assumed to be causal in nature. The state of an actor system at runtime is dependent upon the messages that have been exchanged by the actors in the system; when the actors are procedural, the state is also partially determined by the state of each actor's local variables. The state is, however, distributed; this is a fundamental property of actor systems. The local state of an actor depends upon the messages it has received and, in the case of procedural actors, upon the results they have returned. Actor-based programs tend to have very simple components that are assembled in complex ways; the complexity of the resulting behaviour is a direct result of the complex interactions between simple components.

3.4.3 Extensions to the Actor Concept

Actors have been highly influential, both as a proposal for practical concurrent programming and as a theory of computation. Since the publication of [47], there has been a considerable amount written and published about actors. Agha's work, in particular his book [2] and many of his papers (see the UIUC Web or FTP site) and the paper [3], show that Actors is not, as some might think, a dead area; on the contrary, it still attracts attention. For example, Briot, in a series of papers [14], has shown how the actors model can be embedded to advantage in the more conventional environment of Smalltalk. My own work on reflection [33, 31, 32] has been, in part, inspired by the Actor concept.

Further evidence of the viability of actors can be seen from the work of Yonezawa *et al.* on their ABCL languages [101], and, more recently, the Obliq language [22] of Cardelli, a language designed for distributed programming environments such as the Internet. I will briefly consider each of these developments in turn, for they show a different approach to object-oriented programming languages.

The ABCL languages [101] are actor-based and clearly object-oriented. These languages are procedural in nature in order, according to [101], to make them easier to use. They allow objects to be created by instantiation and objects can contain references to other objects in local variables; local variables describe the local state of an object and are invisible to everything outside of the object in which they reside. Objects in ABCL form visibility barriers. An assignment mechanism is provided to update local variables. There are no global variables. The ABCL languages are pure object-oriented languages, therefore.

Within an object, messages are received and interpreted in terms of patterns. The handling of messages in this way dates back to PLASMA [47] and makes it considerably easier to write message-handling code and to understand what the form of a message is. The patterns are associated with sequences of actions which are performed if the latest input message matches the pattern. The patterns are evaluated in turn until one matches the message. When the pattern is matched, the corresponding action sequence is executed to elicit either a change of the internal state of the object or to send a message to another object (or both). Matching of the patterns is required to be sequential from the top of the object to the bottom ("top" and "bottom" being defined in terms of the appearance of the object on the page). Thus, the reception of a message can cause the internal state of an object to change, just as it can cause the external state of the system of objects to change.

One immediate observation that can be made about an object, and about actors in a notation like PLASMA, and which can be disguised in languages like Act1, [56], is that they resemble an ordered sequence of production rules. A production rule is an *if-then* construct often found in Artificial Intelligence [97, 31, 32]. What makes an actor different from a collection of rules is that such actors have local variables which are used in the component rules.

A distinction is made in ABCL/1 between a *dormant* (or waiting) and an *active mode*. When an object is in the former mode, it is waiting for messages and is inactive. When in the active mode, an object is performing actions and processing messages. If, at the end of processing a message, there are no more messages in the object's input queue, it enters the dormant mode, otherwise it remains active until all of its messages are processed. An object remains dormant until it receives a message. Sometimes, however, an object needs to enter the waiting mode and wait for a particular message or for particular messages. In ABCL/1, this transition is achieved by means of a *select* statement similar to that in Ada [9]. The ABCL/1 select statement is pattern-based and conforms to the same syntax as the body of an object. The idea is that the object enters the select statement which then puts it into a waiting state. If a message that matches any of the select statement's patterns arrives, the object becomes active once again and processes that message.

ABCL/1 enriches the ability of objects when sending messages by introducing different kinds of message-passing style. In addition, there are two ways to send a message in this language. First, messages can be sent in either the *ordinary* or *express* modes. Objects have two message queues, one for each of the two delivery modes. When an object receives a message in express mode, if that receiving object is already active, the actions it is performing are suspended until it has handled the express message. When the express message has been dealt with, the suspended actions are resumed; there is an option to abort suspended actions, but the default is for their resumption. If an object is in the express mode and is, therefore, handling an express message, any newly arrived express messages are placed at the end of the object's express message queue. Ordinary mode messages obey the protocol described in the previous paragraph; the arrival of an ordinary mode message causes an object to enter the active mode if it is dormant; otherwise, the message is placed at the end of the object's ordinary message queue.

The language also introduces three ways in which a message can be sent. The three ways are called *Past, Now* and *Future* in [101]. *Past* message passing corresponds to the normal way of sending messages in actor languages. That is, past message passing is an asynchronous transmission of a message; the message is stored in the receiving object's message queue when it arrives at its destination. Yonezawa *et al.* [101] state that they assume that message arrival order is the same as transmission order, an assumption originally missing from the actor model (a point mentioned above). *Now* message passing is, basically, synchronized message transmission in which the receiver acknowledges receipt; it can be considered as a form of remote procedure call (RPC). The sender and receiver synchronize in order to exchange the message. When the receiver has received the message, it returns a result to the sender of the message and the two objects continue on their separate ways.

The final kind of message passing protocol, the so-called *Future* protocol might not be as familiar to readers as the other two kinds. Future message passing is similar to the Now protocol, but differs in that the sender does not, at the time the message is sent, require an immediate result. The sender continues with its computation immediately. When the sender of the message needs the result, it checks a special variable that is associated with the, as yet, unsatisfied, request; if that variable contains a result, it is employed in the remainder of the computation. This mechanism is similar, but not identical, to the *future* construct employed in some concurrent LISP dialects [41]. In these LISPs, the result of a computation need not be returned immediately but a future can be returned in order to stand for the value in later computations; when the value represented by the future is required, the future is required to compute the value (or *forced*). With futures, the caller demands the execution of the process that will produce the result and waits until the future is able to return a meaningful value; with the future message passing protocol, the producer binds the result to a variable supplied by the consumer and the consumer must wait for that variable to become bound to a meaningful value. The two mechanisms, seen this way, are dual.

The ABCL languages started with a relatively straightforward concurrent programming language. Since then, reflection and distributed programming have been of interest to the ABCL group and later versions [100] have been heavily influenced by the need to perform reflection, particularly in a distributed environment.

The Obliq language was developed by Cardelli at DEC Research [22] as a language for distributed programming. A modern distributed processing environment will be composed of servers of various kinds, one of which will be a *code server*; a server that delivers pieces of code which can be integrated into other applications. Obliq provides support for code servers by permitting pieces of code, methods, to be exchanged between objects. The language is one in which the copying of objects is performed rather than instantiation; messages can be used to change the values stored in an object's slots. The copying operation does not permit the user to add or remove slots from an object. The language is, therefore, close to actor languages and also close to prototype-based languages, though it lacks some of the features found in the latter. The language is completely different from class-based languages because no inheritance structure is defined. Obliq uses a form of delegation. Obliq permits objects to migrate from one site to another, i.e., from one processor-memory pair to another; this has consequences for the variable binding strategy used in the language for the reason that free variables must be captured somewhere.

At one stage in the development of the actor model, messages were also referred to as "actors" (for example, [47] does this). In [3], Agha *et al.* make the observation that there are problems in allowing messages to contain arbitrary code. The reason for this is that they will contain variables which must be bound; if they are unbound, they will constitute "holes" in the messages, and these holes might be erroneously bound to strange values in the receiving environment. Similarly, mobile Obliq objects might contain free variables which might be erroneously bound in a receiving environment. To solve these problems, Obliq employs a rigid lexical scope rule. Thus, free variables in messages and objects are bound to values in the defining environment, not in the receiving one. This permits messages and objects to be sent with impunity across a network.

Obliq shows that actor concepts are still part of current research. Indeed, as time passes, problems observed with actors are being solved. The actor approach has, in addition, been the source of the prototype-based programming approach. The reason is that the concept of delegation employed in prototype languages is a direct descendant of that in actor languages, and the idea of creating new objects by copying and then modifying them is also an actor-based concept. In an actor language, new objects are created by copying existing ones and then sending them messages containing the values of what amount to instance variables (acquaintances, as well as other values).

4. Inheritance and Delegation

4.1 Introduction

Inheritance in its simplest form is performed by classes in class-based programming languages. Languages based upon prototypes support a mechanism called delegation which appears to be more general and, in some ways, more fundamental than inheritance. Inheritance, though, is an extremely important concept and is found in many computer systems (the X-windows system, for example), as well as object-oriented languages.

The simplest form of inheritance, simple or single inheritance was discussed in a little detail in Chapter 2 above (Chapter 2, Section 2.8). My aim here is to introduce multiple inheritance, the generalization of single inheritance and to discuss its properties and problems. I will, as a consequence, need to introduce the concept of a *mixin*, a class that is introduced into the inheritance lattice with the sole purpose of combining superclasses. A discussion of mixins naturally concerns abstract classes, so I consider their behaviour under inheritance as well. As part of the discussion of multiple inheritance, I will present a number of algorithms for performing inheritance, and I will see that there is little agreement as to what the correct approach is. This naturally leads to the question as to whether there are alternatives to multiple inheritance. As a partial reply, I will return to the concept of delegation in prototype-based languages and will see that it is similar, yet better behaved. I will also consider the case of mixins under delegation and will see that they form a natural method for combining properties in a prototype-based language. I will, next, consider an interesting proposal that single inheritance be made fundamental and that other properties reveal an underlying conception in which perspectives are important. I next take a look at a completely different way of structuring programs, block structuring, and briefly examine the concept of a partonomic organization.

The reader is warned that the concept of inheritance has generated an enormous amount of literature. There are different interpretations of single inheritance, and many different proposals for how to go about multiple inheritance, let alone determine what it means. As a consequence, I cannot present all perspectives and approaches. Instead, I have chosen what I believe to be the key aspects and have discussed them; other approaches or aspects are ignored. I hope that I have included sufficient pointers into the literature for

the interested reader to follow them and deepen their understanding of these
concepts.

4.2 Interpretations of Inheritance

Even though inheritance seems well understood, there are still different views
as to what it is. Different views imply different semantics. In this section, we
consider some of these views. We will revisit the view of inheritance as code
sharing.

The most common interpretation of inheritance is to model classification
hierarchies in the chosen application domain. In this case, subclasses define
subtypes, or specializations of their superclasses. The domain itself provides
rules which determine when to create a new subclass; the class hierarchy
should be meaningful when the application domain is understood. This interpretation of inheritance is the one adopted in Chapter 2 above, and it is
the one that is most often cited in textbooks on object-oriented programming.
It is the view that was assumed above when discussing multiple inheritance.
Multiple inheritance is viewed by its exponents as being a natural extension
of single inheritance. The big advantage of this view is that it corresponds
to the application domain in a natural fashion; this makes for a more easily
understood structure and organization of objects.

A second interpretation is incidental inheritance. It was proposed by
Sakkinen [75]. Incidental inheritance occurs when a superclass possesses a
property (data slot or method) which is inherited by a subclass even though
it is irrelevant to the subclass. We have already seen how incidental inheritance occurs if we define a LIFO stack in terms of a DE queue. Stacks usually
operate in terms of addition and removal from one end of a linear data structure; DE queues, on the other hand, allow additions at both ends of the data
structure, but removals at only one end. Consequently, if a Stack is defined in
terms of a DE queue, an extra addition operation is inherited. That extra operation is the one that works on the opposite end to the one at which addition
and removal occurs. This extra operation is incidentally inherited as a result
of the definition in terms of DE queues. (It should be noted that when delegation is used, it is possible to avoid incidental inheritance completely—this is
an issue which is often ignored when comparing inheritance and delegation.)

In Java, incidental inheritance is relatively common. For example, when
creating a subclass of the *java.util.Vector* class, depending upon the application, the subclass can often inherit unwanted operations, for example *re-
moveAllElements*, *removeElementAt*, *toString*, *ensureCapacity* and *clone*.

The third view we consider starts more from the viewpoint of implementation. Inheritance is a way of implementing objects by means of sharing.
Unfortunately, for most accounts of this kind, it can be extremely difficult to
determine when a subclass should be defined; the approach lacks the natural

correspondences that allow the subtyping view to support a natural and easily understood decomposition into subclasses, for the sharing view must rest upon how many instances are to be created and what they are to be used for.

The sharing approach reduces to two alternatives:

- inheritance of specifications;
- inheritance of code.

When inheriting specifications, there is a sub/superclass relation between a class and its superclass. If the subclass is considered a subtype of its superclass, the subclass can be used whenever its superclass can. When inheriting code, on the other hand, a sub/superclass relation does not necessarily exist. There are considerable difficulties in designing languages that support specification and code inheritance with equal ease.

4.3 Inheritance as Subtyping

A problem with inheritance is that it should be hidden from its subtypes (its clients). The way in which a class is derived should not matter to users of that class. Some methods for treating classes are fragile in the sense that the effects of inheritance can be felt when redefining or manipulating objects in various ways (see the discussion of graph inheritance below, Section 4.8, for one such example).

Inheritance can appear in the external interface of a class if one adopts *subtyping*. Subtyping consists of the rules by which objects of one type (class) are determined to be acceptable in contexts that expect another type (class): downcasting is one common example. In statically typed languages like Trellis/Owl [78] or Sather [76, 77], C++ or Java, subtyping rules are extremely important for they determine the legality of programs. In dynamically typed languages (CLOS or Smalltalk) subtyping rules affect the result of type predicates.

As has been seen in Chapter 2, many languages equate subtyping and inheritance. In Trellis/Owl, Simula and Sather, class *Stack* is a subtype of *DEQueue* if and only if *Stack* is a subclass of *DEQueue*. If the designer reimplements *Stack* so that it becomes self-contained and inherits from no parent class, the assumption that *Stack* is a subtype of *DEQueue* would no longer be legal. Subtyping rules *expose inheritance*.

In order to avoid this, subtyping should not be equated with inheritance. Rather, subtyping should be based on the behaviour of objects. If instances of class x meet the external interface of class y, x should be a subtype of y. The example of *Stack* and *DEQueue* shows that the implementation hierarchy need not be the same as the type hierarchy (as defined by object behaviour). In the *Stack* example, *Stack* inherits from *DEQueue*, but is not a subtype of *DEQueue* because it excludes operations from *DEQueue* (in particular the operation that adds elements to the back of the queue), but *DEQueue* is a subtype of *Stack* but does not inherit from *Stack*. The relationships between the *Stack* and *DEQueue* abstractions and implementations are shown in Figure 4.1.

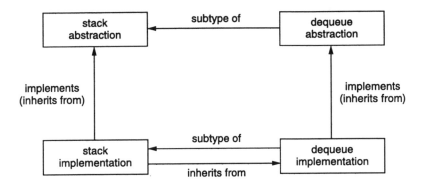

Fig. 4.1. *Inheritance, subtypes and implementation.*

The concept of a type hierarchy can be represented by abstract classes. The virtual or abstract operations of abstact classes document the external interfaces of the abstraction. A subtype of an abstract class is another abstract class. However, as hinted at by Figure 4.1, a single class hierarchy composed of abstract and instantiable classes is inadequate to model, in the general case, both the subtype and implementation relationships.

Behavioural subtyping cannot be deduced without formal semantic specification of behaviour. Without such definitions, subtypes can only be deduced on the basis of external interfaces of a syntactic nature (i.e., operation names and signatures). In addition (or as an alternative), the designer can specify the classes of which it is a subtype. Yet, as demonstrated by the example, the designer should be able to specify that the class is not a subtype of a parent or that the class is a subtype of an unrelated class (which is not its parent). The first case comes about when the behaviour of the objects is incompatible with the interface of parent objects. The second arises when the class supports the external interface of another class without sharing its implementation.

This approach is adopted in Sather [76, 77].

4.4 Inheritance as Code Sharing

According to one view [81], the logical or specificational view, inheritance is a definitional mechanism. The definition of a class is as a construct that represents (or defines) a collection of entities. The definition is couched in terms of their properties and operations. (The collection is finite if we want to consider its realization in a computer; however, we can treat the collection as often being potentially infinite if we remain in the realm of mathematical semantics.)

The definition of a subclass imposes additional constraints upon the properties and behaviours of its superclass. Such a definition amounts to the *specialization* of the superclass to suit the context of the newly defined subclass. Specialization requires that the superclass's properties be made more restrictive and its operations made applicable to fewer cases. The specialization of a class applies to fewer objects than does the class; specialization serves to reduce the number of possible (non-identical) instances that can be created.

This view of class derivation is purely logical. If we were to define it formally, we would have to state that the class definition represents the *intension* of the set of objects it defines, and the set of objects defined is the *extension* of the class. This view entails that logical (mathematical) operations are applied to the definitions of the properties in the superclass in order to derive those in the subclass; similarly, operations are applied to the superclass's operators. (It is worth noting that **inner** and **next-method** are programming devices for operating on class operations.)

This view of inheritance and specialization is not the only one, however. There are alternative views to this. Snyder [81] makes a number of distinctions as to what constitutes inheritance and observes that the logical, specificational view that I have just sketched, is but one of the possible interpretations. Of these interpretations, some are more stringent formally, some less so; the alternative that I will consider is purely pragmatic; the one just considered is one of the most stringent. I will be relatively informal here because I will be returning to the problems of inheritance below (Chapter 4, Section 4.9).

The pragmatic view of inheritance is that it is *code sharing*. Inheritance allows a subclass to share methods with its superclass. Thus, it permits the sharing of the code defined for the superclass with the subclasses of that superclass. Rather than defining new code for the subclass, we just arrange for it to inherit the code it requires from its superclass. In a similar vein, we arrange for a subclass to share all of the non-local variables used by each method; this must be the case, otherwise the method would fail to function. Sharing of variables that are class non-local to each method implies the sharing of the data slots of the superclass. The reader should note the following. At the point where a method is defined, either that method employs no class non-local variables—that is, all of its variables either are defined within the method, or are its formal parameters—or are variables that are global to the program in which the class and its methods are defined. In the more common case, at the point of definition, a method references and updates variables that are defined as slots within the body of the class to which the method definition belongs.

It should be remembered that some languages allow the user to restrict the visibility of class slots. If a slot is invisible, it cannot be directly included in any other construct or method. In some languages, as has been discussed, it is possible to hide slots from the outside world and from subclasses. When a method referencing or updating such a variable is inherited in a subclass, the hidden variable is also shared by the subclass, but it is shared implicitly. Equally, when a method is inherited, it is possible that the method is defined in terms of other methods defined in the superclass, some of which are hidden from view in some way. The method that the subclass shares must also share the hidden methods. The sharing process is, thus, more complex than simply setting a pointer to the thing that is to be shared.

It is important to note that the re-use of slots is not literal sharing (unless the variable is of a kind similar to a CLOS or Smalltalk class variable, or a C++ or Java static variable). It is, instead, a process of copying slot definitions between class definitions. The reader can verify this assertion by means of a simple experiment. For the implementation of a language with inheritance (and for some accounts of its semantics, in particular its *standard semantics*), these properties of inheritance must be taken into account. For most everyday cases, inheritance can be considered as a kind of sharing.

The code-sharing interpretation of inheritance is attractive from the viewpoint of modularity. Modularity is enhanced because methods and variables from outside the inheritance chain are not introduced and code depends only upon those classes that are higher in the inheritance chain than its defining class. Without those classes, its class cannot be defined so a maximal kind of modularity can be enforced. Code sharing is also attractive when one wants to re-use components. The programmer can tell where the definitions of the components are, and all that one need do is to trace the inheritance chain back to an ancestor in order to find the point of definition. Thus, in principle, re-use by extension amounts to the inclusion of the classes in the inheritance chain followed by some specialization.

Sather is somewhat special as far as its class taxonomy is concerned. Sather makes a firm distinction between subtyping and code sharing. In Sather, classes declared as being abstract are permitted to have specializations. A notational device distinguishes an abstract class from a concrete one: the name of an abstract class is prefixed by the dollar "$" symbol, while the name of a concrete class has no such prefix. Class names, it is worth noting, are always spelled in upper case (Sather is case-sensitive).

Abstract classes are defined in terms of method signatures and data slots. Data slots can be marked as constant or as attributes (mutable slots). A method in Sather can be a routine (which is a standard method) or an iterator (see Chapter 2, Section 2.10). An abstract Sather class does not contain routine or iterator bodies. A concrete Sather class is distinguished from abstract classes by the fact that routine and iterator bodies are supplied. In other words, concrete classes in Sather provide *implementations* for their methods.

Concrete classes can be instantiated in Sather. Abstract classes cannot be instantiated.

When deriving one class from another, Sather provides two mechanisms. The first is subclassing; the second is implementation sharing. In Sather, the definition of a subclass is strictly associated with the definition of a subtype. The subtype relation is denoted by the "$<$" symbol (which is becoming something of a standard symbol, for it also appears in Theta [57] as well as in other languages). Thus, in Sather, $\$A < \$B$ denotes the fact that (abstract class) type $\$A$ is a subtype of (abstract class) type $\$B$. Where this relation holds, the derived class ($\$A$) is a subtype of $\$B$.

The alternative is the sharing of implementation. This is only permitted for concrete classes and is indicated by the *includes* relation. A concrete class is an implementation of a type. If concrete class A includes concrete class B, A shares its implementation with B in the sense that methods defined in B are included in A. Hence, concrete class A is able to call the iterators and routines defined in B, as well as accessing B's constants and updating B's attributes.

Implementation sharing does not mean that all methods must be taken intact. It is possible to redefine a method defined in an *included* class.

4.5 Single Inheritance

In Chapter 2, we saw that classes can be related by the superclass. The superclass represents a more general version of the concept than do its subclasses; subclasses represent specializations of a general case. Inheritance gives more specialized entities access to methods and properties that are general. Alternatively, inheritance allows general properties to be inferred by more specialized concepts. In practical terms, visible slots and methods can be inherited by subclasses from their superclasses. What makes the scenario presented in Chapter 2 special is that we restricted inheritance so that classes were permitted only to have a *single* superclass.

Under single inheritance, a search for a method or a slot continues from an instance of a class up along the superclass links until the root of the inheritance tree is reached. If the required slot or method is located, the appropriate operation is performed on it. If there is no such slot or method among the superclasses of the caller, an error (often a compile-time error) is raised. It is important to see that the search proceeds from an instance of a class through the *classes* which form its superclass chain; the request for the slot or method is initiated by an *instance*, not a class. Inheritance, as noted in the first paragraph of this section, is a relationship between (or operation upon) classes, not instances. Indeed, the whole area of inheritance, whether single or multiple, deals with the relationships between classes. This is natural, for classes are defined in terms of inheritance from more general models.

Although it is important to remember that instances are the objects with which we deal at runtime, it is the class that defines the structure of its instances. A class is, in a sense, only a template defining its instances.

The organization of classes under inheritance is of considerable importance. Under single inheritance, each class has only one superclass. On the other hand, a class can have many subclasses. As a consequence, the classes that are defined in terms of specialization (subclass derivation) from a given class form a rooted tree. This tree has an arbitrary branching factor because a class can have many subclasses. However, there is a unique path from each class to its superclass because a class can only have a *single* superclass.

In some languages, C++, for example, there is no most general class from which all other classes are derived. The Java, Dylan and Eiffel languages, for example, are languages which provide a most general class. In these languages, it is advisable to make all user-defined classes subclasses of the most general class so that the newly defined class can inherit methods to perform basic operations. In Java1.1, for example, the most general class is called *Object*. If one does not derive a new class from *Object* or one of its subclasses, the new class does not, for example, inherit the methods to perform serialization (the process of writing a class to an output stream and of reading one from an input stream). If one does not specialize Dylan's most general class, instance allocation fails to work. When there is a single class that is the ancestor of all other classes, user- or system-defined, the entire tree of classes is said to have a *single* or *unique* root; the tree is rooted (every subtree of a tree is rooted by definition, unless it is the empty tree).

In C++, there is no root class in the sense of most general class from which all others inherit slots and methods. C++ programs are organized as multiple trees, each of which is rooted, but each of which is disjoint from all the others. A rooted tree in the sense we are considering, one with a system-defined most general class, has the enormous advantage that downcasting allows an instance of any class whatsoever to be bound to an argument or assigned to a variable whose type is that of most general possible class. This feature makes programming considerably easier in many cases and allows the definition of generic functions without resorting to a template construct (as in C++) or the introduction of generic types (as is done in Ada, for example).

Single inheritance is often powerful enough for the needs of a given program. Single inheritance has the enormous advantage that it is *simple*, semantically and operationally. However, it is sometimes argued, it lacks power and makes the definition of some classes more difficult or *ad hoc* than necessary. An example is the derivation of a class representing waterskiing accountants (which, as we saw in the last chapter, is trivial to describe in a prototype-based language). Under single inheritance, we would need to define a class representing accountants and then specialize it to produce one which adds the waterskiing hobby. Under multiple inheritance, we combine the classes representing *waterskiers* and *accountants* in order to produce the new class.

4.6 Calling More Abstract Methods

When defining a new method, it is very often the case that a new piece of code is written. This code might be completely new and defined especially for the needs of the new class. Other times, the code is written as a specialization of a method that appears further up the inheritance chain; in this case, when the method is all new code, the behaviour of the method is totally new. However, it is often the case that a new method can (indeed should) be defined in terms of the behaviours of one or more methods higher in the inheritance chain and which perform the same function. This occurs when the new method is to play exactly the same role as the other(s) and represents an extension to the behaviour that is inherited. Rather than completely re-write such a method, it would be far better to re-use the existing methods. The ways in which methods can re-use existing methods is the topic of this subsection.

One very common way to specialize a method is to perform some operations before and after the operations represented by the more general method. If the more general method's operation is denoted by S, and the extensions we need to make are A and B, then the method that we need to write is:

$$A; \; S; \; B$$

That is, we perform some operations prior to doing whatever the more general method does, and then do some other things after the more general operations. This arrangement is necessary when it is remembered that a specialization, a subclass in other words, contains more detail than its superclass. One kind of operation that must be done before calling the more general method is to arrange for the data to be of the right kind; equally, after the general operations have been performed, it might be necessary to convert its result into a form that conforms to that required by the subclass.

C++ provides a relatively general mechanism for accessing methods in the superclass. This involves the use of the so-called scope-resolution operator which is written as two adjacent colons ("::"). The left-hand side of this operator should either be left unbound, or should be bound to the name of a class; the right-hand side is bound to a slot in the class named by the right-hand side. When both sides are bound, as in *C1::i*, the expression is interpreted as the slot i in class *C1* (the operator is actually more general, so global variables as well as slots in nested classes can be differentiated, but we are simplifying matters here). If there is no such slot, a compile-time error is raised. This scope operator allows methods in the superclass to be called. If C_1 and C_2 are classes with C_2 being the superclass of C_1, and if both classes define a method m, then if $C_2::(\ldots)$ appears in the method m in C_1, it is interpreted by the compiler as a call to that method m defined in class C_2 (in C_1's superclass, that is).

Smalltalk, LOOPS and Java provide a special method call to invoke methods that are more general. This call, often called *super*, calls the next most general method above the current one with the same name and the same number of parameters (Java imposes the additional requirement that the types of the parameters be the same). In Smalltalk, super functions in a way similar to SELF: it is a receiver for a message, and, as such, is sent a normal message. The *SendSuper* operation in LOOPS operates in a fashion similar to super in Smalltalk. In Java, super is often used in constructors to call the constructor of appropriate type in the superclass of the current class. Here, super takes the form of a 0-arity procedure call. In other contexts, super can be used as the name of the immediate superclass and is written as a class prefix:

```
super.add1(n);
```

this will call the method *add1* in the superclass of the class in which the method is being defined.

The next alternative we shall consider involves provision of a construct or operation to call a higher method. The operation in question is often called *next-method* or *call-next-method* when defined in a bottom-up fashion, and is called *inner* when defined in a top-down one. The *next-method*, *call-next-method* approach is adopted in Dylan and CLOS, respectively. The *inner* approach derives from Simula67 and is used in Beta. I will consider *next-method* and *call-next-method* first.

The operation of *next-method* and *call-next-method* are the same. I will use *next-method* to stand for this operation simply because it is shorter. The *next-method* operation takes no arguments and can occur in a method at any point where it is legal for a procedure or function call to appear. The *next-method* operation is a pseudo-call and stands for a call to another method. The semantics of the operation are as follows. The arguments to the method that calls *next-method* are supplied to *next-method*. The *next-method* operation searches the inheritance chain of the class to which the calling method belongs in an attempt to find another method with the same name and same parameters at a point higher in the inheritance chain. In other words, *next-method* searches for a more general version of the method being called. If such a method cannot be located, an error results. If, however, there is such a method, it is called using the arguments supplied to the original method and to the *next-method* operation. If there is more than one method that is applicable (for the reason that the method has been redefined in more than one subclass), the most specific method is chosen for execution by *next-method*. The results produced by the more general method (if any) are returned to the method that called *next-method*. These results are then available for general use.

It can be seen that, when using a next-method approach, one defines. general methods in the same way in which one would define a procedure. Later, when the need to re-use that method's code is encountered lower in the inheritance chain, next-method is there to call the most specific, more general method.

To make this clear, the following example is offered.

Let us assume that we need to define two queue types, one using the FIFO, the other using the LIFO discipline. Let us assume that the implementation language provides us with a list data type (either by having built-in lists or by defining them in a library). We might start by defining the FIFO class thus:

```
define class FIFO
   slot elems : LIST;
end class FIFO;
```

We need to define an operation to add an element to the queue. We adopt the generic functions approach to methods (the same as in Dylan and CLOS), and so we write the method as:

```
method add_element(q : FIFO, x)
   elems(q) := cons(x,elems(q))
end method;
```

In this case, we supply the queue to be operated upon as the first argument to the method; this allows the method lookup process to determine the class for which the method is defined. The second argument is to be bound to the object to be added to the queue. The body of the method consists of a single line whose effect is to update the queue elements by adding a new element to the front of the queue. The notation *elems(q)* when denoting an l-value (left-hand side of an assignment) denotes an operation which updates the slot *elems* of instance *q* with the result of evaluating the right-hand side of the assignment. On the right-hand side of the assignment, the instance of *elems(q)* serves to return the value of the *elems* slot of the instance *q*. The function *cons* adds a new element to the front of a list. (The assignment can be re-written as *elems(q,cons(x,elems(q)))*.)

When we come to write the LIFO class, we have very little to do, in fact. The class definition is simple: we add no slots to the existing FIFO class. Equally, the methods require little work. In order to minimize the work, we observe that all LIFO operations can be performed on a FIFO provided that we reverse the queue appropriately. In a LIFO queue, we add elements to the front and take them off the front. In a FIFO, we add them to the back and remove them from the front. To make a FIFO queue behave in this way, we need to reverse the list representing its elements and add the element there; in order simply to inherit the *next_element* method from FIFO (thus avoiding the need to define an operation for LIFO), we have to arrange for the elements to be in the correct order—thus, we reverse the queue before exiting the *add_element* method.

The addition operation is, then, simple to write:

```
method add_element(q : LIFO, x)
   elems(q) := reverse(elems(q));
   next-method;
   elems(q) := reverse(elems(q));
end method;
```

where *reverse* is the function which (non-destructively) reverses the elements of a list. We need to perform the first reverse because we want to put an element onto the front of the queue. It has to be on the front of the queue if we are to use the *next_element* method without modification. We reverse the list a second time so that the most recently added element is the first to be removed.

For reference, the *next_element* method is:

```
method next_element (q : FIFO)
   if (empty?(q)) then
      nil
   else
      let elts := elems(q);
      let nxt := hd(elts);
         elems(q) := tl(elts);
         nxt;
   fi;
end method;
```

where *nil* denotes the empty list; *hd* is the function that returns the first element of a list (the head); *tl* is the function which returns the list minus its first element (the tail); the *let* construct introduces local variables; and where, finally, *empty?* is the predicate which tells whether the queue has no elements (this is a method defined for class FIFO and which can safely be inherited by LIFO).

We can allow LIFO directly to inherit *next_element* if we employ the double reverse in *add_element*. Thus, along with *empty?*, we do not need to specialize it to LIFO.

A second example comes from parallel programming. We might define a class to represent a FIFO queue. Such a queue forms the basis of an inter-process communications mechanism. It might be the case either that the queue is needed elsewhere in the program, but not in a way that involves parallelism. It might just be easier to define and test the FIFO class as a piece of sequential program. The semantics of the FIFO queue, in any case, are independent of their operation as part of a parallel program, so defining the FIFO's operations without regard to parallellism makes good sense.

The FIFO class might include the following operations:

- test for emptiness (*empty_queue?(q)*);
- add a new element (*add_element(q,x)*);
- remove an element (*next_element(q)*).

where the names of the methods that implement the operations are shown in brackets. The argument, *q*, refers to the FIFO queue and *x* is to be bound to an object of the queue element type.

The implementation of these operations is relatively straightforward when considering a sequential program. Now, the problem comes of altering these operations (methods) so that they treat the queue data structure as a critical region. Some languages provide tools for parallel programming; for example, semaphores of some kind or monitors might be provided by the language. Java provides monitors and a synchronized construct that implements critical regions; Dylan, in the Mindy and Gwydion implementations from Carnegie Mellon, provides semaphores and events. It is necessary to assume that the object-oriented language used to implement the shared queue provides semaphores and the *wait*, and *release* operations over them. (The two operations acquire and release, respectively, the semaphore which they mention as their argument).

We can now specialize the FIFO queue class. We redefine the class by adding a slot to hold the semaphore controlling access to the queue data structure. We also re-write the methods using *next-method*. For example, we can redefine the *add_element* method as something like:

```
method add_element(q: SharedFIFO,x) is
   wait(q.sema);
   next-method;
   release(q.sema);
end method;
```

where *q.sema* denotes the semaphore that must be defined when the FIFO class is specialized; it is the semaphore that controls access to the queue data structure.

What happens in this revised version of the *add_element* method is the following. First, the method is called and its arguments are bound to an instance of the *SharedFIFO* class and to the object to be added to the queue (note that here we are assuming that methods are multi-methods as in CLOS and Dylan). Next, the method waits on the semaphore, *q.sema*, until the semaphore allows access to the queue data structure. When given access, *next-method* is called. This implicitly passes all the arguments of the method to the next appropriate method in *SharedFIFO*'s inheritance chain, which we assume is the *add_element* method defined for the sequential FIFO class. This call performs the operations required to add an element to the back of the queue. Next, control passes to the call to release the local semaphore to allow other processes access to the shared queue.

The alternative view is the top-down one. This view employs a syntactic construct spelled *inner* to stand for the code represented by a more specialized method. The process of method definition is now almost reversed. The *inner* construct is inserted into the code of a method defined in a class that will become the superclass of the other classes to be defined. The *inner* construct serves as a placeholder for code that will be supplied by methods that are more specific. In the method in which it is defined, inner is a *no-op*, so the following sequence of statements:

    S1; inner; S2

when executed in the method containing it, will have exactly the same effect as:

    S1; S2;

However, if we define a method belonging to a subclass and we write:

    inner: S3; S4;

the effect will be to execute the *inner* statements in the context of the *inner* construct. In other words, the *inner* statement that appears in the subclass's method will be executed thus:

    S1; S3; S4; S2;

That is, the *inner* statement is, in effect, inserted in the superclass's method at the point where the keyword *inner* occurs. Therefore, any *inner* statements are executed between the statements that appear on either side of the *inner* statement in the superclass's method.

The inner statement provides a way of wrapping more code that is more general around code that is more specific. In particular, it allows many statements to be so wrapped because each subclass can provide its own inner statement as appropriate (including no inner statements). The effect of inner is exactly dual to next-method. It also plays the same role. However, with inner, one must define a superclass' methods in such a way that inner statements lower down the inheritance chain can be correctly executed. In our shared FIFO example, this would lead us to define a shared object and then define a shared queue as a subclass. Similarly, the order in which we defined the FIFO and LIFO queues in the first example would need to be reversed.

Some languages, CLOS in particular, go even further than allowing *inner/next-method* techniques for method construction. CLOS, for example, defines a set of method-combining forms. The idea is that a method can be distributed across the inheritance hierarchy with contributions being made at different points and in different superclasses. Method combining forms in CLOS are derived from earlier efforts at automatically providing methods and parts of methods that could be combined to form complete methods. In CLOS, method combiners are methods which are inherited in the normal way, but which specify when they should be executed. The result is a complex method that is composed of elements taken from different classes in its superclass structure.

C++ also supports renaming. Renaming is performed using the "scope operator", (spelled "::"). This is the infix operator that is used in the definition of methods (it is also the same construct that is used to make calls to a superclass). The left-hand operator is a class name and the right-hand one is the method (or slot) name. If the left-hand operand is omitted, the scope is taken to be the most global possible. It makes qualified renaming possible as a mechanism for inheritance; however, such a move can be defeated by the standard inheritance mechanism, so great care must be taken when using it.

Finally, it is necessary to observe that some languages (Java and Eiffel, for example) contain constructs which inhibit redefinition under inheritance. That is, it is possible to prevent users from redefining a slot. In Java, a slot that cannot be redefined is marked as final; in Eiffel, it is marked as frozen. For example, in Java, the definition:

```
final private int importantConstant = 2.5;
```

declares an integer variable that cannot be updated. Similarly,

```
final int add1(int x){ return( x + 1); }
```

declares a method that cannot be redefined in a subclass. The same effects can be had in Eiffel with:

```
frozen importantConstant : Integer is 2.5
```

and:

```
frozen add1 (x : Integer) is
   do
      Result := x + 1
   end
```

with, again, the intent that neither the data nor the method slot can be re-defined in a subclass of the one in which the definitions appear.

When a language incorporates multiple inheritance without some kind of linearization (see below, Section 4.9.3), the *call-next-method* operation leads one into problems for, as will be seen, it is an open question as to which method is the "next" in the inheritance structure. The *inner* statement is in a slightly better position, given that it operates top-down. Here, an extension to the semantics of the *inner* statement will be necessary to cater for the case in which the inherited method does not have an inner statement in its body.

4.7 Multiple Inheritance

Single inheritance has been found to be a powerful mechanism for constructing programs. Sometimes, single inheritance is insufficient and enforces *ad hoc* solutions upon the programmer. For example, if we have a class for accountants and one for water-skiers, the combination of the two under single inheritance requires that we specialize one of these classes, say the one representing accountants, and define a slot to hold an instance of the waterskier class. In many ways, this is not what we want, nor what we intend. If we think in terms of sets, what we require is the intersection of those people who are accountants and those who engage in waterskiing:

Accountants ∩ Waterskiers

If the solution just described in the last paragraph is adopted, the result is different from the above set expression. It makes the waterskiing aspect a part of the new class. (Of course, it could be argued that being a waterskier is just a perspective, an aspect, of a person, just as their profession is a perspective—I will consider this below.) It can be argued that the solution involving the creation of a new slot to hold an instance of a class does not have the appropriate semantics, and for this reason alternative solutions were sought.

The problem of representing those people who are both accountants and water-skiers immediately suggests that the new entity should have two superclasses, not one. Other examples include the definition of a class to represent a digital meter (a visual component that shows a numerical quantity and a slide whose length represents that value) as a subclass of a numerical display and a meter class (see [85]); both the numerical display and the meter are defined in terms of (are subclasses of) a class representing a gauge. The gauge class is, itself, a subclass of a window class. In a representation of the kinds of food that one finds in a supermarket, it would be necessary to represent fruit and vegetables in ways that respect the fact that they are perishable; that is, for each of these types of food, there is a date after which they are to be considered to be no longer edible. To make this representation, it appears useful to define a *Foodstuff* class whose immediate subclasses are *Vegetable* and *Fruit*; the *Foodstuff* class might contain a representation of the unit cost of foods. In addition, we might care to introduce a *PerishableCommodity* class which contains a date (representing the date by which the commodity must be consumed). The *Fruit* and *Vegetable* classes will be subclasses of the *PerishableCommodity* class, as well as of *Foodstuff*. We have another example of multiple inheritance (this example is also due to [85]).

Therefore, the concept of multiple inheritance was introduced into object-oriented programming languages. Early languages that used multiple inheritance were FLAVORS [21] and then LOOPS [15]; more recently, Eiffel [67] and its derivative, Sather [76, 77], as well as C++ [91], and a number of less known languages, have employed multiple inheritance.

As its name suggests, multiple inheritance means inheritance from more than one superclass. In a language that supports single inheritance, a class can have zero or exactly one superclass. It has zero superclasses if it is a root class, and one superclass if it is an interior or leaf class. Under multiple inheritance, each class can have zero or more superclasses. Again, if a class is a root of the inheritance graph, it has zero superclasses, while an interior class has one or more superclasses.

Before moving on, it is necessary to observe that we will concentrate below on the problem of finding or inheriting a single entity, a slot or a method, from an inheritance structure using some kind of multiple inheritance. Although this is the most usual case, it is sometimes useful to be able to perform an operation on *all* ancestor classes, whether direct or indirect. To our knowledge, the only language to permit this and to support it adequately, was LOOPS [15] using its *send superfringe* operation. The operation is possible in C++ or Eiffel (see [67] for more information), or in any language that permits explicit naming of superclasses, and more particularly in those languages that permit the unique naming of all slots and methods. With a renaming operation, it is still necessary to assemble a sequence of the names upon which to operate or which are to be called; this must usually be done when the program is written, so dynamic performance of this kind of operation is not usually possible.

4.8 Multiple Inheritance Graph Shape

When a class has just one superclass, multiple inheritance reduces to simple inheritance. When, on the other hand, a class has more than one superclass, some slots will be defined specially for it as part of the derivation (specialization) process, but it also inherits slots from each of its superclasses. Thus, a slot can be new to the class or can be inherited from a superclass. As a consequence, the inheritance structure in each case has a different topology. Under simple inheritance, the inheritance structure takes the form of a tree. The root of the tree corresponds to the most general class from which all others are derived. Under multiple inheritance, on the other hand, the inheritance structure is often described as a lattice or, more generally, as a rooted DAG (directed acyclic graph). When viewed as a graph, multiple inheritance structures might have more than one distinguished node (root), each corresponding to the most general classes. Sometimes the structure is organized so that there is a single most general class (as it is in Eiffel and Dylan, for example) which is defined by the language.

In general, there are always two ways to view an inheritance structure. The first is to look at the structure generated by all defined classes (be they system-defined or otherwise), while the second is based upon the structure that pertains to a class that is located somewhere in the inheritance structure. Thus, under single inheritance, the class-centred view reveals a chain or linear sequence. The DAG or lattice that is induced by the multiple inheritance relation can also be represented as a tree whose root is a particular non-root (interior or leaf) class; when viewed this way, one sees the superclasses of the class in question; when a class appears as the intersection of two or more paths through the structure from the designated class, it will appear in as many branches of the tree as there are paths to it. This multiple representation of a single class can be thought of as a form of colouring of the inheritance graph.

Inheritance structures are used to find entities that are defined in more general classes. A search through the inheritance structure, be it a single or multiple inheritance structure, must be performed in order to find slots and methods that are not defined locally. This search poses problems for multiple inheritance because there can be more than one path from a class to the place where a slot or method is defined. This is shown in Figure 4.2:

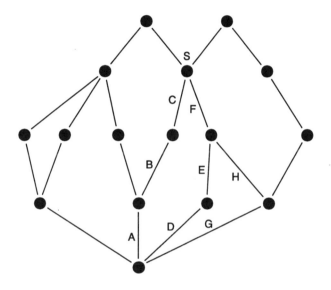

Multiple Paths:
{A, B, C}, {D, E, F}, {G, H, F}

Fig. 4.2. *An inheritance lattice.*

Because a class often has more than one superclass, it can be seen that the search has a much more complex structure than is the case with single inheritance. At each branch point (superclass), a decision has to be made as to which path next to follow (see Figure 4.3).

A decision as to which path to follow next naturally leaves some paths unexplored. Since we cannot know *a priori* on which branch a slot will appear, we must search the lattice exhaustively until either the slot is found or all superclasses have been examined. An exhaustive search implies that every branch must be visited in the search. This implies some systematic method for searching the graph, which, in turn, implies that at each decision point, *either* the unexplored alternatives are recorded so that they can later be explored,

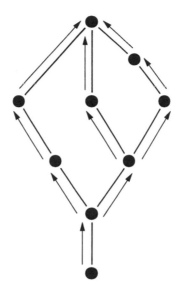

Fig. 4.3. *Decision as to which path to follow.*

or the graph is re-ordered in some way so that the nodes (superclasses) are put into some canonical order.

At this point, we encounter a central problem with multiple inheritance: we need to decide how to search the inheritance lattice. As will be seen, there are different methods for performing an exhaustive search and the choice as to which to employ has proved controversial. Different methods visit nodes in different orders, so the behaviour of multiple inheritance will vary depending upon the method adopted. This means that a slot that will be found early by one search algorithm might not be found until much later by another. This leads to the problem that one search algorithm, by finding one instance of a method, say, early on, can mask off, or render invisible, another instance of that method. This can have the consequence that, say, a relatively specialized method will not be found because a more general one has been encountered along another path through the inheritance structure. This property has the consequence that, different methods will be returned and, therefore, different computations will be performed—the *meaning* of the program can be altered by the search algorithm; moreover, the search algorithm is essential in determining the correctness of programs.

One way out of this problem is to give up the idea that algorithms should be portable from one language to another, so programs must be re-written when moved from one language to another, particularly to a language that uses a different search algorithm or technique.

When two objects in the inheritance structure have the same name, they are said to *clash*. An alternative is simply to make clashes illegal. That is, when the compiler detects a conflict, it flags an error and terminates. This is a weak suggestion, for obvious reasons.

A second alternative is to permit qualified message passing or to allow renaming. Qualified message passing (a more general form of renaming) qualifies the inherited slot or method's name with the name of the class in which it is defined. When this is employed, all names become unique. Thus, it becomes possible to designate each slot or method uniquely; a name becomes available with which to refer to that entity. When potential name clashes occur, they can be resolved by renaming one of the inherited entities, an operation that can be done locally, not in the superclass where the entity is defined.

A rather more far-reaching problem occurs when there is more than one path from a given class to one of its superclasses. A simple form of this is shown in Figure 4.4.

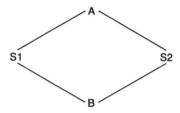

Fig. 4.4. *A common root.*

This is called a *common root*. Let us assume that we are seeking to inherit a slot (or a method) from the class that is a common root. If we employ a search that traverses all paths from the leaf to the common root, there will be as many copies of the desired slot as there are paths from the leaf to the common root. In the case of the example shown in Figure 4.4, there will be two copies of the desired slot, one for each path. Very often, only one copy of the slot is desired, for example in the case of incrementing the value of the slot by one. If we have k copies of the slot, it will be incremented k times unless we are careful to ensure that only one copy is actually modified; being careful in this way requires some semantic support from the language, and this support might not be forthcoming.

The problem of common roots arises in two forms. The first, and most obvious one, is that a subgraph contains more than one path to a single root node, as shown in Figure 4.5. In that figure, we have a collection of classes which are related by the subclass relation and eventually are rooted in a single class (F). A root class is a source of slots that are inherited by its subclasses.

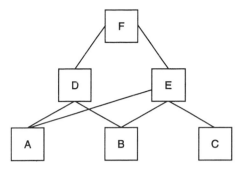

Fig. 4.5. *Another common root.*

Here, the common root is an interior node (F) which also inherits from some superclasses. Comparison of these two cases immediately suggests that the common roots problem is one that is recursively defined.

Let us consider again the lattice in Fig. 4.4, assuming that class F defines slot s. If we consider class A, there are two paths from it to the root class, F: A, D, F and A, E, F. We can compare this with the situation depicted in Figure 4.4; here, A, D, E, E form a diamond, as do B, D, E and F – each is a simple case of a common root. Now consider node B. Assume that F defines a slot s. There are two paths from B to F: B, D, F; B, F, and C, D, F. If we employ a simple-minded inheritance algorithm, the first case will yield two copies of s for inclusion in A, while the second will also yield two copies of s for inclusion in B. In each case, the subclass (A or B) only requires a single copy of s.

Multiple inheritance can, therefore, lead to the replication of inherited slots. Duplicates must be handled in some meaningful way. The problem of common roots has been given different names over the years. Bobrow and Stefik [15] refer to it as the "up-to-joins" problem, while Meyer [67] refers to it as "repeated inheritance". I have called it the "common roots" problem because it results from different subgraphs having a common root node. If we consider the lattice shown in Figure 4.6, we can see an additional complication: that of determining when a common root is encountered.

We must consider the effect of superclass ordering in the superclass specification of a particular class. The question is whether an ordering should be taken into account, or whether it should be ignored; furthermore, a decision has to be made as to whether duplications in the superclass list should be considered significant or a typographical error. The reason for asking these questions is that, as noted above, different search algorithms can visit nodes in the inheritance lattice in different orders. If the search can be influenced by starting it at a particular point, the order in which nodes are visited can be influenced. If one superclass is guaranteed to be searched before another, its superclasses will be visited before those of the remainder, so any slots known to be in that subgraph will be found before slots elsewhere (including similar or identical slots). By this means, one can arrange for a particular slot to be encountered before any others.

The problem with this approach is that it is highly sensitive to modifications to the inheritance lattice. If the desired slot is moved to another subgraph, it will not be encountered as expected; if the class containing the slot is moved or a new class is placed in the path to that class, the slot might not be found as expected due to the delaying nature of the inheritance algorithm. This is where unique names would be of considerable utility. Languages like CLOS [82] take into account the order in which superclasses appear in a class's superclass list; other languages, like Eiffel, do not. From the example in [91], (p. 204), it is stated that "the compiler detects name clashes resulting from using a name defined in more than one base class [superclass]. This implies that unless there actually is an ambiguous use the programmer need not do anything to resolve it."

4.9 Approaches to Multiple Inheritance

We have seen that the class structure above a given class takes the form of a lattice, not a chain. Globally, the relationship between classes is also a lattice, whereas single inheritance imposes a tree structure. We can see the lattice structure in Figure 4.6.

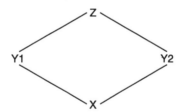

Fig. 4.6. *An inheritance lattice.*

However, we can view this lattice above a given class as a tree as shown in Figure 4.7.

Comparison of these two figures shows that it is possible to transform a lattice into a tree (or that a lattice contains a tree-like local structure). Consequently, we have three fundamental approaches to finding a slot or method in a multiple inheritance lattice:

- extract the appropriate (local) tree and operate on that (*tree* inheritance);
- consider the structure as a graph and operate on that (*graph* inheritance);
- tackle the lattice directly, enumerating its nodes and imposing some linear ordering upon them (*linearized* inheritance).

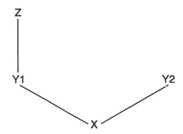

Fig. 4.7. *An inheritance tree within a lattice.*

4.9.1 Tree Inheritance

Tree inheritance involves labelling nodes when conflicts arise. This makes it possible for a class to inherit more than one copy of a slot or method, but under different names. As a consequence, a renaming operation is required. This approach is called *tree inheritance*. This corresponds exactly to the view of the inheritance structure that decomposes it into a number of trees with coloured nodes. Thus, each parent of each class will define a completely separate set of inherited slots (instance variables in particular); if a slot can be reached via a number of paths through the inheritance structure, there will be a separate set of slots for each path.

Unfortunately, tree inheritance radically alters the semantics of inheritance in the presence of shared nodes. Shared ancestors often arise when inheriting multiple classes which are all intended to be instantiated (are complete, in some sense). An alternative would be to define a set of complete classes and one or more *mixin* classes (*mixin* classes are discussed below, but, for now, they can be thought of as classes that define a set of operations that are related to one particular feature and are designed only to be inherited from).

The problem, in essence, is that parents are duplicated. This is Snyder's [81] *undesirable duplicate parent* operation invocation problem. Consider the case of the classes *Point*, *HistoryPoint* and *BoundedPoint*. Instances of *Point* can be moved (they have slots denoting their x and y co-ordinates). Instances of *HistoryPoint* record all movements of the point, and instances of *BoundedPoint* can only be moved within certain boundaries. The problem is to define a point which is bounded and which records its position. Clearly, we can engage in multiple inheritance and make *BoundedHistoryPoint* a subclass of *BoundedPoint* and *HistoryPoint*. The new class will inherit a move method from both parents. This implies that, should both methods be executed, two updates of the x and y co-ordinates will be effected. The two superclasses cannot be sufficiently combined to form the required point using tree- or graph-based multiple inheritance. (Renaming one of the two move methods is a non-solution, note). Linearized inheritance works very well with this problem; indeed, it works better than does graph inheritance.

Tree multiple inheritance is an approach that *deliberately* introduces name clashes. It is concerned with solving the problem raised by the diamond diagram. Graph multiple inheritance works by exposing the structure of inheritance; tree multiple inheritance exploits the issues raised by taking exactly the opposite decisions about naming and conflict.

In tree multiple inheritance, the graph is transformed, as it is in linearized inheritance. In the derived tree, there is a path from the class doing the inheriting to the root for each branch coming from the bottom class (the one doing the inheriting). This involves duplicating some nodes. From this point, all name clashes are treated as equals. No name clashes can occur from slots that are inherited along different paths for the reason that all ancestors in paths that have joins are already duplicated. This solves the encapsulation problems of both graph and linearized inheritance. However, in some examples, in particular where *exactly one* instance of a property only makes sense for a class, tree inheritance does not work well (it leads to a duplication); it needs to be augmented by a unique naming scheme (see the case of Eiffel below).

4.9.2 Graph Inheritance

The second approach is called graph inheritance. It consists of searching the inheritance graph somehow and resolving conflicts in some way. Neither the search nor the conflict resolution methods are specified. Tree inheritance suffers from a number of problems, as we have noted. Here, we add the additional problem of graph inheritance that it exposes the inheritance structure. The concept of encapsulation implies that the way in which a class is ultimately derived should not be visible; only the immediate superclasses should be visible to a class; it should not be necessary, nor possible, to examine the superclasses of each of these superclasses (i.e., the set of ancestors). Consider the "diamond" diagram (Figure 4.8) showing repeated inheritance. If S_1 defines exactly those slots that are in A for itself (i.e., within its own visibility area), any side effects on those slots will be invisible to S_2. If S_1 merely inherits all those slots, all side effects will become visible to S_2. The structure of inheritance is exposed to subclasses.

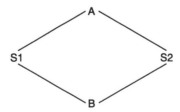

Fig. 4.8. *A diamond inheritance shape.*

Special-purpose methods are used to resolve conflicts. One of these is to redefine the inherited operation in the child class (this is a method recommended by Lipmann [59]); the definition in the child class can invoke the operations defined by the parent classes (using a unique naming scheme, for example). To invoke all the definitions of an operation in the inheritance graph, each class can define an operation invoking the operation on each of its parents and then perform any local computation. The result is a depth-first traversal of the graph.

The problem with graph inheritance is that it exposes the inheritance structure of the graph. This violates the concept of encapsulation of classes. Such exposure tends to occur not when there are duplicate operations, but when it is a tree. In many languages supporting graph inheritance, there is only one set of instance variables (instance slots) instantiated for each ancestor class, regardless of the number of paths by which the class can be reached. This result is usually desirable, but it can introduce problems. For example, in the above example, depth-first traversal with merging was employed, but this can result in some operations being invoked more than once on the same set of instance variables. Consequently, a designer cannot change the use of inheritance within a class without risking breaking some descendant class.

Let us consider the tree structure shown in Figure 4.7. Let us assume that operation o is defined by classes z, y_2 and x, where the definition of o in x invokes o on both parents. Assume, further, that the designer of class y_2 decides to reimplement it to inherit from z in such a way as to preserve the external behaviour of objects of class y_2. Also, assume that y_2 will either inherit o from z or will revise its definition of o to invoke the o defined by z. Operation o in class x will now have the effect of invoking o on class z twice, and on the same set of instance variables (instance slots); if o has side-effects, this might not be a desirable outcome.

In this example, it can be seen that a change in the inheritance structure by a class (y_2) breaks one of its client (inheriting) classes (x). This occurs even though the operations have the same external behaviour. The use of inheritance is therefore exposed to inheriting client classes.

Trellis/Owl [78] signals an error at compile time when a class attempts to inherit an operation from more than one parent. It is an error for a class to inherit operations with the same name from two or more parents only if the operations are actually different (cf. the account of inheritance in Eiffel, below).

The error is a problem because it exposes the inheritance structure to client (sub-) classes. A further example will be useful. Consider the diamond graph in Figure 4.6. If an operation o is defined only by class z, it will be inherited by y_1 and y_2 and then by x; this will cause no error. Now, assume that class y_2 is reimplemented so that it no longer inherits from z (see Figure 4.7) but still supports the same behaviour. Class x will now be in error for it inherits two different operations named o, one from z via y_1, the other from class y_2. (The operations are different but have equivalent behaviour on objects of their respective classes.) So, the change to class y_2 to stop inheriting from z was visible to x, a client of class y_2, even though the external interface of instances of y_2 remains unchanged (the instances have the same externally visible behaviour).

Exposure of the inheritance structure is not always desirable. When this is the case, the same operation exception in the conflict rule must be dropped. This suggests that *ad hoc* solutions must be employed.

4.9.3 Linearized Inheritance

Linearized inheritance is a mechanism which first flattens the inheritance structure into a linear chain without duplicates and then searches this chain in order to find slots (a process equivalent to single inheritance).

With linearized inheritance, the order in which the linearization algorithm encounters superclasses is important. In the case of CLOS, which we will consider in detail below, the programmer can set the order in which direct superclasses appear in a class. This makes the inheritance algorithm select one, rather than any other, conflicting slot. In the case of Figure 4.8, if both S_1 and S_2 define a slot or method x, one or other will be selected according to the superclass order; the other is masked off by the inheritance algorithm. Without additional information, it is impossible to say which x is the correct one, so, in the absence of such information, we must consider them equally good. The choice between them is therefore arbitrary.

A related problem is that inheriting classes are not guaranteed communication with their direct ancestors. The linearization algorithm can insert unrelated classes between an inheriting class and one of its direct ancestors. If the inheritance order produced by the linearization algorithm is B-S_1-S_2-A, B cannot directly communicate with S_2; equally, S_1 cannot communicate directly with A. An implication of this is that there is no way to combine slots; at any point in the linearized graph, there is only one slot that is visible. It is for this reason that CLOS provides such a wide variety of method combining constructs. Method combination does not replace the need for a class to be able to communicate reliably with its direct ancestors.

Inheritance involves a search for slots (and methods). We need, therefore, an algorithm that will give us access to all the superclasses of an input class. Access to the classes should represent a consistent way of accessing those superclasses. The simplest approach to searching the space of superclasses is to linearize their graph and then remove duplicates from one end or other of the resulting sequence.

The simplest of the ways employs a *depth-first* (or *pre-order*) *traversal*. The idea is that we want to visit each node in the inheritance lattice just once and in a particular order, as we put each node (class) into a list when we visit it. Once we have collected all the nodes, we can remove all duplicate references. When we encounter a node, we place it in the list of visited nodes. We need to keep track of the nodes that we have visited, but we allow a node with an out degree greater than one to appear more than once in a visited list. We then take the leftmost path, keeping the others until later. When all the nodes in the leftmost subgraph have been visited, they will be present in the node list. When a subgraph has been visited, the next leftmost subgraph is visited, its nodes being placed in the list. When the last path out of the root node (the class whose superclasses we are trying to find) has been traversed, we have a complete list of all of that class's superclasses. This list can contain duplicates.

Once we have produced a list of superclasses, we need to decide how we want to remove the duplicate class references it contains. There are two ways:

- remove duplicates from the front, or
- remove them from the end.

The first alternative works as follows. Begin with the start of the list. If the first element occurs later in the list, remove those later copies. Continue until all duplicates have been removed. The second works in a dual fashion: start with the end and remove those elements which have duplicates earlier in the list. (Duplicate removal can occur as part of the visiting phase, but it is easier to describe it as a two-phase process.) FLAVORS [21] employed a depth-first search combined with removal from the end, while LOOPS [15] used a depth-first search with duplicates removed from the start of the superclass list. Neither the FLAVORS, nor the LOOPS approach is completely adequate.

Linearized inheritance is a relatively old technique, so it is relatively well understood. However, although it is used in CLOS, and still, therefore, has currency, it suffers from a number of problems.

First, the linearization process inserts unrelated classes between related ones in the sorted superclass chain. This has the disadvantage that the "effective parent" of a class might be a class of whose existence the programmer is totally unaware. This has the consequence that, for example, iteration over ancestors can generate unexpected results.

Secondly, and related to the first problem, is the problem that an entity that is derived through inheritance might be known to be sub-optimal. The optimal entity might be in a part of the class chain that is made inaccessible by an inserted class that contains an entity with the same name, the sub-optimal entity. When the search order can be influenced, as it can in CLOS, there can be some measure of control; however, even when search can be influenced, the order in which duplicates are removed can still intervene and remove an optimal selection from the linearized class chain.

Finally, communication with "real" parents is very hard to establish. The reason for this is, again, that extraneous classes can be inserted into the linearized class chain between the "real" parents. The additional, inserted, classes appear to be parents of the one from which the superchain was generated, but they come from regions of the inheritance graph that are not strongly connected with the originator class. Thus, when engaging in a search along the parent chain, a query might be satisfied by a class other than a genuine parent of the class from which the search started (assuming a reflexive superclass relation). The *send super* operation and method combination mechanisms were introduced in order to support communication with "real" parents.

4.10 Implemented Multiple Inheritance Techniques

4.10.1 The CLOS Search Method

The CLOS extension to Common LISP defines a specific method for inheriting slots ([82], Chapter 28). This same method is used in Dylan [6]. The algorithm is complex, but avoids the problems described above and that can sometimes arise with depth-first searches. The algorithm is explained in Chapter 28, Section 1.5 of [82] (pp. 782-784) and in [35]. I repeat it here almost *verbatim* (with explanation as appropriate). The algorithm works by producing a list of superclasses that is then ordered. It is noteworthy because it is a sophisticated version of a linearized inheritance technique, but one that makes the problem with joins somewhat easier to handle. I present the algorithm in detail in order to show the reader how complex these things can become.

First, we observe that a class together with a list of its immediate superclasses (those mentioned in the superclass list or specification that forms part of its textual definition) forms a total ordering and is called the *local precedence list*. It is a total ordering because a search for a CLOS slot will begin with the class and then move along the class list from left to right (the order of the superclasses in the list is arbitrary, but they must be ordered somehow, simply because text is linear). The *class precedence list* for a class C is a total ordering on C and its superclasses that is consistent with the local precedence orders for C and each of its superclasses. In other words, for each class S that is in a superclass of C, the class precedence list respects the ordering induced by the local precedence list of each S.

In the class precedence list, a class precedes its direct (immediate) superclasses and a direct superclass precedes all other direct superclasses specified to its right in the superclass list in the class's textual definition. For every class C, define:

$$R_C = \{(C, C_1), (C_1, C_2), \ldots, (C_{n-1}, C_n)\}$$

where $C_1, \ldots, C_n$ are the direct superclasses of C in the order in which they appear in the textual definition of the class C.

Let S_C denote the set of C and its superclasses, and let R be defined as:

$$R = \cup_{c \in S_C} R_c$$

A partial ordering might or might not be generated by R; this depends upon whether the R_c, $c \in S_C$ are consistent. It is assumed that they are consistent and that R generates a partial ordering. When the R_c are not consistent, R is inconsistent.

To compute the class precedence list for C, it is necessary to use a topological sort on the elements of S_C with respect to the partial ordering generated by R. When the topological sort must select a class from a set of two or more classes, none of which is preceded by other classes with respect to R, the class selected is chosen deterministically, as described below. If R is inconsistent, an error condition is raised.

Topological sorting works by finding a class C in S_C such that no other class precedes that element according to the elements in R. The class C is placed first in the result. Remove C from S_C, and remove all pairs of the form (C, D), $D \in S_C$, from R. Repeat the process, adding classes with no predecessors to the end of the result. Stop when no elements can be found with no predecessor.

If S_C is not empty and the process has stopped, the set R is inconsistent. If every class in the finite set of classes is preceded by another, then R contains a loop.

Let $\{N_1, \ldots, N_m\}$, $m = 2$, be the classes from S_C with no predecessors. Let $(C_1, \ldots, C_n)$, $n = 1$, be the class precedence list thus far constructed. Class C_1 is the most specific class, and C_n is the least specific. Let $1 \le j \le n$ be the greatest number such that there exists some i where $1 \le i \le m$, and N_i is a direct superclass of C_j; N_i is placed next.

This rule selects from a set of classes with no predecessors. Its effect is that classes in a simple superclass chain are adjacent in the class precedence list and that classes in each relatively separated subgraph are adjacent in the class precedence list. For example, let T_1 and T_2 be subgraphs whose only common element is the class j. Suppose that no superclass of j appears in either T_1 or T_2. Let C_1 be the bottom of T_1; let C_2 be the bottom of T_2. Suppose that C is a class whose direct superclasses are C_1 and C_2 in that order. The class precedence list of C will start with C and will be followed by all classes in T_1 except j. All the classes in T_2 follow next. Class j and its superclasses appear last.

Like the depth-first enumerations, this algorithm involves some knowledge of how the inheritance lattice is structured. This is typical of many multiple inheritance algorithms, but it also requires that the programmer be aware of how the algorithm works. This is a burden on the programmer, except in the simplest cases.

4.10.2 Multiple Inheritance in C++

C++ [91] also recognizes the problem of repeated inheritance. The solution adopted in C++ is to introduce a new kind of superclass, the *virtual* superclass. Before this introduction, C++ already supports different kinds of superclass: *public, protected* and *private*. The intention behind this division is the restriction in visibility of the superclass's public slots (method and data members, in C++ parlance). With a *public* superclass, all of its public slots are public in the subclass; with a *protected* superclass, inherited public slots become protected in the subclass, and similarly for *private* superclasses.

When a superclass is marked as being *virtual*, the compiler is instructed to use only one copy of the named superclass. The *virtual* marking can be combined with the *public, protected* and *private* markings and has the same effect in terms of visibility. However, a *virtual* marking ensures that, no matter what the visibility of the public slots of the virtual superclass, only one copy of them will appear in the subclass being defined or in any of its subclasses.

In fact, the story is not quite as simple as the last paragraph would suggest, for what really happens is that a class which is a direct subclass of a class that will be repeated must mark that superclass as virtual. This can be made clearer with a diagram (see Figure 4.9).

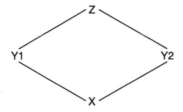

Fig. 4.9. *Diamond inheritance structure—shared super.*

In the figure, class X inherits from classes $Y1$ and $Y2$. Classes $Y1$ and $Y2$ have class X as their superclass. Class X is, therefore, a shared superclass. If inheritance worked in the normal way, slots in X would be duplicated. However, in C++, if classes $Y1$ and $Y2$ mark X as a virtual superclass, only one copy will be inherited. C++ forces the programmer to recognize that a superclass will be repeated when its immediate subclasses are defined. If this is not done, the programmer must, at some later stage, return to those classes and identify the shared superclass. This clearly requires good documentation.

The above strategies can be combined with the "scope resolution" operator (the "::") operator. Although nothing is stated in [91], it would appear that C++ employs graph inheritance combined with renaming.

4.10.3 Multiple Inheritance in Eiffel

The Eiffel language [67] permits multiple inheritance. The approach to multiple inheritance that is employed in Eiffel is different from those we have previously seen. Rather than demanding that the inheritance process find exactly one instance of a slot or method (a "feature" in Eiffel parlance), the language permits multiple copies of a feature to be returned. There are, according to Meyer [67], two cases that must be addressed:

"Depending upon the context, either solution may be the right one, and you will need some leeway for choosing between them in any particular case:
1. In some circumstances you may use repeated inheritance precisely because you like a feature of an ancestor so much that you want two of it.
2. Often, however, one copy is enough". ([67], p. 169)

Thus, Eiffel is designed to permit the programmer to decide whether one or more (two, according to the language definition) copies of a feature are to be included by multiple inheritance into a subclass. Further down the same page, Meyer states explicitly that:

"Not only would it be too restrictive for the language definition to specify either solution 1 or solution 2 for all cases of repeated inheritance: forcing developers, for each case of repeated inheritance from a class A, to select either one of these solutions for all the features of A would also be impractical. In reality, you need replication for some features and sharing for some others" ([67], p. 169)

Eiffel, therefore, provides a mechanism that provides the programmer with the required flexibility. This is called the *Repeated Inheritance Rule* ([67], p. 170). The rule states that if a feature is inherited under the same final name (name in the subclass being defined), a single feature is included (the multiple copies are *shared*); otherwise, the feature is included as many times as there are new names for it (this is referred to as *replication*). In order to make this rule work, Eiffel provides a mechanism for renaming features that have been inherited.

Eiffel, unlike many of the other proposals considered in this chapter, permits the programmer to choose between *tree* and *linearized* inheritance.

The Repeated Inheritance Rule suffers from a problem. Because features can be arbitrarily renamed, it is possible for a feature to be inherited in a form that represents the result of renaming. This can lead to naming conflicts in different branches of an inheritance lattice (different features can be given the same name). In order to remedy this, Eiffel has a Repeated Inheritance Consistency constraint. The constraint is defined thus:

"It is valid for a class D to be a repeated descendant of a class A if and only if D satisfies the following two conditions for every feature f of A:
1. If the Repeated Inheritance Rule implies that f will be shared in D, then all inherited versions of f are the same feature.

2. If the Repeated Inheritance Rule implies that f will be replicated in D and f is potentially ambiguous, then the Select subclause of exactly one of the Parents of D lists the corresponding version of f, under its final name." ([67], p. 191)

Eiffel's select construct is a means to remove ambiguity in inheritance declarations. Consider the case of class A which defines a method called f. Class A has two subclasses, B and C, each of which redefines f. Class B redefines f as a method that prints "yes", while C redefines it as one that prints "no". Now consider a class D which is a subclass of both B and C. Class D will inherit both versions of f; clearly, they conflict in their behaviours. Eiffel allows renaming of components that are inherited from particular sources, so it is possible to rename the instance of f that comes from B as b_f, and that from C as d_f (in fact, as the language definition makes clear, such a simple renaming is invalid in Eiffel).

The problem is that this relies upon the order in which the renaming is performed. In a simple case such as this, where the origins of features can be determined with ease, there is no problem with such renaming. However, the standard case is far more complex, and determining where things come from is not easy. Furthermore, the order in which classes are listed in a subclass can be significant, particularly because this affects search order in the superclass lattice. In the case under consideration, there are too many interpretations of f, not too few; banning the case is, according to Meyer, not a serious option.

Whenever a repeated descendant (such as D here) inherits two or more separately redeclared versions of a feature, or the original and a redeclared version, the Repeated Inheritance Consistency constraint requires that D select exactly one of them. This is where select is used: it acts as a redefinition of all of the conflicting inherited versions (f from both B and C in this example). This means that f is bound to d_f under the above renaming—d_f is the selected version.

One reason why the problem arises is that Eiffel is a dynamically bound language and both B and C are of the common type A. Thus, any variable that is declared to be of type B, say, is also of type A; equally, any variable declared to be of type C is also of type A. Therefore, any variable declared to be of type B or C is automatically of type A. As a consequence, anything of type B can be assigned to a variable of type C and vice versa. It is not, therefore, possible to discriminate between d_f and b_f in the example presented above, for they can be considered to be of the same type. Since the order in which the lattice is searched is significant, the first instance of f that is encountered can serve the role of the first renamed f in D. As long as we can identify the origin of a feature, reliance upon search order is possible. However, in cases that are more complex or in which we cannot know the order, such reliance is misplaced, for a feature might be derived from a source other than the one we believe it to be. If, for example, we have four classes divided into two subclasses and two supers such that each of the subclasses inherits from both of the superclasses, there is no particular way for a feature to be inherited. If the origin cannot uniquely be determined, it becomes impossible to determine which of a repeated collection of features is the intended or "correct" one. Thus, the select construct is introduced with the effect of stating that the feature being selected is the one chosen for use in the class. The feature that is selected is guaranteed to be derived from the superclass specified. Some Eiffel syntax should make this clearer:

```
class D inherit
    B
    rename
      f as bf
    select
      bf
    end;
    C
    rename
      f as df
    end
    ...
end  -- class D
```

This has the effect of making b_f, the version of f inherited from B, the version of f that is used in class D.

4.11 Mixin Classes

We have already encountered the concept of an abstract class. This is a class for which it makes no sense to create direct instances. An abstract class serves as a place-holder in an inheritance graph, defining those properties and behaviours which are required by many other classes, but, when taken on their own, should not be instantiated. Examples of abstract classes abound in Computer Science.

The inheritance graph has, as one of its linearizations, one which is shown in Figure 4.10:

It will be recalled that there is more than one possible linearization of this graph and that classes are inserted into the linearized form by the search algorithm so that a class is often separated from its direct superclasses. Above, we considered this to be a disadvantage. It is possible to generalize this to a new form of class, one that has no apparent ancestor, but which does not invoke parent operations in any meaningful fashion. Classes of this kind have been named mixin classes because they rely on the linearization in order to be "mixed in" at the appropriate place as a class that inherits from a class providing the required operations. This means that it is possible to create mixins that can be mixed in to a set of different superclasses (base classes

Fig. 4.10. *A linearization.*

in mixin terminology). A number of authors have suggested that mixins are useful and highly flexible building blocks with which to construct inheritance hierarchies. An alternative approach to multiple inheritance is based upon the mixin as the only mechanism used to create inheritance hierarchies. This is called *mixin-based* inheritance [18, 17, 46].

The classic example of a mixin is a class that adds colour attributes to a variety of base classes.

In mixin-based inheritance, a mixin is not a class and multiple inheritance is a consequence of, and not a supporting mechanism for, the use of mixins. In this approach, mixins are the only abstraction mechanism for building the inheritance hierarchy (see [18, 17, 46, 27, 87], as well as [86]).

Let us consider the following model of inheritance. We consider inheritance as an incremental modification mechanism that alters a parent to produce a result. The result is often some kind of combination of the parent plus its modification. Such a model is fundamental to the model of inheritance proposed by Bracha and Cook [18] and is used as the basis for the introduction of mixin-based inheritance. In that paper, it is also shown that mixin-based inheritance subsumes those mechanisms provided by Smalltalk, Beta and CLOS for inheritance. We can, following Steyaert ([86], p. 118), write the inheritance as a modification process for a parent, P, and result R under a modifier M, as:

$$R = P\Delta M = P + M(P)$$

While it is the case that in conventional inheritance of whatever form, the modifier, M, has no independent existence, being usually part of the result, mixin-based inheritance is based upon the intuition that one can view the modifier M as an abstraction which has an existence that is separate from the parent and result—i.e., it is a kind of operator. Under this interpretation, modifiers are called *mixins*. The composition operator, Δ, is called a *mixin application*. The class to which a mixin is applied is called the *base class*. Classes can only be extended through the application of mixins in *pure* mixin inheritance. The base class is typically accessed through a pseudo-variable in the same way that a subclass has access to its superclass, even though the composition operation takes the base class as an argument. In statically typed languages, this has the implication that a mixin must specify the names and types of the attributes a candidate base class must supply; for this reason, mixins are occasionally referred to as "abstract subclasses".

Mixin-based inheritance, as described above, is based on the model of inheritance as an incremental modification mechanism. The concept makes explicit wrappers and wrapper application. Steyaert [86] generalizes mixin-based inheritance in three ways. First, his mixins are based on a more general formulation of the concept of a wrapper in which wrappers can have more than one parent. The concept of a wrapper with multiple parents was introduced by Cook [28]. In Steyaert's work, multiple parents are used to solve name clash problems in multiple inheritance hierarchies when interfaces are merged. Secondly, the use of mixins is extended to object-based inheritance. This is similar to the implicit anticipated delegation of Stein *et al.* [83]. Thirdly, mixins can be viewed as named slots in objects in the same way that objects and methods are; this permits an object to exercise some control over the way in which it is extended. This leads to an abstraction method that can control inheritance hierarchies. It also implies nested mixins as a natural consequence of permitting mixins to be slots.

4.12 Alternatives to Multiple Inheritance

It should be clear from the above that multiple inheritance is far from being a settled issue. Differences still exist as to how to perform searches among the multiple superclasses and how to resolve the problem of avoiding the duplicate slot or method names that can result from a superclass search. The most obvious alternative is to resort to single inheritance (as is done in Beta, for example) and to employ some other technique as appropriate, as we saw in Chapter 2 when we considered Beta's block structure and its ability to represent nested classes. Here, we consider the concepts of *perspectives* and *interfaces* as two popular suggestions.

4.12.1 Perspectives

An alternative that derives from the knowledge representation literature is the concept of perspectives. This appears in the FRL work of Roberts and Goldstein at MIT [73], as well as in Braspenning and Bakker's INCA [8]. The idea underpinning a perspective is that it represents some facet of the object as seen from some viewpoint. Our example of the water-skiing accountant would be organized as a class representing accountants which has a perspective representing the water-skiing hobby. If it is necessary to know about the hobbies of an accountant, the perspectives are examined and the one representing hobbies is accessed. This would represent the multiple inheritance from classes *Accountant* and *Water-skier*.

Thus, a class or object is associated with one or more perspectives. If perspectives are represented as kinds of class (as they might be in an implementation of INCA), their inclusion within an ordinary class, C, might be performed by having a slot that is to contain a list of perspective names. The slots of the various perspectives are then merged in instances of C. This requires a special annotation in the definition of a class, but, as Eiffel shows, annotations can be used to very good effect when they are well-motivated.

Perspectives are special kinds of class. They engage in inheritance themselves and can, therefore, inherit slots from their superclasses. They can also have perspectives themselves, assuming that the underlying structure is regular (as it should be). In the case of a class representing an accountant, we would, presumably have a *Hobbies* perspective which would, presumably, hold a set of references to *Hobby* objects. But a class representing an accountant will also have more than one perspective, for we have *Person* as an accountant, as a person with hobbies, as a parent, as a tax-payer, and so on. Some of these can be inherited from the class's superclass (tax-payer), but many will not, and some will depend upon who, exactly, the person being represented is. This is an issue which suggests that individuals be represented by their own classes; this was an argument that led to the proposal of prototypes, so we will not go further into the issue.

The Beta language contains a mechanism that allows perspectives (or aspects) of an object to be represented in a fashion that does not require a completely new syntactic construct, nor a new semantic concept. Instead, it permits the explicit definition of classes (or Beta's equivalent of classes) to occur as the values of slots. Thus, Beta permits the definition of nested classes (as does C++ and Java). This gives Beta an extended block structure and allows different, separate, aspects of an entity to be given a relatively straightforward representation. The block structuring principle allows for a degree of modularity and information hiding. Because the components are classes, they can be directly instantiated and manipulated as such.

4.12.2 Interfaces in Java

Another alternative approach to multiple inheritance can be seen in Java. Java is intended to be a much-simplified version of, and improvement upon, C++. It omits pointers and multiple inheritance. Instead of multiple inheritance, a Java class can achieve the same effect by inheriting from a single superclass and implementing one or more *interfaces*. An interface is a construct that collects into a single unit the specification of the variables, constants and methods that, when implemented, will perform the functions the interface is intended to perform. An interface, let us stress, is not a class but a specification of the data and operations that achieve some effect. A class which implements an interface must provide definitions for the methods specified by the interface; these methods, as well as any constants and variables specified by the interface, can be inherited by the subclasses of the class which implements them. Since it can implement an unbounded number of interfaces, a Java class can gain the effect of inheriting from multiple sources.

The interfaces approach works relatively well. In versions of Java before 1.1, interfaces could only contain method prototypes (using ANSI C/C++ terminology). In version 1.1 and after, they can contain constants and variables as well as method prototypes. This allows some specification of a state to be acquired by implementing classes. This is important because inheritance not only provides access to methods, it also provides components to be included in the state.

4.13 Delegation and Prototypes

We saw how delegation works in the case of prototype languages in the last chapter. In these languages, there is no class structure and no inheritance lattice. As we saw, new objects are created from old by cloning or by merging. Cloning is a more common technique and depends upon the existence of a single parent.

Prototypical objects were originally proposed by Lieberman [55]. In that paper, Lieberman assumes that an object will usually be composed of more than one prototype:

> "To create an object that shares knowledge with a prototype, you construct an *extension* object, which has a list containing its prototypes, which may be shared with other objects, and *personal* behavior idiosyncratic to the object itself. When an extension object receives a message, it first attempts to respond to the message using the behaviour stored in its personal part. If the object's personal characteristics are not relevant for answering the message, the object forwards the message on to the prototypes to see if one can respond to the message. This process of forwarding is called *delegating* the message" (pp. 215-216, original italics).

Thus, we see that Lieberman explicitly construes an object as being composed of one *or more* prototypes, the object being able to serve as a prototype in later constructions. Therefore, delegation should occur between an object and many others (its prototypes).

The idiosyncratic behaviours exhibited by an object can contain components which engage in *computed delegation*; i.e., computations which decide to which objects delegation should occur (we mentioned this in the last chapter).

Thus, the range of delegation behaviours that are permitted of a prototype is relatively extensive. This suggests that delegation can be a more dynamic mechanism than inheritance; it also suggests that relationships exist between an object and its many prototypes in a fashion related to those between a class and its superclass.

Under delegation, when an object needs a slot or a method, it delegates to one of its parents. In the case of a method, it is executed in the requesting object's context; a slot is merely retrieved. The process of delegation, at least in its conventional interpretation, would involve messages being sent to the prototypes that are the parents of the sender. In a sense, this kind of delegation involves a search through the supers of the requesting object. Viewed in this light, delegation does not admit of a comparison with multiple inheritance for delegation is related entirely to single inheritance.

If, however, we consider the Actors approach to computation [47, 2, 1, 3], we see a more general approach to delegation that is more closely related to multiple inheritance. In Actors, the fundamental unit of computation is an Actor, a side-effect free module which executes in parallel with all other actors and which interacts with them via a message-passing protocol. In Actors, if an individual actor receives a message to which it cannot respond, it delegates the message to another actor. If the first actor to which the message is delegated is unable to respond (perhaps, itself engaging in delegation in order to determine this), the original, delegating actor can attempt to delegate to an arbitrary number of other actors in an order determined by that actor. Thus, we have a situation in which a single object, an actor, is able to delegate messages to other actors; this corresponds to the notion of multiple inheritance. We could construe multiple inheritance as the sending of messages to the multiple superclasses of the sending object.

In the multiple delegation case, the actor determines the order in which it delegates to the other actors. In a more generalized prototype language, a prototype can delegate to an arbitrary number of other prototypes. It is most natural to delegate first to those objects (prototypes) which were involved in the creation of the delegating one. These objects are more likely to contain information that is central to the delegating object's structure. However, there would appear to be no reason why a prototype could not delegate to any appropriate prototype in the system. The limit on such behaviour is the appropriateness of the prototype to which the task (message) is being delegated. The order in which delegation is performed can also vary. A strategy requiring delegation to the most appropriate prototype first, followed in descending order by those less likely to produce results is one approach. If delegation is needed in order to synthesize a new entity, the prototypes that are able to supply data and operations appropriate to its construction will receive messages—note that such dynamic creation of entities is extremely hard to perform in a class-based language.

An efficiency problem was identified by the SELF team with respect to the slots shared between prototypes. They observed that strict cloning would involve making a complete copy (usually a shallow, not a deep, copy) of a prototype before subjecting it to modification. This is the approach taken in the Kevo language [93, 94], a Forth-based prototype language for the Apple Macintosh. Kevo is a remarkable achievement, supporting reflection (see Chapter 8), multi-tasking and a graphical user interface. The cloning operation in Kevo involves taking copies of objects and then modifying them. This leads, naturally enough, to many copies of slots being present in the system at any time. As far as the SELF team was concerned (see [25]), this is a waste of memory, while Kevo makes it a virtue. The Kevo experience suggests that for many objects, the amount of memory consumed in copies is not that great, however the additional expenditure of memory is performed.

The SELF team decided that this duplication wasted memory. Cloning should, therefore be restricted. For each prototype, a *traits* object is created. This object represents everything that is essential about an object. In a sense, it is a kind of class from to which delegation can occur. When delegation is performed, the traits object will respond with values that are typical of an entire class of objects, or with methods that are general for the entire class. Since whatever is put into the traits object must be common to all objects of that kind, it seems sensible to expect that a traits object will be composed of constant slots, access methods and general methods. It can be argued that traits objects merely re-introduce classes into prototype-based languages.

For example, if we consider an object representing a point in a two-dimensional space, its traits object might contain a method to convert from Cartesian to polar co-ordinates, and a method to perform the inverse computation, as well as a method to print the point's data (its two co-ordinates).

In [84] Stein (pp. 138-146) argues that inheritance is a more general mechanism than delegation. It is possible to argue the converse: i.e., that delegation is more general than inheritance. The status of delegation with respect to inheritance is, therefore, controversial.

4.14 Aggregation

The message that is to be derived from the concept of part objects is that they provide a mechanism that is as powerful as multiple inheritance, but with less conceptual overhead (and with a simpler semantics). They also show how aggregation can be simulated in Beta. Aggregation is a technique that we have not yet mentioned, but is used in a number of systems, Microsoft's OLE, for example. Aggregation is another alternative to inheritance, one that is closely related to, but distinct from, delegation.

The concept of aggregation is founded on the idea that components of an object can be obtained via either naming or message passing. In the case of naming, one object names the components of another object and refers to these remote components by means of these names. This means that one object has access to at least the interface of the other object. If aggregation is performed by means of messages, we have a structure closely related to delegation. If the aggregating object wants a component, it sends a message to the object which contains it; the receiving object then returns a message that contains the desired object (so, in the case of a method, it is executed in the context of the delegating—or aggregating—object). When an object based on aggregation is used, it must be used in conjunction with the objects whose components it references; clearly, an aggregate object depends upon the other objects for its operation. This suggests that an aggregate object is related to a container object (in OLE, aggregations are containers).

If naming is used to refer to objects and components, a single address space is implied; if messages are used to gain access to objects and components, there can be multiple address spaces (hence a distributed application). Neither of these assumptions is necessary, provided that adequate support and translation mechanisms are provided.

Conceptually, the same remarks that apply to delegation apply to aggregation. In this sense, aggregation is a variety of delegation. However, for an aggregation to be formed, more than one object is required. This contrasts with objects under inheritance and delegation where we can have a well-formed program composed of a single object (this object does not engage in inheritance or in delegation).

Consider the case of a *DE* queue which is based on a *FIFO* queue class. The *DE* queue type will be defined in terms of an add to the front and an add to the back method, an empty test, and so on. Some of these operations are inherited from the *FIFO* class, but some are newly defined in the *DE* class. If we now try to define a stack (a LIFO stack, that is) in terms of the *DE* class, we encounter the problem that we need to exclude, or prevent the inheritance of, some operations (e.g., the add to the back operation). Further examples of this kind can often be found in the use of Java's API classes (I have frequently needed to hide unwanted methods). Given that such an anomaly occurs, it might seem that simple subclass derivation is not the correct way to handle the problem. Aggregation can be employed, together with aliasing or redefinition, as the following examples show (the reader familiar with Beta should note that I have simplified the language a little in order to avoid unnecessary details).

In Beta, use of part objects can be made so that some operations are hidden because they are not exposed in the containing class.

If the *Stack* class is defined as:

```
Stack : (# d: DEQueue;
           push : d.enterInFront;
           pop : d.removeInFront;
         ...
        #)
```

the part object, *d*, can be made accessible via the path notation.

Now, if we assume that the *Stack* class will be almost the same as the *DEQueue* class with the exception that there is no *enterInFront* method, a part object can be used in the definition of push:

```
Stack : (# d: DEQueue;
             push : (# ? #)
             pop : d.removeInFront;
                 . . .
         #)
```

We can also engage in a complete redefinition of *DEQueue*'s operation:

```
Stack : (# d: DEQueue;
             push : d.enterInFront(# ? #);
             pop : d.removeInFront;
                 . . .
         #)
```

This redefines the *enterInFront* method that is originally defined in the *DEQueue* pattern: the outermost definition over-rides the one in the original class. This technique ensures that we have the right definition of the method for our use.

Aggregation plus renaming can also be used to implement the kind of multiple inheritance that has been used in C++ [92]. Assume we have a pattern *T*, such that:

```
T : (# a : A;
        b : B;
     #)
```

This aggregates objects *a* and *b* which are instances of *A* and *B*, respectively. Assuming that *A* has slots *x*, *y* and *z*, and *B* has attributes *s* and *z*, the slots available to *T* can then be accessed by:

$$a.xa.ya.zb.sb.z$$

In order to avoid naming conflicts and to avoid compound identifiers, renaming needs to be performed. (Beta provides other facilities to assist in automatic name-conflict resolution, but they are not relevant to the current discussion).

The essential point, the one which the reader should remember, is that aggregation is an alternative to inheritance, particularly when locally defined classes are permitted. In the above examples, aggregation helped in a more natural definition of the Stack class (pattern, in Beta terms) than is possible just using inheritance (the reader is invited to compare the Beta solution to that in [35]. The developers of Beta argue that part objects are an extremely useful addition to an object-oriented language, one which alleviates a number of difficult problems.

5. Methods

5.1 Introduction

Methods often seem to be the forgotten part of object-oriented languages. The emphasis seems very much to be on inheritance and polymorphism, not on what methods are and how they are derived. This chapter reviews the position of methods in object-oriented languages and how they are located.

Methods are the representation of operations in an object-oriented programming language. The slots of an object represent the properties or data that the object encapsulates and methods represent the operations that are defined over these slots. They are procedures and functions which are associated with an object via its class or prototype and are intended to perform the operations defined for that object or class of objects. Methods are the procedural component of object-oriented languages of all kinds.

Because they are the procedural element, methods often tend to be overlooked. In C++ and Java, methods are very similar to routines in C, the major difference being that methods have access to a pseudo-variable called *this* which refers to the class in which the method is defined; *this* allows a method to access the data slots of the objects over which they are defined. A pseudo-variable with the name *self* is used in Smalltalk, LOOPS and many other languages for exactly the same purpose; it is often implemented as an additional parameter which is automatically added to each method's formal parameter list; the pseudo-variable is always bound to the object to which the method belongs when that method is called. In prototype-based languages, the *self* variable is bound to the object which is calling the method, it should be noted; it does, however, serve exactly the same purpose as in class-based languages.

The Beta language [54] has a novel approach to methods and classes. It treats them both as aspects of an over-arching concept, the pattern. The difference between a class and a method is essentially that a method can be executed. The representation allows slots to be added to basic methods in exactly the same way as if method definitions were ordinary class definitions. This allows methods to be annotated in various ways, for example describing the situations in which they should be used (this is reasonable because a method object can only describe or define the method; it can never be the method).

The method representation adopted in Beta suggests that it should be possible in a rigorous fashion to consider methods as first-class objects. In CLOS and other languages that use generic functions, methods are often implemented as objects, but they tend to be treated in different ways. One way in which we could do this is to examine the types in the signatures of method objects and to organize them in those terms; this is very much the way in which generic functions and multi-methods are organized. However, such an approach still ties methods with classes and does little to clarify the use of inner or super statements when methods are treated as separate from classes as they can be in some languages. In Beta, it is possible to define free-standing method patterns which should naturally be treated in terms of their family relationships; the inner statement allows such methods to be defined so that they can be specialized in a way that is not directly related to containing classes. Similarly, in CLOS, sets of multi-methods can be defined that are not systematically related to classes, but which are internally consistent and admit of a classifying construct such as a class; multi-methods are also used in Cecil [24]. Until we are able to define such methods in a more flexible way, we will merely concentrate on the ways in which methods are associated with classes and prototypes.

It is clear that methods must interact with objects in a number of ways. Principally, methods must be associated with objects in some way in order that they be found and applied to the correct entities. In many languages, there is an exact correspondence between a method and a set of classes (it is possible, as will be seen in Chapter 6, that two methods can have the same name and appear in different classes); for example, in CLOS, multi-methods are associated directly with classes (considered as types). When a method is defined in a class which has subclasses, that method is available to all subclasses of its defining class via the inheritance relation. This means that the operation represented by the method is defined for the subclasses. It also means that the code that is the runtime representation of that method is shared among all of the defining class's subclasses; it is not necessary for a class to redefine a method unless the inherited behaviour is not what is wanted in the subclass (such redefinition is possible in most class-based languages). This immediately leads to a question (which is asked in Sather [76, 77] and, to a lesser extent, in Eiffel [67]): why define the code (body) of a method until it is needed? Classes which do not specify method bodies should be considered abstract for they cannot be fully instantiated (full instantiation implies that all operations be defined). In Sather, unless a class is to be instantiated, its methods are not completely specified; instead, only their *signatures* (see below) are defined. Later, when an instance of a class is required, the implementation-specific parts are stated by the programmer. This has the consequence that code sharing, which is automatic in most object-oriented languages based on classes, now must be a matter of explicit choice. The normal situation is for code to be shared because complete methods (signatures and code) are inherited; this allows one to treat inheritance as if it were just a mechanism for code sharing (see [81] for a discussion).

The interaction between inheritance and methods is of considerable importance because it is possible in subclasses to *redefine* methods that have been defined in ancestor classes. In typed languages, there are interactions between this redefinition and the type system.

In a similar fashion, it is possible to *overload* the methods that are defined in ancestor classes. Overloading is another property that is intimately connected with a language's type system.

Section 5.2 deals with the relationship between methods and objects, while Section 5.3 considers the relationship between object constructors and methods. Next, in Section 5.4, the concepts of environment and closure are introduced in order to motivate a discussion of higher-order functions and methods. As part of this, the *block* construct in Smalltalk and SELF is discussed and shown to be an extremely powerful construct—it is used in both languages in the definition of conditional and iteration constructs. Section 5.5 considers the interactions between methods and inheritance. Finally, static and dynamic method binding are discussed and two key implementations of dynamic binding are presented.

5.2 Methods and Objects

Methods are typically associated with objects in object-oriented programming. In class-based programming, they are associated with classes; in prototype-based languages, they are associated with prototypes. When defining a class, it is typically the case that methods must also be defined. If we recall the ADT model of class-based programming, it can be seen that methods represent the operations to be performed by the ADT represented by the class. When defining a new prototype, new behaviours are added in order to differentiate it from other prototypes, in particular the prototypes from which it is derived. When object-oriented programming is viewed as a modelling technique, methods are the behaviours of the objects that are required by the model.

In a great many languages (Smalltalk, Java, C++, Eiffel, Sather, Beta) methods are defined for the class in which they reside. Methods can be overridden as part of the construction of an inheritance hierarchy, and over-riding methods are associated with new classes that are lower in the hierarchy. The relationship between methods and objects (typically classes) is clearly very close, even though methods with slightly different behaviours might be associated with the same name at different points in an inheritance hierarchy. For example, we might have a class which represents a container and which has an addition method to add elements to that container. In a derived class, we might want to keep a count of the number of items we have added to the container, so we subclass the original class and redefine the addition method so that it increments a counter every time it is called and then adds an element to the data structure. These two methods will have the same name and the same signature (this is required in C++ and Java, for example).

The signature of a method is the complete specification of its type. In Java/C++ notation, a function which inputs two integers and returns no value would have a signature:

$$int \times int \rightarrow void$$

for example; a function which inputs an instance of InputStream and an integer, returning an integer would have signature:

$$InputStream \times int \rightarrow int$$

(again, in C++/Java notation). We will return to the concept of the signature in Chapter 6.

A constraint in many languages is that the signatures of derived methods must be the same as in their parent class. This means that if we have a method m in a class, C, and we then define a subclass, C_1, of C, and we redefine method m, if we want the version of m in C_1 to over-ride that in C, the two must have the same name and same signature.

The most significant alternative to this direct attachment of methods is the generic function and multi-method combination found in languages of the LISP group and in Cecil [24]. The underlying ideas are that method specification can be separated from class definition and that a method can have different implementations depending upon the types of its inputs. This approach also makes the interface to methods explicit. Thus, when using generic functions and multi-methods, the programmer first specifies the interface which the method will present and then defines instances of the method which depend upon their input types.

The specification of the generic function is a specification of an interface. It does not include any code. A generic function is a template, therefore. To define a generic function, a name is supplied (the name of the method) and the arguments are specified. The arguments must be correct in number and are specified as arbitrary names. There are no type specifications for a generic function's arguments. The reason for this is that the arguments will be associated with types when the methods are defined. Until a method is defined, a type cannot be associated with an argument; furthermore, a generic function cannot specify types because that might anchor the function at a particular place in the space generated by the classes in the program or system. When it is defined, a generic function specifies the corresponding method's name and its arity.

The next stage is to define methods that implement their generic function. Method definition is the same in this approach as it is in others: a procedural entity is constructed. When defining a method, its body is constructed in the normal way, and its arguments are defined. The name of the method must be the same as the generic function which it instantiates and the number of arguments must be the same (LISP, like some other languages, allows, amongst other kinds, optional parameters and these are taken into account by the method standard defined for CLOS). Types can be specified for each argument. In LISP, it is legal for a type to be omitted; in such a case, the formal parameter can be bound to a value of any type—it is a *polymorphic* variable (in fact, CLOS defines a root type, t, from which all types are derived; all formals which are not associated with a type are assumed to have t as their type).

There can be more than one method (actual method) for each generic function. This is the reason why they are called *multi-methods*. At runtime, it is necessary to determine which multi-method to apply. This is done as follows. When a call is made to a method, the type of each argument is found in turn. When the types have been determined, the method with the same input types is chosen for execution; if there is no method whose input types match, either an error is signalled or a default method (if there is one) is called.

Although conceptually accurate, the search for a method would actually be performed in a way that does not wait until all types become available. Instead, it is performed incrementally. First, all methods whose first formal argument has the same type as the actual argument are retrieved (plus any methods which either have an unspecified type for their first argument or which have a first argument of root type). The second argument's type is used to reduce the set by eliminating those methods which do not have a second argument of type matching that of the second actual parameter, and so on recursively. This does involve a space overhead, but techniques exist [51] to speed up retrieval.

The generic functions approach separates the definition of operations from the classes to which they apply. It suggests that methods should be treated as independent, possibly polymorphic, entities which can be represented in their own right. This is an interesting possibility, one to which we will return later (see Chapter 8, below). Meanwhile, it is worth noting that Cecil [24], a language not of the LISP group has adopted multi-methods and generic functions.

5.3 Object Constructors and Methods

There is a considerable interaction between object constructors and methods. In particular, the way in which parameters are passed to methods interacts with objects.

Under the *call-by-value* (*leftmost-innermost*, or *applicative order reduction*) scheme, values are passed into procedures; thus, any expressions which are supplied as parameters must be evaluated in order to produce a value to which the procedure can be applied. Given the following function definition:

```
function add1 (int n) : int is
      n + 1
end function;
```

the following call:

```
add1((2 * 3) + 1)
```

(assuming that *add1* is the function which adds one to its argument) will be evaluated as follows. The expression supplied as an actual parameter $(2*3)+1$ is evaluated to produce 7. This value is then bound to the formal parameter, n, and the body of the *add1* function is executed to produce 8.

This scheme works very well for simple types, for arrays, records and pointers; it also works well for functions and procedures. Arrays and records can be represented by pointers to blocks of store; they can also be copied bitwise from the caller to the called routine's stack. Procedural objects are often represented as pointers to their primary entry points or as pointers to closures.

The question arises as to the effect of a call-by-value scheme upon objects. Clearly, if objects are represented by pointers, all that needs be done when calling a procedure is to pass the pointer as an argument. If objects are not represented by pointers, the entire object has to be passed to the called procedure. Here is where potential problems are encountered, for call-by-value implies that a local copy of the parameter object is made. A problem with this is that, C++, by default, for example, employs a technique called *memberwise initialization*; it does *not* employ a bitwise copy of objects. This process copies each built-in or derived data slots from one class object to another. Component classes are subjected to the same process and not copied; this can lead to sharing of values where no sharing was intended.

If a C++ class contains a pointer and defines a destructor method, memberwise initialization is, in general, insufficient. The reason for this is that the destructor method is applied to every instance of a class, not just those created by a creation method. This fact leads to the possibility that an instance can be deallocated when such an operation is not wanted.

The solution in C++ is to pass a reference (constant pointer) to a class which is being passed as a value parameter. This is combined with a technique which explicitly initializes a new instance of the class from an existing one. This initialization technique employs an explicit mechanism for initializing the slots of the instance that is being created. This ensures that all slots are correctly initialized. The mechanism employed is not unrelated to that employed when defining class-specific assignment operators.

If, on the other hand, *normal-order reduction*, or one of its implementations (*lazy evaluation, call-by-reference, call-by-name*, etc.), is employed to pass parameters, the problems with object initialization no longer occur. The reason for this is that the address of the actual parameter is passed to the called procedure when call-by-reference and call-by-name (using a *thunk*) are used. These methods, therefore, simplify the calling process somewhat. When using lazy evaluation, a number of techniques can be used. For example, a *promise* might be constructed. A promise is like a thunk in that it is a function of no arguments (strictly, a closure of a zero-adic function) which, when called, evaluates its body and returns the result. Thus, the object is "wrapped" in a function which can be called at any subsequent point in the evaluation of the program. Promises are not the only way to perform lazy evaluation; functional languages have been implemented using a variety of techniques that ensure lazy evaluation (mostly based on the concept of graph reduction). What is essential for lazy evaluation is to ensure that explicit destructor methods are not employed until all references to an object have been removed.

5.4 Environments and Closures

5.4.1 Introduction

When discussing methods, it is essential to examine the following concepts:

- environments;
- closures;
- continuations.

Here, we will be interested in the first two concepts. The reason for our interest is that they allow us to determine how free variables are handled by a method and they allow us to relate code to free variables and, thereby, to provide a construct which allows us to treat methods as first-class entities. First-class entities are those computational objects to which methods can be applied and which can be returned from methods. Here, note, we understand "method" to include primitive operations such as addition; we do not, of course, expect to be able to add two environments or continuations, for we still need, in this chapter, implicitly to respect a type discipline of some form.

When we are able to apply methods to methods and return methods from methods, we have higher-order constructs and we have gained considerable amounts of notational power. However, we do not need to go as far as to make closures (methods) first-class entities when we introduce the concepts of environment and closure. What we also get, by considering these concepts, is a better understanding as to what is required at runtime in representational terms. We also gain an understanding of what it is that is inherited when a class inherits a method or what is involved in method delegation in prototype-based languages. Furthermore, the question arises, as a natural consequence of examining the relationship between methods and objects, as to how slots are bound; in so-called "impure" languages, the additional question arises of how non-local variables declared outside all objects interact with methods. Such questions can be answered by a consideration of the concepts of environment and closure.

5.4.2 Environments: A More Formal Definition

Most languages make a distinction between those variables which are local to a procedure and those which are not. In the λ-calculus, as well as in the Lower Predicate Calculus, this distinction is made. Variables in the λ-calculus can be free or bound. If a variable is bound by a λ operator, it becomes bound, otherwise it is free. Thus, in:

$$\lambda x.fx$$

the variable x is bound by the λ, while f is free (not captured, or abstracted, by a λ). On the other hand, in:

$$\lambda x.\lambda y.fxy$$

variable f remains free for the entire expression while y is bound in $\lambda y.fxy$ and x is bound in $\lambda x.\lambda y.fxy$. In the sub-expression $\lambda y.fxy$, we say that x is free for y in $\lambda y.fxy$; this means that within the scope of y, x is free. Freeness for a variable is more fundamental, for, in a programming language, all variables are bound at some level (even global variables are bound by the outermost scope).

In a programming language, arguments are bound to functions and methods in a way directly analogous to the λ-calculus. Variables can also be declared inside a method; this corresponds to nesting of λ-expressions. If a variable is supplied by a scope that encloses the definition of the method (function or procedure), that variable is sometimes said to be *free* for the method. Variables defined as slots in a class that contains a method are free for the class's methods.

It is well known that free variables fix the value of an expression in the λ-calculus. Similarly, the free variables fix the value of a procedure, function or method in a programming language. Furthermore, a method's free variables need to be supplied in order for it to execute correctly. The interpretation of methods as λ-calculus expressions indicates why this is so. Consider:

$$\lambda x.x + n$$

This is the *add-n* function. When we call the function, supplying 5, say, as its argument, we add n to 5. Even though we have no idea what x is, we know that for any value of x, the result of applying this function to it will yield a value of $x + n$. However, unless we know the value of n that is bound into the function, we cannot say what the exact value will be for any value of x. Furthermore, we need n to be associated with a value (bound to a value) before we apply the function to a value of x. To see this, consider:

$$(\lambda x.x + n)2$$

If we apply β-reduction, we obtain $2 + n$, which is not in normal form. Unless n is bound to some value, we cannot, strictly, apply β-reduction to obtain a result (at least, one in normal form). In a programming language, free variables must be supplied prior to evaluation or reduction so that the evaluation process can proceed.

When describing the evaluation of a method, it is conventional to collect all references to free variables and treat them as a mapping from identifiers to values; the identifiers are the names inside the method by which the variables are known, and the values are the values that are bound to those identifiers. This mapping is called the *environment*. In languages like LISP and Scheme, the environment is often implemented for each function; the environment can then be manipulated by the interpretational mechanisms for the language (or those components of compiled code that deal with variables). The environment holds copies of non-local (global or free) variables; in some languages (e.g., Scheme), environments are not shared, so the copies can only be updated by the method in whose environment they appear, with the consequence that special apparatus must be used to update global variables. No matter what the language is, each method (procedure, function) must have an environment to map its identifiers to their values.

When a method needs the value of a free variable (a non-local variable, that is), it looks that variable up in its environment. In block-structured languages, looking up free variables involves a search because it is necessary to examine all enclosing scopes to see whether the desired variable was defined there. If the search fails to find the variable (and, hence, its value), the variable is unbound and an error raised, otherwise the variable's value has been found. In most current languages, the environment is mixed with the runtime stack (if it is a framed one) and variables' references are made in terms of it. Local variables are found in the topmost frame on the stack. Pointers point to the various lower levels where the relevant declarations can be found; in some implementations, a separate array of pointers called the display is used to access non-local (free) variables (see [4]).

Any computation involves a number of environments. Methods create environments to capture their free variables. At the level of the widest scope, there is the global environment; this contains bindings for such things as mathematical constants, standard file designators (*System.in*, *System.out*, *System.err* and so on). This is the global environment. It is part of every method's environment.

A method can be considered to be an environment and a pointer to its code. The environment contains the binding for the method's free variables (at all enclosing scope levels). To run a method, the code is executed by the processor and local variables are typically manipulated via a stack. The environment-code pointer pair is called a *closure*. In order to run a closure, a stack is required and the code must be handed to the processor. Thus, a closure represents a method in a quiescent state; more accurately, we can say that a closure is a meaningful code fragment (a block, say) that is ready to execute.

Higher-order functions in languages like MK, Haskell, LISP, Scheme and Pop11 are represented by closures and each of these languages provides a mechanism for creating and applying closures. In these languages, functions are first-class entities and can be passed as arguments to and returned from functions.

One use of a closure is to fix an argument's value. For example, the *addn* function can be defined as:

$$\lambda n.\lambda x.x + n$$

(I have added the extra abstraction in order to emphasize the fact that, in a program, there must always be a top-level binding—there are *no* true free variables). We could define a closure which binds n to 1 by:

$$(\lambda n.\lambda x.x + n)1 \Rightarrow \lambda x.x + 1$$

and thereby define the *add1* function. When applied to an argument, the λ-expression on the right returns a value that is the successor of the argument's value. The effect of the definition of *add1* is to reduce the number of required arguments because one of them has a fixed value. What has happened is that part of the left-hand side's environment has been frozen to a particular value (hence the name of the operation in Pop11). Since it is a closure, the function on the right-hand side can be passed into and out of functions at will. This allows code to be parameterized with operations, thus increasing the power of the language.

5.4.3 Blocks in Smalltalk and SELF

Both Smalltalk [40] and SELF [25] employ a kind of closure object in a number of contexts, in particular the provision of control structures; indeed, closures have been used in both languages to provide relatively exotic control structures such as co-routines. We will describe these structures, called *blocks*, from the Smalltalk viewpoint for the reason that it is a more frequently encountered language; the similarities between the languages are such that the description holds good for SELF and Omega [11] as well.

A block is a sequence of operations (expressions, statements, or *actions* in Smalltalk terms) whose execution can be deferred. In Smalltalk syntax, a block is a sequence of expressions separated by periods and delimited by square brackets, so:

```
[index <- index + 1.]
```

and:

```
[index <- index + 1. array at: index put: 0.]
```

are both blocks.

When a block (or, sometimes in the literature, *block expression*) is encountered, the statements it contains are not immediately executed. Instead, their execution is deferred. The value of a block expression is an object that can execute the expressions it contains at some later time and upon request. The computation of the value represented by a block expression is performed when the block expression receives the **value** message. Thus, the two following expressions have identical results:

```
index <- index + 1
```

and:

```
[index <- index + 1] value
```

both increment the value of index by one.

When a block receives a **value** message, the expressions it contains are sequentially executed.

A block expression can, therefore, be created and its execution can be deferred until some later time. In order to make this possible, blocks must be *first-class* objects. That is, blocks must be treated like ordinary values such as integers, strings and characters. In Smalltalk, when a block is encountered by the compiler, it is compiled into an object; objects in Smalltalk and SELF are first-class objects and are treated as values, so they can be stored, passed as parameters and returned as results. What makes blocks different is that they must be executed in order to produce a (non-block) value. Blocks are analogous to *closures* in other languages.

The following code fragment (from [40], p. 31) shows how a block can be stored in a Smalltalk array called *actions*:

```
actions at: 'monthly payments'
   put: [HouseholdFinances spend: 650 on: 'rent'.
         HouseholdFinances spend: 7.25 on: 'newspaper'.
         HouseholdFinances spend: 225.50 on: 'car payment'.]
```

Smalltalk associative arrays have a method **at: put:** which places the second argument (the one prefixed by **put:**) in the location specified by the argument prefixed by **at:**. Thus, a block expression is stored in array *actions* at a place specified by 'monthly payments'. To retrieve the block, the **value** message can be sent to the array:

```
(actions at: 'monthly payments')value
```

The retrieved block can then be executed.

The following example (taken from [40], p. 33, but my commentary is slightly different) shows in more detail how blocks work. Consider the following code sequence:

```
incrementBlock <- [index <- index + 1].
sumBlock <- [sum + (index * index)].
sum <- 0.
index <- 1.
```

```
sum <- sumBlock value.
incrementBlock value.
sum <- sumBlock value.
```

This sequence is evaluated as follows (we ignore the evaluation of integer-valued objects). First a block is assigned to *incrementBlock* and one is assigned to *sumBlock*. The variable *sum* is initialized to zero, while *index* is initialized to one. Next, *sumBlock* is sent the **value** message; this causes its expressions to be evaluated and return a value which is assigned to *sum*. Then, the block stored in *incrementBlock* is sent a **value** message and it is executed. Finally, *sumBlock* is sent the **value** message, causing its evaluation, and the result is stored in *sum*. If we follow through this evaluation sequence assigning values as specified above, when *sumBlock* receives the **value** message, it returns the value one. Next, the evaluation of *incrementBlock* yields two. The final evaluation of *sumBlock* then returns five (sum is one, and index is two).

The evaluation of this sequence is very much as one would expect. However, there are some points which are worth noting. First, the two blocks are defined in terms of free variables (recall that the values of free variables fix the meanings of expressions). However, the variables are defined inside the block and then initialized at a subsequent point in the code sequence. The second point is that blocks can be repeatedly evaluated. The free variables in the two blocks store intermediate results between evaluations.

It is possible for a block to declare local variables (they are called *block arguments*). Syntactically, Smalltalk block arguments are prefixed with a colon and are separated from the rest of the block by a vertical bar:

```
[ :array | total \leftarrow total + array size]
```

and:

```
[ : newElement |
    index \leftarrow index + 1.
    List at: index put: newElement.]
```

A common use of blocks with arguments is to implement functions that can be applied to all elements of a data structure (cf. the use of LISP and Scheme λ-expressions and ML *fn* in mapping functions). Many objects representing data structures like lists or sequences respond to the **do** message. The **do** message takes a single argument block as its argument. When the object receives the **do** message, it executes the **do** message's argument once for each of the elements it contains. Each element in the data structure is bound to the block's argument (so the block is applied to successive elements of the data structure). In the following example, the sum of squares of the first five prime numbers is computed (a list of values between #(and) is a list in Smalltalk):

```
sum -> 0.
```

```
#(2 3 5 7 11) do:
    [ :prime | sum    sum + (prime * prime)]
```

(the example shows, once again, how a block can be repeatedly applied). In this example, it can be seen that a block is being used in a higher-order context. Furthermore, the block is being used to implement a new control structure.

A block can have more than one argument, for example:

```
[ :x :y | (x * x) + (y * y)]
```

A block with more than one argument must have a corresponding number of **value:** keywords in the message that is sent to evaluate it. The above example would require two **value:** keywords; the two arguments of the message specify the values of the block arguments in order. The last example can be evaluated by the following message:

```
value value: 2 value: 3
```

which evaluates to $(2 * 2) + (3 * 3) = 4 + 9 = 13$.

Smalltalk and SELF take the block to be a fundamental structure. They both use it in the implementation of non-sequential control structures. The Smalltalk equivalent of a *for* loop requires a block:

```
2 timesRepeat [sum <- sum * sum]
```

More famously, Smalltalk defines its conditional and conditional repetition (while) in terms of blocks. Objects with boolean type respond to two methods with selector **ifTrue:ifFalse:**, each selector taking a block as its argument. The interpretation is that the object **true** sends its value to the first argument, while **false** sends its value to the second. We can see this in operation in the expression to compute the parity of a number (parity is a test for evenness):

```
(number \\ 2) = 0
    ifTrue: [parity  0]
    ifFalse: [parity  1]
```

First, the modulus (remainder) is computed by the \\ operation; the remainder is tested for equality with zero. If the result is zero, we assign zero to parity; if it is non-zero, we assign one to parity. The boolean object returned by the equality test responds to the message with selectors **ifTrue:ifFalse:**,, each of which is bound to a block. It is possible to use **ifTrue:** without **ifFalse:** in a message (and vice versa).

In an analogous fashion, the **whileTrue:** and **whileFalse:** selectors can be used in a message sent to a block; the other argument to these selectors is also a block. Thus, schematically, **whileTrue:** has the form:

```
[block] whileTrue: [ block]
```

(**whileFalse:** has an identical structure). In order to evaluate such a construct, the recipient block (the first argument) sends itself a **value** message and returns a value. If that value is true, it sends the other block a **value** message and then repeats the process. Should the value returned by the first block be false, execution terminates. The operation of **whileFalse:** is the exact converse of this.

Smalltalk makes other uses of blocks. As noted above, they are all variations on higher-order functions for they allow segments of code to be passed between expressions. The concurrent execution primitives are based on the use of blocks; the reason for this is that a block's execution is deferred until it receives a **value** message. Blocks allow complex and novel control structures to be defined. The downside is that completely incomprehensible code can be produced.

5.4.4 Block Structure in Beta

The Beta language [54] employs an explicit block structuring by permitting classes to contain nested class definitions. This, as we noted in the last chapter, is something it shares with C++ and Java, but the role of local classes is less worked out in these other languages. In the particular case of Beta, this can mean the nested definition of classes and methods. Because Beta employs a similar representation for classes and methods, both of which are called *patterns*, it supports what amounts to nested procedure definitions as well as nested class definitions. (A consequence of this is that a Beta implementation must support *closures*.)

Block structure follows the standard scope principles for block-structured languages. This has the implication that contained definitions are normally invisible to their container. However, Beta employs a scope referencing method akin to Ada, so that, by means of an hierarchical name, a nested class, attribute or method can be accessed. This allows Beta programs to define well-formed components and to manipulate them in an enclosed space; we saw how this could be effected in Chapter 4 when we considered aggregation. As we saw there, access to methods is an essential aspect of aggregation.

Another consequence of the Beta approach, one that is less obvious, is that a class can contain a method that defines local classes, not just instances. This enables the programmer to be very flexible in their processing.

Block structuring makes classes more organized and gives principles for accessing components. It localizes the applicability and effects of method applications.

5.4.5 Higher-Order Methods

In pure object-oriented languages like Java, Eiffel and Sather, it is impossible to define an independent procedure; all one can do is to define methods. As we noted, Smalltalk, SELF and impure languages treat procedures or their analogues as first-class entities. Methods belong to objects (classes, typically), so, in order to define a method, one needs to define a class. Therefore, if it is desired to pass a method into a method in one of these languagess, it is necessary to define a class to hold the method that will be an actual parameter. This requires a uniform naming policy for the potential argument classes.

For example, if we want a class that has a method that could perform certain operations on a data structure, but they are too numerous satisfactorily to include as part of that method, one way round the problem is to define the operations in the classes on which they operate. These operations can be passed into the main method as part of the class to which they apply. In an interpreter for production rules, for example, the actions that rules perform can be extended, in some systems, so, in an object-oriented implementation, we would define a class for each action and have an *execute* method in each class. The *execute* method takes a number of parameters and implements the operation performed by the action. In this way, the main execution method defined for the rule class (we assume that rule execution is taken care of by the rule's class) takes the action class as a parameter and calls the *execute* method when the action is to be executed.

The alternative to this would be to use a case (switch) statement. However, this approach has the disadvantage that, whenever a new action is added to the interpreter, the case statement has to be modified and recompiled. Using the class-based approach, new actions can be defined without having to modify the rule's execute method—all that needs to be done is for the new action to be represented by an appropriate class; only the new class need be linked into the interpreter program.

It is possible to define higher-order operations in this way. We could define the twice function

$$\lambda f.\lambda x.ffx$$

in terms of methods and object. This requires the class to pass its method for f into this method as an additional parameter. (Note that this removes a level of recursion from the resulting definition.) This requires us to define a separate class for each operation. While this affords some advantages, it does increase the number of classes considerably and it does, of course, require a considerable amount of extra effort in defining new classes. Nevertheless, it is the only mechanism available in languages such as Sather, Eiffel and Java.

In a language like Smalltalk or SELF, blocks are available. We have already seen how Smalltalk uses blocks to implement conditional and iteration structures; similar structures are implemented in similar ways in other languages. Omega [11], for example, is defined in such a way that blocks simplify its structure and semantics. We can define a two-arm conditional in an Algol-like syntax as follows:

```
define cond2 (pred, thenpart, elsepart) =
```

```
begin
  if (call pred) then (call thenpart)
  else (call elsepart)
end
```

Similarly, an iteration construct can be defined (again in an Algol-like syntax) as:

```
define while-iter (pred, body)=
begin
  bool cntrl;
  l1: cntrl := (call pred);
  if cntrl then begin
    (call body)
      goto l1;
    end
end
```

(we have used a low-level syntax in order to emphasize how such a construct might be compiled and to show how we need not rely upon an identical construct being provided by the language). In each case, the arguments to the routines are all assumed to be blocks. The operation call is assumed as a primitive which calls a block; it is our analogue of the **do** message in Smalltalk. (We do not use a Smalltalk-like set of constructs because we want to show how such an approach can be adopted by another language; we are attempting to be language- and implementation-independent.)

The two examples above show how blocks can be used to implement program structures with a little support from an underlying language. The examples show that closures can be used to implement anonymous blocks of code which are to be passed as arguments to other closures. Because a closure can be passed as a first-class entity, it can be used to implement a great many structures including co-routines. The addition of closures into a language affords that language considerable flexibility. It is possible to pass routine pointers as arguments in C++, but closures in the sense of the Smalltalk, SELF, Omega or LISP sense cannot be defined and manipulated, for the reason that, as noted below, there are some problems that arise from their inclusion.

By passing a block into a low-level procedure or parameterizing constructs in ways akin to Smalltalk, SELF and Omega, must make procedural closures a first-class concept in the language. This fact has a number of implications for the language. The language must not only explicitly represent closures or blocks, it must also provide mechanisms for their manipulation; manipulation of blocks or closures implies that methods can be higher-order in the more conventional sense of that term. There must be ways of creating blocks when required and for determining whether a closure is required for future evaluation. There are choices to be made as to where closures are allocated; if they are allocated in the heap, there can be performance penalties to pay.

There is a trade-off between the admittedly high utility of closures and the implications of their inclusion. Once a decision as to the representation and allocation of closures has been reached, it is worthwhile to consider whether the chosen representation and allocation policies should not be adopted for all closures, not just those that are to be passed as actual parameters.

The approach to higher-order functions exemplified in this section has its origins in early work on functional programming (see [19] or [45] for more examples). Not only does it permit the parameterization of syntactic structures in such a way that they can be modified or adapted at runtime, it also opens the way to lazy evaluation. When evaluating its arguments lazily, a function only evaluates those expressions supplied as arguments when a value is needed. In a conditional, it is essential to evaluate fully the predicate expression for it is necessary to determine which sub-expression to evaluate next (the sub-expressions provided to represent the then- and else-parts of conditionals). If the predicate evaluates to true, the then-part can be evaluated; the else-part is, in this case, not evaluated (it could be passed, unevaluated, to another function if required). Blocks naturally lead to the examination of the implications of lazy evaluation, a task which we defer for it remains very much a research issue.

5.5 Methods and Inheritance

The interactions between methods and inheritance are discussed in this section. The method hierarchies in Theta [57] are considered first, followed by the method combiners of CLOS.

5.5.1 Method Hierarchies in Theta

The Theta language [57] introduces a hierarchy among its routines. The language distinguishes between methods and routines; the language also makes a distinction between modules and classes. In Theta, classes define new data types while modules collect items together in the familiar way; classes obey a reflexive class-subclass relationship which is interpreted in terms of type and subtype. In this language, it is possible to define free-standing routines; that is, there is notionally a separate semantic category for methods and for routines. The language is covariant, which explains why the subtype relationship is reflexive, and is strongly typed (see Chapter 6 for more details on types in object-oriented languages).

The covariance of Theta also has an interesting implication for the language: it becomes possible to arrange routines in a hierachy. The hierarchy is derived from the types of the formal parameters of the routines. Although it is not used by other structures in the language, and it can be used in type checking at compile and at runtime, this is an example of how a constraint on parameter type can be related to the inheritance structure of a language. This relationship then allows the classification of another part of the language. It also points to the fact that there will probably be a number of equally viable alternatives should it be decided to employ hierarchical structures to classify free-standing routines and to classify methods.

5.5.2 Method Combination in CLOS

CLOS defines a set of *method-combining* forms, of which *before* and *after methods* are the easiest to explain (the concept of before and after methods, as well as wrappers, was first introduced in FLAVORS [21]; FLAVORS is still available as part of Franz LISP's Allegro Common LISP distribution and is still in use). The idea is that code can be written which will alter the behaviour of a called method. The kind of method that we have so far considered is called a *primary method* in CLOS; it is the method that does all the work. However, it might happen that, at some stage in the definition of classes belonging to a particular inheritance hierarchy, we need to do some things before we call the primary method; we might want to do some things after we have called the primary method; we might even want to do things before *and* after the primary method is called. The primary method might be perfectly useful on its own, a fact which precludes addition of code to the beginning and end of the method's body. CLOS, and FLAVORS before it, permit the user to define *before* and *after methods* to perform these tasks.

When a primary method is called in CLOS, a search is made up the inheritance chain to find all the before methods that have been defined for this method. If there are any, they are called in the order most specific to most general. When all before methods have been called, the primary method is called and the major computation is performed. Next, a search is made for the after methods. If there are any such methods defined for this primary method, they are executed in increasing order of specificity, the reverse of before methods (they are executed from most general to most specific). Before and after methods wrap around a primary method, providing additional (additive) functionality.

At any point in the inheritance chain, before and after methods can, in principle, be defined for a primary method. This is true even if the primary is inherited. This allows the programmer to define code that will run before or after the primary without needing to define a primary method.

CLOS provides more of these method-wrapping methods. For example, it provides a *progn* combination which executes methods in order and returns the value returned by the last method (the *progn* combiner is a descendant of the *wrapper* combiner in FLAVORS), as well as combiners that perform arithmetic on the results. CLOS even allows the programmer to define new method combiners for themselves. There is much that can be said about method combiners, but we do not have space here; the interested reader is therefore advised to consult [82].

The method combiners discussed so far are all procedural in the sense that they directly operate on some notion of a state. That state is implicitly provided in the case of *before*, *after* and *progn* combiners. There are other combiners, however, that work in a more declarative way. Method combiners are the only way to access ancestor classes in a linearized multiple inheritance scheme such as that used by Common LISP. Otherwise, because of the arbitrary arrangement of ancestor classes, it is not possible to access ancestors in a principled fashion.

5.6 Static and Dynamic Binding

A natural consequence of the organization of a class hierarchy is that methods are to be found at various levels in the structure. The obvious and universal method for program construction involves either the redefinition of methods that appear higher in the inheritance structure (over-riding) or the use of these higher methods in the bodies of methods that are defined at lower levels or as local methods in their own right (inherited methods). The second of these options involves a search for the specified method and it is possible for more than one method to be retrieved during the traversal of the inheritance structure. The first option also interacts with inheritance for, when over-riding, it is essential to determine precisely which method is being over-ridden. Under single inheritance, matters are simple, but some forms of multiple inheritance make matters more complex, as was seen in the last chapter with respect to the general case of a slot. The third case, method inheritance, is most fundamental, for it is necessary to inherit at least a signature in order to over-ride a method (this is necessary in order to verify that the over-riding method's type is correct), and it is necessary to inherit the method proper if it is to be employed locally or to be used as an inherited method (used complete, in a sense).

The problem that faces us, here, is that of *binding* the correct method to the 'hole' for it in the current class. When a method is to be inherited, it must be located. The location of a method can be static in the sense that the desired method is stated explicitly and statically, or it can be dynamic in the sense that the name of the method is specified, together with its type, and the system is expected to locate the method to be used.

The process of method location is related to that of *downcasting*, as described in Chapter 2, because downcasting is the process of mapping a superclass onto a subclass (supertype to a subtype, i.e.); downcasting, therefore, involves a search which is similar to inheritance. However, inheritance interacts with the methods defined in higher classes in an inheritance structure. In particular, there is the question of how to find a method. Let us set this in a context.

Consider two classes, C and C_1. Assume that C defines a method m. Assume also that C is the superclass of C_1. Class C_1 inherits m in the usual way; all instances of C_1 can call m because it forms part of the definition of their class.

Now, let us assume that class C_1 defines a method m for itself. Perhaps the new m is defined using next-method. We will adopt the convention that we will write m_1 to refer to the version of m defined in C_1. Thus, when we define:

```
v1: C1;
   ...
v1.m( ... );
```

The call to m is a call to m_1, the specialization of m defined in C_1.

These two cases should be obvious and should be clear to the reader. Now, consider the following case. Let us assume that we have two variables, v and v_1, defined as follows:

```
v:C;
v1:C1;
```

Moreover, let us assume that we have a method defined as:

```
method foo (c : C) ... c.m( ... ); ...
```

Finally, assume that we call *foo*, supplying an instance of C(v) as its actual parameter:

```
foo(v)
```

Clearly, inside the body of *foo*, c.m will refer to the m defined in class C. All is, therefore, as we would expect.

Now, what happens if we call *foo* and supply v_1, an instance of C_1?

```
foo(v1);
```

Which version of m is called? Is it m or m_1?

We can argue in one of two ways. We can argue that the actual parameter specifies C as the class of the argument, so we must expect to call the method that is defined in C (the method we call m). Since C_1 is a subclass of C, any instance of C_1 must also be of type C. The other argument says that we have supplied an instance of C_1, not an instance of C, so we must apply the method defined in the subclass (the method we call m_1). Which of these arguments is correct?

The answer is that both are correct and neither is—it depends! It depends upon the language. Each argument gives a different way of associating methods with instances of classes.

The first argument gives an approach called *static* or *early* binding. Under static binding, the method to be called is the one associated with the class that appears as the type of the formal parameter. Thus, in the case of method *foo*, for the reason that the formal parameter c is defined to have type C, the method call inside the body of *foo* must refer to method m (the method

defined in class C). Thus, the method $c.m$ inside the body of *foo* is bound to
the method defined in class C. This binding can occur as soon as the type of
the formal parameter is known and is, for this reason, called *static* binding.

The alternative approach is called *dynamic* or *late* binding. Under this
approach, the choice as to which method is actually called is delayed until
the call is to be made. This takes place at runtime. When the call is made,
the class of the object which has been passed as the actual parameter is
determined and the method associated with that class is the one that is
called. That is, when the call is made, the method m that is associated with
the class of the actual parameter is bound to $c.m$. Since an instance v_1 of class
C_1 has, in this example, been passed to *foo*, $c.m$ is bound to m_1. Because
binding is performed when the actual type of the formal parameter, c, is
known (i.e., when v_1 is bound to c), the process is called *dynamic binding*.
It is useful to note that dynamic binding is also a technique for handling
polymorphism.

The difference between static and dynamic binding can be seen in the
following example:

```
V: C;
V1: C1;
V := v1;
v.m( ... );
```

(the assignment assumes that downcasting between non-heap allocated instances of a class is permitted). Now, which m is called? Under static binding, the m defined in C will be called. Under dynamic binding, it will be the
one in C_1. The binding of the class to v in the assignment is critical to the
behaviour of the program. We could also cite the following case in which an
instance of a subclass is bound to an element of an array whose element type
is the superclass (again, a binding problem):

```
a1: array(...) of C;
v1 :C1;
a1(2) := v1;
a2(2).m(...);
```

Again, static and dynamic binding will yield different results.

Many languages (Smalltalk, Java, Sather, Eiffel, for example) employ dynamic binding, while others, notably C++, opts for static binding.

In C++ static binding is the default, but methods can be defined as
dynamically bound by means of the *virtual* construct. When defined as virtual
in a superclass, a method with the same name must be defined within each
subclass and it must have the same number of parameters; each parameter
must be of the same type in the subclass as in the superclass. (In other words,
the method defined in the subclass must have the same *signature* as the one
in the superclass.) When a call is made to a method that has been declared
to be *virtual*, the class of the instance that has been bound to a parameter,

variable or container element is used to determine the method that is actually called.

The C++ view is that static binding constitutes an "optimization" technique because it does not impose the overhead of using a lookup (or dispatch) table when determining which method to execute. Instead, calls to static methods are compiled into direct calls to the methods involved. The C++ programmer is required to determine which methods to "optimize", for those methods to be dynamically bound must be explicitly marked as being *virtual*, while statically bound methods are unmarked. (Some languages are able to employ runtime tests to determine which methods can be statically bound.) Often, though, static binding can give the *wrong* results in an object-oriented context because it will invoke the method associated with the type of the reference to the object, not the object proper. Given that dynamic binding is a property that is almost always seen as a defining property of an object-oriented language, the reliance on static dispatch in C++ is questionable.

The way static binding works is as follows. The compiler uses the type of the instance reference to access the class of the object which is statically declared as being bound there. It then compiles a direct call to the method, inserting the instructions comprising the call sequence directly into the object code.

Most modern languages adopt dynamic binding while older statically typed ones generally prefer static binding. Static binding is easier to type check and generates simpler code. However, static binding does not allow one to specialize behaviours as one would wish: one always has the behaviour associated with the superclass. Dynamic binding allows the behaviour associated with the class of an instance to be exhibited.

For dynamic behaviour to work, there must be some runtime mechanisms for associating an instance with its type and for associating an instance with the methods of its class. Both of these requirements impose a slight overhead which static binding avoids. The former requirement amounts to determining what the type of an object is. The second requirement forces each instance of a class to be associated with a table of methods for its class; when a class is compiled, this table is constructed. The table can contain pointers to the entry points of those methods that are locally defined. The table will include pointers to those methods which over-ride methods defined higher in the class's inheritance chain. In our example, the table for C will contain a pointer to m, while the table for C_1 will contain a pointer to m_1. In some implementations, the method table also contains pointers to the methods that are inherited; in others, the table contains a pointer to the superclass's method table. The second approach avoids the first's need for runtime search at the cost of additional storage (which must be allocated on a per-subclass basis, and which, therefore, might be more costly than a simple pointer chase). The runtime representation of instances of each class must contain a pointer to the appropriate method table, in addition to containing a reference to their class (type). (We might care to implement method tables and instances as objects in their own right—this is a fascinating proposal, and we will return to it below in Chapter 8, Section 8.3.4.)

There are at least two ways to implement dynamic binding. We will consider the mechanisms adopted in Smalltalk ([40], pp. 561 *et seq.*) and in C++ ([90], pp. 74 *et seq.*).

In Smalltalk, when a message (method call) is received by an object, the message's selector is looked up in the method table associated with the class of the object. If the method selector is present, the associated *Compiled-Method* object is called and the method is executed. If the method selector is absent, the superclass of the class is located and its method table consulted. The search through the superclass chain continues until either the specified selector is found or the end of the chain is encountered. If the former holds, the method is executed; if it is the latter that is true, a runtime error is raised—there is no such method. This is clearly a dynamic process, but does it implement dynamic binding? The answer is in the affirmative. The Smalltalk scheme first directs the message to the current object and then continues up the inheritance chain if the method is not locally defined. If Smalltalk were typed (it is not), this scheme would work and would implement dynamic binding because it performs the method search on the *object* not on the class corresponding to the reference to the object. Dynamic binding must work on objects, not on types, because it calls the method associated with the object currently bound to the reference, not with the static type of the reference. Smalltalk implements dynamic binding.

C++ defaults to static binding as a "default". Its *virtual* function (method) mechanism allows dynamic binding to be implemented at low overhead. The basic idea in C++ is that the virtual functions in a class define an array of pointers to the functions. This implies that a call to a virtual function is just an indirect call through the array. The array, called the *virtual function table*, is implemented once per class and contains pointers to the virtual functions for the class. The array collects the pointers to the virtual functions that are defined, possibly by inheritance, for the class. The compiler has to determine which virtual methods are defined for each class; it also has to be rebuilt whenever the virtual methods for a class are changed. The advantage of the approach is that it is fast.

The process works at compile time. Virtual methods are collected by the compiler as it scans the inheritance structure for a class. This scan directly structures the virtual function table, but does not insert any pointers to the code which implements the virtual methods. A pointer from the structure which represents instances of the class at runtime is set to point to the class's virtual function table—there is only one such table stored at runtime *per class*. Later, when the entry points of the code implementing the virtual methods are known, they are entered into the table. Before the entry points are known, the compiler can generate code to call virtual methods by indirecting off the virtual function table.

6. Types I: Types and Objects

6.1 Introduction

It is impossible to examine any kind of programming language without a discussion of types. Even languages such as Scheme, LISP, Smalltalk, or even Basic, which are considered by many to be "typeless", must admit of a typed account. One reason for this is that the untyped (type-free) λ-calculus has no consistent models, thus demonstrating that untyped languages produce unpredictable results (normalization cannot be guaranteed). A second reason is that the operations in such languages, say that of addition, are typed: for the addition function to be correctly applied, its arguments must be numbers. Addition has to be redefined if an addition operator is to be applied to, say, strings; such a redefinition would result in a concatenation function. Thus, it makes no sense to say that LISP, Scheme, Basic, and so on, are "typeless" or "untyped", for they are more correctly described as being dynamically typed (or, more strictly, their variables, parameters and function returns are more correctly described as being dynamically typed). The reason for this is that types play an essential role in the evaluation of the expressions of such languages, but the type of an arbitrary expression is determined dynamically at runtime rather than statically at compile time.

We are used to the concept of compile-time type analysis and assignment based upon our experience with languages such as Pascal, Ada, the Algols, and others. Java and C++ are examples of class-based languages which are statically typed. Many modern object-oriented (typically class-based) languages such as Eiffel and Sather, Beta and Theta, require a compile-time type checking process to be undertaken. However, and this might come as a surprise, some languages have a semantics which renders compile-time type checking only a partial check on the program text. This is not for reasons of separate compilation, but for properly semantic reasons. As will be seen below, some languages require *both* static *and* dynamic checking because of constraints imposed upon method argument types. We will discuss this and its implications in depth below.

On the other hand, prototype-based languages have often been dynamically typed; SELF, Obliq and Kevo are all dynamically typed, although Omega [11] is statically typed. Dynamic typing seems to fit better with the general ideas of prototype-based programming; it appears that prototype-based programming is better suited to exploratory or experimental programming than with production methods. In addition, the concepts of cloning and aggregate formation seem to be at odds with the concept of static typing. We do not know of an example of one that is even partially statically typed. We are aware of JavaScript's facilities for prototype-based programming; however, these features are coupled with *inheritance*, not delegation, a property it shares with Omega [11].

The Omega language introduces types into a prototype-based language, [11]. In Omega, every prototype corresponds to a type and vice versa. Omega uses inheritance between prototypes rather than delegation, so a subtype hierarchy is defined by inheritance between prototypes. Omega prototypes can be replicated by cloning just as in other languages. Omega prototypes can be altered by copying and modification prior to instance formation. These last two sentences justify the sense in which Omega is considered a prototype language. The reader is advised to consult [11] for a complete discussion of this interesting language.

It is often construed that there is an intimate connection between classes and types; prototypes, it will be remembered, take a different approach and define collections that are more loosely defined. In this chapter, we concentrate on the relationship between classes and types as evidenced in Eiffel, C++, Java, Sather, Beta and Theta and other languages. In the case of Beta and Sather, it is necessary to observe that there is a further distinction between implementation and type, but we do not consider that here.

The identification of classes with types is extremely common and is derived from the analogy with Abstract Data Types that was discussed in Chapter 2. In some languages, the concept of type and subtype is mixed with the concept of the definition of code and its re-use. In a similar vein, when considering polymorphism, some languages, again thinking of C++, identify redefinition and overloading. The confusion, which probably results from too much operational thought, can lead to a lack of clear distinction between concepts in some languages.

It will be clear that the chapter is almost exclusively about concepts in class-based languages. There is no reason why a prototype-based language should not be equipped with a type system, particularly one which permits the definitions of new types. The fact is that, to my knowledge, there is, at present, no such language.

One significant reason for emphasizing class-based over prototype-based languages is that they typically lack type definition facilities. This has the consequence that slots can hold methods or values of primitive types or can hold references to objects (prototypes). Objects can be defined in a way analogous to that in class-based languages, but this does not necessarily guarantee that the object pointed to by a slot is related to the desired prototype object; it is necessary to resort to programming conventions and to other devices, whereas in a strongly typed, class-based language, slots are typed and the correspondence between types and slots can be verified. Furthermore, the cloning operation is one which typically occurs at runtime while subtype definition is part of the compilation process; thus, one cannot be guaranteed that a desired object will actually be constructed at runtime.

There is no inherent reason why a prototype-based language should not include type definition facilities (Omega allows slots to be typed, for example). However, the concept of a type appears to go against the grain; moreover, the relationship induced by delegation between prototypes does not correspond to the type/subtype relation found in typed languages. The reason that typing seems to go against the grain of prototype-based languages is that the relationships between prototypes are richer than the simple sub/supertype relation; prototypes are based upon similarity along a variety of dimensions, not just one. However, because of the richer, metric-based similarity concept in prototype languages, the notion of imposing a unique type upon an object appears impossible; the most one can do is to say that *when regarded in such and such a way, an object is closer to X than to Y*. Such an approach does not appear to suit the stricter scheme assumed for class-based languages which conform to conventional type disciplines much more readily. This view of object similarity has implications for such matters as object transformation and correctness and require new ways of construing these processes and properties.

6.2 Inheritance and Types

We have already discussed the connection between classes and Abstract Data Types (ADTs). Classes and ADTs encapsulate their data and allow operations to be defined in a modular fashion over these data. Operations are always bundled together with data, so there is encapsulation at that level. In addition, classes must be instantiated in order to be of use; similarly, a type must be instantiated in order to produce a value that can be manipulated by a program. Classes and types are often thought of as the same thing, and this is a prevalent view in object-oriented language design. It is important, therefore, to consider what happens under the type view when we engage in subclass definition (often called *derivation* or *type extension*).

It should come as no surprise that the classes-as-types view treats subclasses as subtypes. In the original work on ADTs, no mention of subtypes was made; occasionally, the idea of a part-of relationship between ADTs is hinted at. However, when we define a subclass of a given class, we are specializing the definition of the type, so we are forming a subtype. The relationship between a class and its subtypes is akin to that between, say, the concept of integers, non-negative integers and natural numbers. For the integers, we have all whole numbers between $+\infty$ and $-\infty$, the operations of addition, multiplication, subtraction and a kind of division (remainder—we only have a full version of division when dealing with $\Re$). For non-negative numbers, we have all the integers between 0 and $+\infty$ (inclusive), but have operations addition, multiplication, remainder and a kind of subtraction (positive difference) defined as

$$n \Diamond m = |n - m|$$

(where $|x|$ is the absolute value of x). Finally, we have the naturals, the whole numbers, n, such that $0 < n \leq +\infty$, and the operations addition and multiplication (we could define subtraction and division operations, but would have problems when deciding what to do with $n - n$ and n *rem* kn, for arbitrary natural k). What we note in each case is that the range of objects with which the type deals is increasingly restricted and we also see that, in each case, we progress towards an increasingly impoverished set of operations (we also move from a relatively complex algebraic structure, a field, down to a simpler one, a group). A similar effect is seen when considering successive subclasses of a given class.

When we consider the relationship between a class and its subclasses, the subtype relation is often brought to mind. One reason for this is that we normally expect it to be possible to substitute instances of subclasses for instances of a class (their superclass). A subclass is a more constrained form of its superclass; equally, a subtype is a constrained form of its supertype, hence any property which holds of a superclass must *a fortiori* hold of any of its subtypes.

The concept of a *subtype* is closely associated with that of *type extension*. The reason for this can be seen if we return to the basic picture of what a type is. We can consider a type to be a set of entities and a set of operations (axioms). Application of one of the operations to an element of the set yields another element of that same set (the set is closed under the application of the operations). We can extend an algebra by introducing new operations (new axioms). This makes the operation set applicable to fewer cases, note, so the extension is more specialized than the original. The axioms of the type from which an extension has been derived still obtain in the extension; there are more theorems that hold in the new type (algebra), but the original set of theorems are still true in the extension, as they are in the original algebra. The type extension operation corresponds to the derivation of a subclass from a class.

At this point, it is essential to record that the subtype and supertype relationships are often considered to be reflexive. That is, a class, C, is always considered to be a subtype or a supertype of itself. This convention should make understanding many of the issues relating to sub/supertype relationships easier to understand (particularly variance).

What we have seen is that classes can be substituted in limited ways and that instances of a subclass can always be treated as instances of a superclass. This allows us to pass parameters whose class is a subclass of the declared type; we can bind variables in other contexts in a similar fashion. This amounts to a limited form of *polymorphism* (from the Greek, meaning "having many forms"). It allows operations to be applied to objects of a type that is different from the one they were designed for, provided that certain conditions are met (upcasting being the primary one).

Operations normally specify the number and type of their formal parameters; they also specify the type of their outputs as necessary. If we define an operation which will perform the same action, but which is able to accept inputs of types other than those which have been specified (modulo constraints on well-typed expressions), we have an example of a polymorphic operation. We will discuss polymorphism in object-oriented languages in more detail in Section 6.8, below; for the time being, we note that polymorphism is introduced for methods as a natural consequence of inheritance.

6.2.1 Telling What the Type Is

We have seen that if a language uses dynamic binding, it is essential for the type of instances to be made known at runtime. This imposes constraints on the representation of instances at runtime; in particular, it requires that instances contain a reference of some kind to their class (type). Semantically, we need a runtime function, say, which, when applied to an instance, yields its class (type). The provision of this function as part of the language (as a predefined or library function) is also extremely useful in practical terms.

Very often, it is useful to know what the type of an object (instance) is so that some operations can be performed on it. For example, if one is constructing an interpreter for a language, an abstract syntax tree might be constructed as the runtime representation of the program being interpreted. The nodes of the tree might be represented by instances of classes, each class representing a different type in the abstract syntax. Thus, there will be a node for conditionals (**if**, **case** or **switch**, perhaps **select**), and one each for the various iterative constructs (**while, until,** etc.). Each node will have certain methods in common, but some nodes will need to be treated differently. If we have an expression language (like LISP, Scheme, Dylan, Icon, or Algol68), we can define an *evaluate* method for each node class. (The *evaluate* method will need to be dynamically bound so that we evaluate the right node.) This method will evaluate the subtree dominated by the node currently being evaluated and will also have to access various kinds of non-local variable and, perhaps, a symbol table.

To evaluate an expression in the language, we call the *evaluate* method of the topmost tree in the abstract syntax tree. Control percolates towards the leaves of the tree as the *evaluate* methods call the corresponding methods in their subtrees. Eventually, a result is returned.

On the other hand, we might be writing an interpreter for a statement language; that is, based upon a division between statements and expressions (e.g., Algol60, FORTRAN, Pascal, Ada, and C in its most common usage—C is based upon expressions which are "converted" to statements). Statements are usually described as constructs that transform the state of a program.

For example, the **if** statement of Algol60 and Pascal is used to determine which of a maximum of two states is to follow the state in which evaluation of its conditional expression occurs. Expressions are considered to be value-producing entities. Values and states are considered to be different kinds of entity in statement-based languages. Expression languages do not make this distinction and every construct returns a value (even iterative constructs).

The division between statements and expressions in a statement-based language causes some problems for the hypothetical interpreter writer. Whereas in the expression language, every node was associated with an *evaluate* method, we are now faced with the problem that some nodes (nodes representing expressions) have an *evaluate* method, but others (nodes representing statements) do not. (To be fair, in both kinds of language, declaration nodes behave still differently.) Nodes representing statements control the state of execution; they do not produce values. There is a seeming problem for it is impossible to define an evaluate method that can be applied to every node in the tree. Some nodes will return a value, others not. We could define an *execute* method and allow every node to be associated with it. The *execute* method performs the same task as *evaluate* but does not return a value; instead it updates the state as appropriate. However, a decision is now required as to whether an expression is a kind of statement or vice versa. If one looks at the semantic equations of most languages, no such distinction can be made. It seems more reasonable to maintain a distinction, at least if theoretical purity is desired, between the two kinds of node. This implies that, at runtime, it will be necessary to make a distinction between nodes that represent statements and those that represent expressions.

In C++, such a distinction is the job of the programmer, for the language contains no constructs that will allow type discrimination. Here, one normally associates an integer with each type and defines a method that returns the type of the object. This is clearly a messy and error-prone technique. Other languages, happily, provide better methods for telling the type of an object at runtime.

In a dynamic binding language, object types must be represented at runtime. In so-called untyped, or (more correctly) dynamically typed languages (LISP, Scheme, Icon, Basic) objects are tagged with type information so that expressions can be correctly evaluated. We should, therefore, expect that languages from these two families will provide constructs for runtime type discrimination and this is, indeed, true. LISP and related languages employ runtime type tags so that primitive routines can determine whether the data that has been supplied to them is of the correct type. Common LISP, therefore, provides a number of functions and predicates for returning and testing the type of an object; Scheme, however, at least in the R4RS [26] version specifies no function for returning the name of an object's type. In Common LISP, though, *type-of* returns the name of the type of its argument, and *typep* returns true if the name of the type of its first argument is the same as its second argument. One slight problem is that some objects in Common LISP. are of a type whose name is not necessarily what one expects, and implementations vary as to the names which they assign to some of these types. For example, *t* and *nil* (true and false, or true and the empty list, depending upon context) are both of type *symbol*, while an integer is of type *fixnum*; floating point numbers can have a variety of implementation-dependent names.

Other languages adopt an approach to type discrimination based upon the provision of predicates to test the types of objects, and upon functions which return the names of types (note that type names are returned, not the type itself–see below for discussion). Java supplies a predicate, *instanceof*, which takes two arguments, the first being an instance of some class, the second being the name of a defined class. Thus, an example call of *instanceof* might look like:

```
instanceof(foo,AClass);
```

The call to *instanceof* will return true if and only if the first argument, *foo*, has a type whose name is that supplied as the second argument, here *A Class*. It is important to note that, by transitivity of inheritance, the class name that is provided as the second argument can be the name of an ancestor of the class that is actually the class of *foo*. Thus, when using *instanceof*, one must exercise a little care.

In addition to type-handling functions, Common LISP provides a case-like construct, called *typecase*, for testing types. This construct is also defined in Modula-3. The provision of this construct exemplifies the second major approach to type discrimination. The construct is similar to the case statement that is familiar from Pascal and Ada. Whereas in an ordinary case statement, branches are labelled with literal integer constants (or symbolic names standing for integer constants), the branches are labelled with the names of types. Thus, in a neutral, Algol-like language, we might have:

```
typecase foo of
    when integer    A;
    when integer_ptr  B;
    when boolean    C;
    otherwise D;
end typecase;
```

We assume that *foo* is some object or variable whose type we wish to determine. The branches of the *typecase* are labelled by the types *integer*, *integer_ptr* and *boolean*. If *foo* is of type *integer*, action *A* is taken and control falls out of the construct. If, however, *foo* is of type *integer_ptr*, *B* is performed. If the type of *foo* is something other than *integer*, *integer_ptr* or *boolean*, the (optional) *otherwise* branch is taken and *D* is executed.

The basic control flow of the *typecase* construct can be seen to be similar to the more familiar case statement.

The example shows that a user-defined type, in this case *integer_ptr*, can appear as a type name (a class name in an object-oriented language). It would be of little use for a construct such as this to fail to recognize the range of types that can be defined in the programming language. Therefore, the name of any type, whether it is predefined (defined by the language) or user-defined, can serve as the basis for discrimination.

There are variations on the *typecase* theme, naturally enough. For example, in Dylan, there is a *select* expression which normally can be considered as a multi-branch conditional of a fairly standard kind. Rather than operating as a variety of case expression, Dylan's *select* acts more like *cond*, the so-called *McCarthy conditional* in LISP because the branches are labelled with the names of predicates which are applied to the value returned by the control expression. The control expression can be annotated so that different kinds of value can be obtained. For example, in:

```
select(foo by instance)
   ...
end select;
```

the control variable, in this case *foo*, is evaluated in terms of its type. The expression containing *foo* is evaluated in order to determine the class of which *foo* is an instance. The control expression, by means of this qualification, returns a value that can be used to satisfy predicates defined over type names. The select expression in Dylan can contain a default case, as can *typecase*.

These two approaches to type discrimination are not the same. Some might believe that the simple approach based upon predicates and type name-returning functions would be more flexible and, therefore, more easily used. Others might argue that a construct like *typecase* is better because it insulates the user from all inessential details regarding the way in which type names are represented at runtime. We believe that the second argument is better and that *typecase*-like constructs are preferable to the other methods. One reason for this is that it does not require the programmer to pass around objects standing for the names of the types in the program. It must be noted that only the names of the types are thus manipulated; real types cannot be handled in such a way. However, when using the functions and predicates approach, it is important to remember that type names are introduced into the programming language as a new domain of denotable values. Unfortunately, there is little that can be done with these names: they can be supplied to predicates and functions and returned from functions. It is very rare for a construct in the language to be provided that returns the referent of the type name (the definition of the class whose name it is, for example). Thus, a new domain of values is introduced into the language, thus complicating its semantics, but this domain is of very little utility for the reason that there is very little that can be done with these values. The *typecase* approach reduces this. It is, and will always be, necessary to have some way to refer to types within a program: names, particularly of classes, are the obvious and most efficacious choice. We need to refer to types (classes) in order to create instances of them as well as to discriminate between them. However, unless we are able to manipulate types (classes) like other types (integers, reals, etc.), the impact upon the language of the need to manipulate and test these names should be restricted as much as possible. The *typecase* construct acts as such a limit; it restricts the area within a program in which type names are used. The alternative allows type names to be regarded as ordinary values, able to be passed between expressions. Thus, under the functions and predicates approach, type names can appear almost anywhere in a program.

6.3 Polymorphism

Polymorphism is one of the more important concepts in object-oriented languages. When introducing class-based languages in Chapter 2, I briefly introduced the idea that an instance of a class can be substituted at runtime for an instance of one of its subclasses. This process, called downcasting, is one of the topics discussed in a later section (Section 6.8), so further discussion will be deferred except to observe that downcasting is a source of *polymorphism*.

The term polymorphism was introduced by Strachey [89, 88] in the 1960s while working on the CPL language. The word itself is derived from the Greek and means "taking many forms". Strachey's intuition was that a procedure could be defined so that the number or types of its arguments differed. The "meaning" of the procedure remains the same, but the number or types of its inputs vary. Polymorphic procedures often require many definitions of a procedure; this entails that the same identifier is used to name a set of procedural objects, each of whose signatures is different from the others.

6.3.1 Signatures

A signature is the complete definition of the input and output types of a procedure or function, so:

$$int \times int \rightarrow int$$

is the type of integer addition, while the predicate (function) which tests whether a character is in upper case has the signature:

$$char \rightarrow boolean$$

and the logical *and* operation is:

$$boolean \times boolean \rightarrow boolean$$

The $\times$ symbol represents the Cartesian product of types and $\rightarrow$ represents a function with inputs on its left-hand side and outputs on the right. It is usual for a procedure to have exactly one signature. A polymorphic procedure is associated with more than one signature, there being one signature for each valid ·collection of types.

For example, an arithmetic function could be defined to accept pairs of integers, pairs of reals, one each of real and integer, two complex numbers, one complex and one real number, and so on; the result of the function would, correspondingly, be altered depending upon the input types. Each definition of this function has the same name. The compiler (or interpreter) is faced with the task of determining which form of procedure to apply given a set of inputs; this can be determined statically at compile time. If the concept of a procedure which has more than one signature is considered, it is a short step to the introduction of type variables. That is, to the introduction of variables whose domains are types themselves. Type variables can be bound, typically at compile time, to types, thus requiring types to be denotable values in a fashion analogous to the usual ones (e.g., integers, reals, booleans). It is quite reasonable that we might write a new polymorphic arithmetic function with the following signatures:

$$
\begin{array}{ccccc}
int & \times & int & \rightarrow & int \\
int & \times & real & \rightarrow & real \\
real & \times & real & \rightarrow & real \\
complex & \times & complex & \rightarrow & complex \\
complex & \times & complex & \rightarrow & real \\
complex & \times & real & \rightarrow & real
\end{array}
$$

However, type variables allow one to define a much simpler signature. Given type variables, α and β, we can define a signature:

$$\alpha \times \beta \rightarrow \alpha$$

When compiling, we examine the actual types of the call to the function (the types of the actual parameters) and instantiate the type variables accordingly; the case in which α and β are identical must be taken into account. This account of polymorphism is often called *genericity*, and was first used in functional languages.

We could define three primary kinds of polymorphism, as follows:

1. *Genericity* employs type parameters (hence, type variables) in the definition of a prototype or template routine or class which is then instantiated by supplying appropriate values (types) for its type parameters.
2. A form, sometimes called *inclusive polymorphism*, formed by a partial ordering on types. Such a relation is automatically induced by the inheritance relation obtaining between parent and children classes. If S is the parent or ancestor of C, a method m defined for S is equivalent to a family of methods, one for every type below its point of definition.
3. *Ad hoc* polymorphism. This is formed by the production of a new behaviour for each element of a set of related signatures (as in the polymorphic arithmetic function above). This is often called *overloading*. The

choice as to which behaviour to select is based upon the types of the arguments supplied to the procedure.

In the definition of *ad hoc* polymorphism, we intend that a single name is associated with a set of signatures whose cardinality is greater than one. The behaviours might be related as in the case of overloading the addition operation, but are different because of the differences implied by different signatures. When considering *ad hoc* polymorphism in a class-based language, it is important to differentiate *overloading* and *redefinition*. Redefinition replaces a behaviour that is inherited by a new one of more specialized type; the signature of a redefined method is typically different from the method whose behaviour is being redefined.

It is worth noting that slots and (local) variables can have signatures. The signature of a variable is its manifest (declared) type.

6.4 Genericity

Genericity has always been available in the Ada programming language for procedure and package definitions. Genericity is the basis for the function and class templates in C++, and it is used in Eiffel in order to implement generic classes. Genericity is considered to be a kind of polymorphism because it takes a piece of code—a class, procedure or function—which implements an algorithm or collection of algorithms in a type-independent fashion (or: in terms of an abstract, most general type) and which employs a type substitution mechanism to produce instances which are specialized to particular types. Viewed in one way, genericity introduces a form of overloading. Viewed in another, it permits the generalization of a component by abstracting from specific types. What makes genericity different is that it introduces explicit *type parameters* or *type variables* into a language to support type substitution or instantiation. Because it is a process based upon substitution, relationships between actual types under instantiation cannot always be maintained.

In languages of this kind, type parameters are introduced via special constructs. In C++, procedural objects and classes can be parameterized; in Eiffel, only classes are subject to type parameterization. In Ada, any type declaration, under appropriate circumstances, can be parameterized; the appropriate circumstances are provided by the generic constructs (procedures and packages—modules).

The idea underpinning type parameterization is that type parameters are to be bound to actual types. An actual type, here, is represented by the built-in types of the language (integer, character, boolean, etc.), together with types defined by the user as classes. In some contexts, an actual type can also be an array or record structure. The actual type is bound to each type parameter and the construct can then be instantiated and checked for correctness. A problem with genericity is that instantiation of the parameterized construct does not guarantee correctness of the result; it is necessary, as a second phase, to verify the resulting construct. A parameterized construct is similar to a template. The checking that must follow instantiation consists of type checking (the template can easily be checked for syntactic well-formedness); it is necessary to verify that the operations performed on the actual types in the instantiated construct can be performed, that result types are as expected, and so on.

It is usual to employ genericity in constructs that define routines and that define classes or types. Classic examples of parametric types are lists, trees, sets and maps. We require lists of integer, lists of real, lists of arbitrarily complex structures. Rather than define a list type for each of these cases, it is best to define a single, parametric type. Thus, we might define such a list roughly as follows:

```
class list[T] is ...
   head() : T;
   tail() : list[T];
   cons(o :   T) : void;
      ...
end class;
```

where *head*, *tail* and *cons* are methods which return the first element, return the list with the first element removed, and which adds a new element to the list, respectively (in the LISP family, they are called *car*, *cdr* and *cons*, respectively). The class is given the name *list* and a type parameter is specified inside square brackets. The type parameter represents the type of the elements to be stored in the list; thus, we require (constrain) the list to hold objects that are of some type we are referring to as T (we assume that type quantification is universal). When appropriately instantiated, instances of this class will hold elements of some actual type. The type parameter is given an arbitrary name, here we have called it T, but it could be *ElemType*, *T1*, τ, or anything else (in the functional language Hope [20], there was a convention that type variables had Greek names, and in Miranda [95] they are denoted by asterisks).

The methods are defined as follows, each is associated with a name (*head*, *tail*, *cons*) and each is assigned a signature. The *head* and *tail* methods have no arguments, hence their formal parameter list is empty. However, they return values. In the case of *head*, it returns an instance of the element type, so its return type is specified as T. The *tail* method returns the list with the first element removed, so it returns an object of type *list[T]*. Finally, the *cons* method adds an object to the list, so it has a formal parameter, *o*, whose type is specified as T. The *cons* method works by adding an element to the list represented by the class, so no value is returned (to get at the elements, one needs to call the other methods).

This defines a parametric type, *list[T]*. We need an operation to instantiate the type. This is done by supplying an actual type to the template. Given *list[T]*, we might have some construct of the general form:

```
intlist : list[integer];
```

to perform the instantiation. This will create an instance of *list[T]* by supplying the integer type as the actual type. The elements of intlist will be integers.

It is possible for parametric types to have more than one type parameter. Parametric types can have an arbitrary number of type parameters; they have as many as are necessary to define the type correctly. We could define a type to represent pairs of objects by:

```
pair[T1,T2]
```

This type has two type parameters, one for each of the component types. The pair type can be instantiated as:

```
pair[integer,integer]
pair[integer,real]
pair[real,real]
```

and so on. Each instantiation assigns a type to the type parameters. In the first and last cases, the two type parameters have been assigned to the same type: *integer* in the first case, and *real* in the last. This is perfectly legal and the actual type will be substituted for the appropriate type variable.

It is also possible to define parametric types in terms of parametric types. For example, when parsing natural language, some parsers will return all legal parse trees, letting a later stage resolve any ambiguities that have been encountered (e.g., the sentence "The boy saw the girl with a telescope" has two legal parses: one in which the boy uses the telescope to see the girl, and one in which the girl has the telescope). To implement this, a list of trees could be created. This implies that we have a new parametric type which could be defined as something like the following:

```
list[parseTree[NodeType]]
```

This defines a list whose element type is a parametric type called *parseTree*. The *parseTree* type has the parameter *NodeType* which represents the type of the nodes that will eventually be stored in the tree.

Given that parametric classes define classes and that they can be instantiated to produce instances (objects to be manipulated), it is interesting to ask whether parametric types can act as the roots type hierarchies just as ordinary classes can. In Eiffel [67], this is permitted, so we can have one parametric type appearing as the superclass of another (the subclass will be parametric by inheritance, of course); it is also permitted in C++ [91], although one is somewhat discouraged by the ungainly syntax. The Theta language [57] also permits parametric types to form hierarchies. Note that, when parametric types can form subclasses, it is possible for the superclass of a parametric type to be a non-parameterized class. If a type hierarchy contains type parameters, it can be instantiated in many ways; this means that the hierarchy will be more generally applicable than otherwise. It also allows for the partial instantiation of class and their subclasses; this restricts their general applicability, but it creates a hierarchy that can still be modified by means of instantiation, an operation that has many benefits over explicit construction.

In the languages Ada, C++ and Eiffel, type parameters are employed in a restricted form. There are no features for treating type parameters as arguments to operations other than definition and instantiation.

Before ending, it is worth noting that there is no inheritance relationship between $A[X]$ and $A[Y]$, even if there is such a relationship between X and Y. To make such a claim is an error (cf. Eiffel and Java which make such claims).

6.5 Overloading and Overriding

Overloading is an operation that has often been included in programming languages for many years. For example, routines that write values to files must be polymorphic for the reason that they must take inputs of different types in order to permit integers, characters, reals, and so on, to be written. This is an example of overloading. The compiler implements the write operation in terms of one procedure for each type; the compiler selects the actual procedure to be used to implement the write operation based upon the type of the argument to the call to the generic write operation. Addition, in most languages, can be performed over a variety of different numeric types. In C++, there are the int, float and double types, as well as short, long and unsigned forms of integer. Addition is always denoted by the symbol "+". This is another familiar example of overloading; again, the compiler selects an implementation based upon the type of the arguments to the generic operation. As far as the programmer is concerned, there is only one procedure or operation in each case; there is more than one routine that implements the operation, each routine having a different (unique) signature but the same name.

An oft-cited property of object-oriented languages of all types is their support for polymorphism. This derives from two sources in class-based languages:

- method over-riding or redefinition, and
- method overloading.

In the former case, there are often constraints on method signatures, while, in the latter, there are frequently none.

It is important to distinguish properly between over-riding in the sense of redefinition and overloading. C++, for example, confuses these cases, as does Java. The Eiffel report [67] is very careful to avoid any confusion and the language contains explicit constructs for differentiating between renaming and redefinition.

A method, m_1, redefines another method, m_2, when m_2 is defined in a superclass of the class in which m_1 is defined and both m_1 and m_2 have the same signature or related, but their behaviour is different. Redefinition is the redefinition of an inherited method's behaviour. The signatures of the original and the redefined methods need not coincide. Under redefinition, the redefining entity renders the redefined one invisible to the class performing the redefinition; the redefining entity *over-rides* the original, in other words. This is a key point about redefinition: it is the replacement of an inherited item by a new one that differs in some significant way; we have also uncovered the relationship between over-riding, overloading, and soon, with overloading; it is a knot that is often left untied.

When methods are redefined, the relationship between the original and the redefined method might be important semantically. This is controlled by the language's *variance* rules (we discuss it in more detail below in Section 6.7.1). Here, we note that many languages (C++, Java, Smalltalk, for example) impose no constraints upon the types in overriding method signatures. Eiffel, Sather, Beta and Theta impose constraints upon signatures. Constraints on signatures are important because they impact upon the ease with which the language can be used and they have implications for the correctness rules for programs. In general, though, the constraint that an over-riding method must have the same arity as the one which it over-rides.

It is important to note that *anything* that can be inherited can be re-defined: data and methods can be redefined. Redefinition can involve the replacement of a signature either of a method or of a data slot; it can in-volve the replacement of the body of a method while its signature remains invariant. In languages like Eiffel that contain pre- and post-conditions, these assertions can be redefined in a subclass; for example, a pre-condition can be strengthened or weakened.

On the other hand, overloading applies to methods only. For example, the addition operation "+" can have a signature:

$$int \times int \rightarrow int$$

as well as:

$$int \times real \rightarrow real$$

where the behaviour is that of adding its arguments and returning the sum as a result. Similarly, printing routines can be supplied for a variety of types, basic and otherwise; their signatures must, necessarily, differ, but the result of applying each is, in an appropriate sense, "the same", namely the printing of a value. In overloading, the definition that matches the argument types most closely is used as the body of the routine that is actually called; to make overloading work, the types of the actual parameters must be computed in order to select the appropriate behaviour or definition.

The simplest case of overloading occurs when methods with the same name but different signatures are defined in different classes; thus, in a class representing character strings, we might define a method called *write* and in a class representing a rational or complex number, we also define a method called *write*. The method that is actually called at runtime will depend upon the type of the object supplied to it as an actual parameter; this, in a statically typed language, can be performed at compile time. Overloading can also occur in the same class as that in which the method being overloaded is defined; it can occur in a subclass of the defining class. It is important to distinguish simple overloading from redefinition because overloading does not render the overloaded method invisible at the point where another case of that method, one with a different signature, is introduced. It is necessary to observe that both write methods are visible to derived classes and to other contexts (unless they are overridden by redeclaration).

From these definitions, it can be seen that, in dynamically-typed languages like Smalltalk, there can only be method redefinition. Method overloading cannot occur in terms of the language because the types of arguments are determined at runtime; overloading is, in such a language, *implicit* because methods respond to arguments of different, though legal, types in the correct way. In other words, in a dynamic language, overloading is an entirely implicit process. (One might also consider the matter as being that dynamically-typed methods are always implicitly ready to select an implementation that is appropriate, provided that the actual arguments have types that are legal for it.)

In [67], Meyer describes the difference between *redeclaration* and *redefinition*; indeed, he sees the process of replacing an inherited item as being far wider than in many languages, C++ and Java in particular. Redeclaration is, Meyer argues, more general a concept than redefinition, the latter being a special case of the former. In both cases, new features (slots, methods, etc.) are not introduced, but the new item simply *overrides* the original declaration of the inherited entity.

In Eiffel, it is possible to introduce a feature (slot, method) that is marked as being *deferred*; that is, its definition is not supplied at the point where that feature is declared. This gives a mechanism for defining abstract classes and deferred features must be given a complete definition in some subclass of the class in which the deferred feature is defined. When this is combined with redeclaration, it is sometimes the case that two or more features must be merged into a single one; alternatively, the inherited implementation of a feature might be discarded or undefined. The former joins two or more features to form a single, new one. The latter is a way of producing new deferred features from instantiated ones. In order to effect a join, it is necessary, in Eiffel, to rename and then to undefine the unwanted features and to rename or re-define the required one. In order to make a feature deferred, it is necessary to employ the *deferred* annotation.

Before we look at root classes, it is worth mentioning a peculiarity of some LISP-derived object-oriented languages, CLOS and Dylan being the best examples. In these languages, it is possible to define what CLOS refers to as an *eql* parameter. This parameter specifies that its argument must be identical to the value specified for the parameter. For example, if we have a procedure p with a parameter of the form:

```
v eql 100
```

When p is called, the actual parameter that is to be bound to v must have the value 100 or an error is called.

This might seem either a variation on default parameters or just plain silly. However, *eql* parameters are extremely useful and cater for a case in which one wants to select a method based on the value of a particular parameter. In the context of a generic LISP function, or in the context of a polymorphic method, *eql* methods come into their own. As we have seen, when a polymorphic or multi-method has many implementations, it is necessary to choose between them according to their input types. The question arises as to how discrimination within a type can be effected. That is, given a method m with a signature Σ, say with:

$$\Sigma = (\alpha \times \beta \times \gamma) \rightarrow \delta$$

method m can be applied to a triple of values of type:

$$(\alpha \times \beta \times \gamma)$$

This is clear. What happens if we want to discriminate between two values, say b_1 and b_2 of type β? With the standard scheme found in most languages, such discrimination must be made with a conditional within the body of m. This might be inconvenient at times. Recognizing this, CLOS supports the *eql* parameter which allows dispatching on values of a type. To discriminate between the two values of β, we might write method signatures as follows:

$$m1 : (\alpha \times (b_1 \equiv \beta) \times \gamma) \rightarrow \delta$$
$$m2 : (\alpha \times (b_2 \equiv \beta) \times \gamma) \rightarrow \delta$$

We define a method for each discriminated value in addition to the other methods that make use of polymorphic definition. The two new methods use eql methods (*eql* is denoted, here, by the $\equiv$ symbol) to discriminate between b_1 and b_2.

We can now consider the role of root classes in class-based languages.

6.6 Languages with Root Classes

Some languages come with a root class. Their inheritance graph for objects that can appear in user programs has a single root. In Common LISP, CLOS identifies this class with the value t, the value true. In Java, the root class is called *Object*, and in Eiffel it is called *ANY*. In these languages, all user objects are indirectly derived from the distinguished root class. This makes it possible for the root class to define structures and methods that can be employed by all other objects. One example is to put some of the instance initialization code into root class methods; another is to put instance printing methods in the root class. In Java, the root class is declared as implementing the interface required for object serialization—that is, the conversion of objects to and from a representation suitable for storage on a medium such as a disk file; this can involve traversal of the graph of objects if the object being serialized contains component objects. Thus, any class derived from the root class automatically inherits methods for serializing and deserializing objects.

Root classes also have the advantage that methods can be defined in terms of the root class and downcasted to particular subclasses. For example, we can define a list class and implement a method which adds an element. The element is to be passed to the method as a parameter. The type of that parameter can be given as the root class. Assuming that the method to add an element to a list is called *cons*, and that the root class is called *Object*, we could define the method roughly as follows:

```
method cons (elem : Object) is ... end method;
```

This method can be applied to an object of any class that is derived from *Object*. This means that it is possible to construct lists that contain elements of any type derived from the root class. We have a kind of polymorphism because downcasting is used when the method is called.

The existence of a general root class imposes the requirement that *all* user-defined classes must be derived from the root class. This has the implication that variables of the root type can be declared, and procedure and method parameters can be declared as being of that type. This automatically ensures that an instance of *any* class can be assigned to such a variable or passed to such a procedure or method. Similarly, if the root class is specified as the return type of a function, that function can return a value of any class whatsoever. This is a feature that is particularly useful in the definition of container classes (list, set, etc., classes). This is a form of polymorphism which allows variables, parameters and functions to refer to any object that is defined.

In pure object-oriented languages like Smalltalk, all objects are represented as instances of classes. Under such a scheme, elementary values such as integers, characters, booleans, and even methods are represented in terms of classes. If there is a root class, elementary values, as well as these additional types of object, can be represented and manipulated more easily when a root class is present.

6.7 Polyadicity and Default Parameters

As noted above, one can conceive of procedures with the same name but with different numbers of arguments. One might want to define an addition or multiplication function which accepts a variable number of arguments. A one-adic addition function (function in one argument) would return its argument, while a two-adic one would behave as expected; an n-adic one would compute the sum of its inputs. Similarly, a one-adic multiplication function would be the identity on its input; the two-adic version acts as expected, while an n-adic one would return the product of its arguments. Such functions are said to be *polyadic*. All arithmetic functions in Common LISP are polyadic; the language provides a number of mechanisms for defining polyadic functions, thus affording a considerable flexibility, albeit at a higher cost in procedure call.

Polyadic procedures are polymorphic, but their polymorphism is restricted to variation in the number of arguments which are instantiated when the procedure is called. Polyadic procedures very often are defined in terms of a core of *required* parameters and a collection of *optional* ones. When a call is made to such a procedure, its required parameters must be instantiated; that is, for each required formal parameter, there must be a corresponding actual parameter. Binding of optional parameters is less strict. When called, an optional parameter might or might not be instantiated; this implies that the number of actual parameters supplied to a call to a polyadic procedure can vary.

Immediately, we are led to a problem: when an optional parameter is omitted from a call to a polyadic procedure, what is the value that should be employed in the body of the procedure? If a required parameter is omitted, an error *must occur* because the procedure is defined in terms of its required parameters. The answer is that default values must be supplied, either by the language or by the programmer. In Common LISP, the default value for all optional parameters is *nil* (the empty list); this standard default makes the task of defining polyadic procedures easier for one does not always have to worry about defaults. In other languages, an explicit default must be given (it can be optionally given in Common LISP, of course). C++ and Ada allow default parameters to be specified, but, in each case, a default value. Thus, in Ada:

```
function add(n : in integer, m :in integer := 1) returns
                integer is ...
```

and in C++:

```
int add(int n, int m = 1);
```

are equivalent polyadic forms of an integer addition function. In each case, a default value is supplied.

In languages that are statically typed, a default value of the appropriate type must be supplied. The constraint on the value is required in order that the procedure's signature will be well-typed according to the language's typing rules. In languages which require additional, runtime type checking, default values must satisfy all type-checking constraints imposed.

The types of the formal and corresponding actual parameters, required or optional, must match according to the well-typing rules of the language under consideration. Polyadic procedures are permitted to have different numbers of actual parameters, but the types must always match. In this sense, polyadic procedures represent a restricted form of polymorphism.

Default values for parameters can be defined in PL/1, a language that was initially defined just before Strachey introduced the concept of polymorphism and which has been revised since then. Polyadic procedures can be defined in Common LISP (and hence CLOS), Ada, C++ and Eiffel. In each case, a default value is associated with optional parameters.

In object-oriented languages, default parameters are often used in defining constructor functions. If a class constructor can, in principle, accept between one and three integers, it is possible either to define three separate constructors, or to define a single polyadic constructor with one required parameter and two optional ones. Optional parameters can also be used in ordinary methods where a well-defined default value is known. Otherwise, the interaction between polyadicity and classes (and prototypes, for that matter) is weak; polyadic methods are really just a notational convenience.

6.7.1 Variance

Variance is a set of rules which govern the way in which methods can be over-ridden. Variance is interesting because some rules can endanger the type-safety of a language (Eiffel is one such language). There are three standard sets of rules:

- covariance;
- contravariance and
- agnosticism or non-variance (*sic*).

The first two terms and their implications are considered in detail in the next few paragraphs. The concept of "agnosticism" or "non-variance" are not standard terms; they both denote an empty set of variance rules. Many languages, Smalltalk, Java and C++ among them, are agnostic or involve "non-variance".

Covariance and contravariance are properties of typed languages, specifically typed class-based languages. To understand them, let us consider the following case. Assume that we have two classes, S and C, where S is the superclass of C. Each class defines a method, m. In S, m is defined as:

```
m(arg :A) ...
```

While in C, m is (re)defined as:

```
m(arg : B) ...
```

An important design issue is what restrictions are to be placed on the type of argument to m. That is, what are the restrictions that must be placed upon A and B? There are at least the following possibilities:

- No restrictions are imposed;
- Type B must be a descendent type of A;
- Type A must be a descendent type of B, and
- Type A and type B must be the *same* type.

The second case is called the *covariant rule*; the third the contravariant rule. There is no standard name for the first case: agnosticism, non-variance, are just two of the names that appear in the literature (agnosticism appeals most to me).

The covariant rule is so-named because, in the child class, the types of the arguments in redefined methods are children of the types in the parent's method. Inheritance "varies" in the same direction for both cases. Contravariance gets its name from the fact that inheritance "varies" in opposite directions for methods and classes. Of the two, contravariance might seem, at first blush, to be the more theoretically attractive. In object-oriented languages, polymorphism means, *inter alia*, that a slot or parameter can be bound to objects of any child type of their declared type. When polymorphism is combined with dynamic binding, the *actual* type of an object will trigger the corresponding method. That is, the method that is *actually* called depends upon the *actual* type of the object that is bound to a slot or parameter; the actual type might be the declared type or one of its descendants.

Under contravariance, we can bind an instance of a descendent type to a slot or parameter and all method calls will still function correctly for the reason that a descendant can cope with the arguments at least as general as those of its ancestor. A child object is, in every possible sense, a valid instance of the ancestor class because we are using inheritance to implement subtyping. Let us unpack this a little to see what is meant.

If we have a pair of classes such that one is the ancestor of the other according to the inheritance relation, we know that the child can be substituted for the ancestor if inheritance is interpreted as subtyping. The reason for this is that slots defined in the ancestor, as well as methods, are valid for the child. In other words, the child class knows how to respond to messages requesting reading or updating of slots inherited from its ancestor; similarly, the child knows how to invoke the corresponding methods. In this sense, the child is a valid instance, in every sense, of its ancestor. If we consider the two as types, then a subtype can always be substituted for a supertype. In both cases, viewing inheritance as the subtype relation is the critical step.

Covariance implies that static type checking might be insufficient in the worst case. It is for this reason that we have qualified statements about the relationships between classes and types and subclasses and subtypes. Contravariance is a completely type-safe rule when applied to parameters. The opposite case holds for return value types; covariance is a type-safe rule when applied to return value types, and contravariance causes problems.

Unfortunately, many real problems require covariance. The following examples taken from the Eiffel FAQ [68] demonstrate the use of covariance. Consider the following definitions:

```
class PLOT is
    method add(arg : DATA_SAMPLE) is ...
```

and:

```
class PLOT_3D is
    superclass(PLOT);
    method add(arg: DATA_SAMPLE_3D) is ...
```

where PLOT is the superclass of PLOT_3D and DATA_SAMPLE is the superclass of DATA_SAMPLE_3D. This example requires covariance, under which rule it works well. The example would fail if a PLOT_3D object were bound to a PLOT slot and we then tried to add an instance of DATA_SAMPLE to it (call its *add* method on an instance of DATA_SAMPLE, that is). The reason for the failure is that the example implements code reuse and not subtyping, while, at the same time, applying a method defined in the superclass to an object of the descendent class as if the descendent object were a true subtype.

```
class HERBIVOR is
    slot diet: LIST[PLANT];
    method eat (food : PLANT) is ...
```

and:

```
class COW is
    superclass(HERBIVORE);
    method eat (food : GRASS) is ...
```

where PLANT is an ancestor of GRASS. This works exactly as we would wish. The compiler must prevent us from binding a COW object to a HERBIVORE slot and trying to make it eat a PLANT. However, we should not be doing this.

It is also illuminating to consider the container object bound to the *diet* slot. There is no need to redefine this slot in descendent classes. The reason for this is that in the covariant redefinition of the argument of the *eat* method, the *diet* slot will always contain an object that can be eaten (e.g., instances of GRASS for instances of COW). If we had contravariant redefinition of the argument of eat, it would be necessary to make the type of the diet container more general.

Sather employs the contravariant rule. It also uses separate mechanisms for subtyping and code reuse. It only allows dynamic binding on genuine subtypes. One consequence is that Sather programs will contain concrete types in an attempt to model covariant problems. Unfortunately, in Sather, a concrete type is one that cannot be further subtyped (subclassed), thus reducing the potential for reuse.

Eiffel, on the other hand, like Beta, uses the covariant rule. In Eiffel, any type can admit of subtypes, subject to checks made by the compiler. Because they implement the covariant rule, both Eiffel and Beta treat the examples above correctly.

C++ and Java are, with Smalltalk, agnostic about the relationships between types. CLOS and its relatives employ a totally different approach, but are still to be regarded as agnostic.

6.8 Downcasting and Subtypes

Subclasses have a significant bearing upon the generality and utility of instances of classes in a class-based object-oriented programming language. The type structure interacts with other facets of the language, as we will now see.

The first point to note is that if C_1 is a subclass of C_2, then all instances of C_1 are also instances of C_2. This impacts upon such matters as parameter passing and variable assignment (including assignment to array elements and slots). Let us consider the case of parameter passing in methods. Let us assume that variable v_1 is declared to be of type C_2:

```
v1 : C2;
```

If we have a method with the following formal parameter specification:

```
c.meth( ..., v : C1, ...)
```

then we can call c.*meth* with v_1 as an actual parameter:

```
c.meth( ..., v1, ...);
```

The reason for this is that all instances of C_1 are also instances of C_2 because C_1 is a subtype of C_2. Given that C_1 is a subtype of C_2, it makes sense to permit any instance of C_1 appear where an instance of C_2 is required.

Just as instances of C_1 are permitted to appear as actual parameters corresponding to formal parameters which have been declared to be of type C_2, so assignment between the two types is permitted:

```
v1 :C1;
v2 : C2;
v2 := v1;
```

This is a legal assignment in many statically typed object-oriented programming languages. On the other hand, given the above variable declarations, the assignment:

```
v1 := v2;
```

is not typically legal for the reason that an instance of a class is not an instance of any of its classes (the equivalence *only runs upwards, not downwards*).

When an assignment of an instance of a class to a variable, v, whose type is a superclass of the instance's type, access is only permitted to those slots in the instance which are found in the superclass. For example, if C_1 has slots s_{11} and s_{12}, and methods m_{11}, m_{12} and m_{13}, and its superclass C_2 has s_{21} as its only slot, and m_{21} as its only method, only s_{21} can be accessed after the assignment. Similarly, methods m_{11}, m_{12} and m_{13} are all invisible and cannot be called from v. (The same applies if v is a formal parameter or if v is a pointer to an instance of C_1.) What happens when assigning to a variable of more general type is that the internal structure of the subclass which is not inherited from the superclass is hidden from use.

The same happens when we pass an instance of a subclass via a parameter whose type is declared to be a superclass. It also happens when we point to an instance. Let C_1 be a subclass of C_2 and let *ptr* be a pointer to C_2. We can point to an instance of C_1, but only those slots in the C_1 instance that are inherited from C_2 can be accessed via *ptr*. This amounts to an *implicit type conversion*. We are seeing an object of one type as if it were of another. Indeed, this implicit type conversion is called *upcasting*.

Upcasting is the process of casting (converting or coercing) the type of a variable from a sub- to a superclass. The reason that *only* the slots in the superclass are visible (accessible) is that only those slots would be visible if one *actually* had an instance of the superclass. Upcasting can be applied to variables, array elements, formal parameters, result parameters and pointers; it can also be applied to slots.

The converse of upcasting is *downcasting*. In downcasting, a variable (etc.) is bound to a value which is an instance of a class that is a subclass of the variable's original class. Thus, if C_1 is a superclass of C_2 and v_1 is a variable of type C_1, and v_2 a variable of type C_2, then the assignment:

```
v2 := v1;
```

downcasts the instance of C_1 to C_2. What we should see is those slots defined in C_1 (i.e., the whole of v_1). The problem comes when we want to access slots defined in C_2. The variable v_2 holds an instance of a class that does not have these slots, so what is to be done? Are default values to be used? Is an attempt to access those slots an error? Indeed, should access be permitted once downcasting has occurred? Downcasting is useful because it allows symmetric binding of classes. The problems just mentioned indicate that it might be a concept of relatively limited utility.

The concept of *self-adjusting* covariance is of some interest, although it is not often encountered. The *like Current* parameter annotation in Eiffel and the *Same* pseudo-type in Omega [11] are two examples of this concept. The symbol *Same*, in Omega [11], refers to a pseudo-type; the *self* variable is of this pseudo-type. In Omega, the *Same* type is defined as follows. If a prototype P contains a method m, expressions of type *Same* can be assigned to variables of type P and the ancestors of P. Such assignments are safe because the method m can only be executed as a result of a message to an object of class P or to a descendant of P (which will inherit m). Expressions of type *Same* can be assigned to variables of type *Object*, the root type for Omega. The rule also applies to methods of monomorphic type. The receiver of a monomorphic type P is always known to be an object of type P, therefore the type *Same* has the same meaning as P within methods of P ([11], p. 143). Reference to the class in which a method is defined is also the defining characteristic of the *like Current* declaration in Eiffel.

6.9 Review

The identification of classes and types, together with the concept of separating types from implementations, provide rich and powerful tools for the construction of new types. However, in the final review, there are some problems which are often ignored. It is possible to define product and sum types in an object-oriented setting. Sum types are defined by introducing a branch in the type mechanism and are manipulated by means of downcasting. Product types are defined in terms of arrays or by the definition of a simple pair type, together with their injection and projection functions. Arrow types appear to be supported by methods. However, it will be seen that the support for arranging methods into hierarchies (as noted in the last chapter) is very poor; the best language, in this respect, is Beta. It might be argued that the programmer, should they want such operations or representations, can implement them if they want. However, this is a matter of implementation. It is possible, though tortuous, to implement objects in FORTRAN-IV or in macro assembler if one *really* wants; we are dealing with Turing equivalent structures, so implementability should come as no surprise. What is required is a notational mechanism for such definitions. In each of the above, we are constrained to *implement* these types in terms of new objects; we introduce new objects into the program's abstraction hierarchy, sometimes at locations which are awkward in the sense that they interact with the rest of the program's organization (this is one place where mixin inheritance can play a role).

What object-oriented programming gives us is encapsulation and subtyping, together with automatic method finding (not selection all the time in Eiffel). A branch in the type hierarchy gives us a sum type, but at the cost of a new class. Products are restricted to Cartesian products and must, again, be implemented by new objects. It could be argued that the organization of methods into an appropriate hierarchy is an application- or domain-specific matter; it would be a start if we could base such abstractions upon a pre-existing set of relationships.

Finally, we come to the notion of the type itself. It is, of course, central to efforts in programming language design. In a class-based language, types correspond to the natural objects in the application domain. What we do is to define new classes according to our intuitions about the organization of the domain. We are typically unable to define constraints that must apply, relationships that obtain between classes or, better still, between instances. The ability to form complex objects from more simple ones in ways that differ from the subtyping and inclusion (part-of) relations is also required. These relations stretch the concept of type.

However, if we consider the Miranda [95] or Haskell [49] languages, we see a mechanism for type definition.

7. Types II: Types and Objects—Alternatives

7.1 Introduction

In this chapter, we will take the notion that classes are types very seriously. We will attempt to discover some of the confusions that are possible when this equivalence is assumed only partially, as is the case in many current class-based languages.

First, in Section 7.2, the relationship between types and implementations are examined in greater detail. Section 7.3 discusses how implementation details can be hidden. Section 7.4 is concerned with type operations and how they relate to classes. Finally, section 7.5 is about containers and objects; it is primarily about modules and their relationship to classes.

7.2 Types and Implementations

Our view of types is that they are algebras and, therefore, composed of a collection (often a finite set) of operators (an *operator domain*) and a collection (often a finite set) of objects upon which the operators act.

In class-based programming, classes are equated with types and instances of types are equated with objects. Classes *define* new types. Classes can be *instantiated* to produce objects; objects are *elements* of the type defined by their class. The instances of classes constitute the objects of the type defined by the class to which they belong. Classes define an abstract collection of entities and the operations which can be performed upon them. Instances of classes, objects, belong to the type. A variable or a pointer which can refer to an instance of a class, or an array whose elements can be instances of a class, input parameters to a method or procedure or the value represented by the return value of a function or method can take the type which is represented by the class of those instances (or instances of the ancestor types of their type). It is, strictly speaking, incorrect to talk of the *type of an instance*, for an instance is an object which comprises part of a type. Thus, a class introduces the operations and objects from which that type is defined. Instances of classes belong to that class (obviously!) and are of the type defined by that class; the type is a property of the instance. Because of the definitional nature of the class construct, objects are uniquely associated with classes (hence types) when they are created; the association is static in the sense that, if we view the extension of a class, the type of the elements of the extension is already determined.

When reflection in a typed class-based language is considered, it becomes necessary to assign types to classes *as well as to* instances of classes (objects).

The reader should note that there are other views as to how the concept of *type* should be interpreted in programming languages in general and in class-based languages in particular.

Given this view of types, the process of constructing a class-based program is one, therefore, of constructing new types and instantiating them to produce objects which can be transmitted between instances of other types, between program components and which can have variable slots updated to reflect their changing state. Instances correspond to values of the types represented by their class. However, as part of the process of class (type) definition, it is very often the case that implementation details must be provided; this is so that the class can be executed when instantiated. A notable exception to this is the definition of an abstract class; here, methods are only equipped with signatures, not definitions.

The process of programming with classes involves the construction of new types, whose properties are transmitted to subtypes (to subclasses) and the definition of implementations which are propagated in a similar fashion. If we regard the specification of a class's signature as the definition of its interface and the definition of the code bodies for methods and iterators as the definition of its implementation, when subclasses are defined, both the interface and the implementation are propagated to them from the classes upon which they are based. The definition of a class's signature amounts to the specification of the types of its data slots and the specification of the signatures of the methods it defines. One reason for this lack of clean separation between interface and implementation is so that any class (except an abstract one) can be instantiated at any time; another is that, by maintaining the two together, all relevant information is defined in one place and can easily be seen by a programmer (perhaps less of a pressing need with the advent of more powerful support tools); another, and rather more cynical view is that the two are not separated because the need for separation has not been perceived.

It has already been noted that the Sather language makes a distinction between types and implementations. Sather distinguishes two concepts for what, in other languages, is considered to be inheritance, and, hence, a single concept. These concepts are subtype definition and implementation inclusion. Subtype definition consists of the definition of a new abstract type which, as an abstract type, cannot be instantiated. When an implementation is required, the Sather programmer must define a concrete type which is permitted to include other concrete types. In effect, Sather distinguishes between implementations and types (represented by abstract classes).

Snyder [81] has discussed the implications of separating subtyping and implementation inclusion. Very often, inheritance in class-based languages is used as if it were a relationship between implementations, a conflation which can cause confusion and, without proper control, can lead to programs that are difficult to understand and which reveal too much information about implementations (we consider an example where this must be avoided in the next section, Section 7.3). In [81], Snyder considers the relationship between classes defining a DE queue and a stack. He observes that one can be made into a subclass of the other with relative ease. If the stack class is implemented in terms of the DE queue (i.e., the stack is defined as a subclass of the DE queue), there is a superfluous operation which adds an item to the "end" of the container holding the stack (we assume that stack elements are added to the "front" of the container). This implies that the relationship between the *implementations* of the two classes is not that of inheritance in the sense of subtyping. Instead, it is one of implementation inclusion because the implementation of the DE queue can be defined from that of the stack by the addition of the operation which adds items to the "end" of the container. However, the DE queue class represents a subtype of the stack class; it is a subtype because it has more structure in the form of the additional method. The relationship between the *interfaces*, or type definitions, is the converse of that exhibited between the implementations.

With care, subtype and implementation can be kept in step; this is an implementation matter, of course. Semantically, we have an interpretation of inheritance that conflates—or even confuses—implementation and subtype. There are other reasons why we might want to separate an interface description from an implementation, or subtype definitions from their implementations. One important case is that in which a type has more than one implementation. The CORBA standard for distributed objects [79] makes such a possibility explicit.

In most object-oriented languages, an interface is typically associated with a single implementation. For example, a list type will have an interface specification which defines the operations that can be performed on it (see below for an example, Section 7.3). In C++, for instance, the implementation of a class is fixed once and for all when it is defined; a similar case obtains for Java, Smalltalk and for many other languages. However, we might want a representation (implementation) of lists in terms of cells stored in a heap or in terms of fixed-size vectors. The choice as to which implementation is most appropriate depends upon factors such as: is there an *a priori* upper bound on the length of the list, must access time be constant (and hence worth wasting some memory on a suitable implementation), can cells be recycled, is there sufficient time to access a heap, and so on. The balance of these factors will determine which implementation is to be preferred. In a similar fashion, a set can be implemented as a vector, a list, a table or a tree, depending upon the properties of the elements to be stored. If there is an ordering relation defined over the element type, a tree-based representation can be used for sets; if the elements are generated in a particular order, a list-based representation might be best. In some cases, more than one representation might be used so that the user-level operations can be most effectively performed.

In a language like Ada, it is possible to have multiple implementations of a type. This is made possible by the package structure, but it requires each type to be named in a different way. An extensive set of data type definitions is given by Booch [12]. The types are distinguished by their different implementations and each is given a different name in order to denote properly what the type does and how it operates. A similar approach is, of course, possible in languages like CLOS, Dylan, Smalltalk, Eiffel, Java and C++. The major problem with this approach is that it requires new names to be thought up each time. Names are only arbitrary labels, but the problem runs deeper because types are referred to in program text by their names. If we want to alter the implementation of a type, we must, under this scheme, redeclare all relevant variables so that they are of the new, not the old, implementation—*the basic or underlying type is the same.*

In languages making distinctions between *private* and *public* slots and methods, like C++ and Java, it is possible to hide the implementation of a type by making all implementation details *private*. Using the *private* slots and methods as a basis, *public* methods, typically, can be defined which provide the interface that is desired for the type. Using this approach then, implementation can be hidden completely from the user, while the interface is totally visible. This is one approach to the separation of interface and implementation, but it is not particularly attractive because the two must co-exist in the same class definition, whereas a full separation will consist of an inheritable definition of the interface and a completely separate implementation.

In languages that permit the definition of *abstract* classes, implementations can be separated from their interface in the following way. An abstract class is defined which provides the desired interface. The methods and, perhaps, data slots of the abstract class define the interface that is to be presented. The implementation of this class can be provided by one or more concrete subclasses. The subclasses can employ the *public/private* distinction described in the last paragraph, if desired. Using abstract classes, the interface can be independently inherited along a chain of subclasses. These subclasses can all be abstract, thus defining a sequence of progressively more detailed interfaces. In parallel with these interfaces, concrete classes can be defined to provide various implementations of the interfaces that are defined at various levels in the inheritance structure. This is one clear and effective method for separating implementation from interface. This approach partially solves the problem, but it still introduces a number of separate types, each with different names, so they are considered to be distinct but related types. The fact that they are derived from a single root class allows polymorphism to assist in the construction of the final product. The use of abstract classes is shown in Figure 7.1.

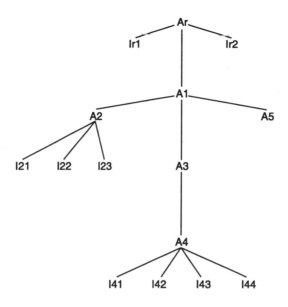

Fig. 7.1. *Abstract classes and multiple implementations.*

The figure shows how there is a central "trunk" and various "branches" emanating from the trunk. The trunk represents the simple inheritance chain produced by successive specializations of the original abstract class. The original abstract class defines the interface. The branches represent concrete classes which implement each successive interface (abstract class).

On a much more speculative note, the separation of implementation from interface and, in particular, the provision of different implementations opens the way to the runtime selection of implementation. This becomes possible when a language or system is equipped with reflective properties (see Chapter 8). Such properties allow it to examine its own state and to make decisions about such matters as the choice of which implementation to adopt at any given point in the execution of the program. For example, if there is little space or time, a list might be represented by a vector. If the list becomes too long for the vector, the program might decide to adopt a heap-based implementation based upon small, simple cells and convert the existing data structure into the new one. It is not necessary, to do this, to have all code in compiled form at the same time, for the program might employ dynamically linked libraries or dynamic compilation.

We now turn our attention to a matter related to implementation and interface, but of a different nature.

7.3 Hiding Implementation Details

The focus of attention in this section is on classes whose sole use is the implementation of a more "important" class. These implementing classes make no sense outside of the definition of the class which they help define and should, ideally, be made inaccessible to all but the implementer of the more "important" class.

Even with a separation of interface from implementation, it is not always desirable for *all* classes or types to be visible to *all* other components. Sometimes it is desirable to hide a class or type from potential users. This is possible in Ada by means of the package mechanism; hidden types are defined as being private to the module; it is also possible in Java where a class can be made private to a package. Dylan also provides the same functionality, as does CLOS. C++ and Smalltalk fail to provide any such mechanism; in these languages, all classes are public and can be instantiated anywhere (the namespace construct in the new version of C++ is an attempt to address this problem). Most of the languages just cited restrict class visibility using an additional language construct. Eiffel does not have modules in the language; implementations of the language often include a directory concept called a cluster which permits selective export of classes—this is, though, an *extra-linguistic* mechanism and can be omitted. If a language permits the nested definition of classes, private types can be handled by internal definition; this, however, severely restricts access to the internal class (unless mechanisms similar to those in Beta are provided). However, the problems with nested class definitions are, among others, that the nested class has direct access to the implementation of the class in which it is defined and that the contained class can only be instantiated when the container is. These arguments suggest that nested classes are not to be preferred.

One simple case where type visibility matters is in the definition of a list type (trees of various degrees are also simple examples). What we would ideally prefer is an interface that represents a list of some type (we assume a class definition mechanism that supports parametric polymorphism). In order to support that definition, we need a class to represent the cells that form the list. Taking the simplest case, a cell will be composed of a head containing the data value and a tail containing a reference to the next cell (or *nil* or some other distinguished value denoting termination—*NONE* and *NOTHING* are two names found in the literature). It is very rarely the case that the user wants the cell type to be visible. What is required is often something like the following:

- the ability to test for the empty list;
- add a new value to the list;
- obtain the value in the head;
- obtain the list represented by the tail;
- search for a value in the list;

- append two lists;
- apply a function or procedure to each value in the list (either updating or producing a copy);
- copy the list;
- return the number of cells in the list (the length);
- reverse the list.

Sometimes, destructive operations are defined for lists; these operations alter the list structure by manipulation of pointers and by setting values directly into the head slots in cells.

Despite the remarks about destructive operations, none of the above operations is described in terms of the cells that are used to represent the list. Instead, the higher-level concept of the list is employed. To avoid belabouring the point, the interface to the list class is defined entirely in terms of operations on the list, not on operations involving the underlying cell type. The cell type is used only for implementation and *not* for specification. An iterator for lists can be written in one of two basic ways: in terms of list operations, or in terms of the underlying representation. The former implementation maintains the abstraction and is to be preferred.

(If we wanted to define a list type suitable for use in LISP, we would have to define a *dotted pair* type and then base the list type upon it; the dotted pair is a legal, if a little uncommon, type in LISP. We would need to expose the dotted pair type even though we would still define the list interface much as above. We would also need operations to access the underlying representation. Such operations could be provided by the list type (via what amounts to a type change) or simply by viewing the list as dotted pairs.)

Types that are introduced simply to make the implementation of a type or class possible should not be made visible to everyone. In the older edition of C++ or in Eiffel without clusters, this is often necessary; in other languages, module mechanisms help restrict visibility. The cell type, in the case of the list type, should not be visible to other components for it is *only* used to implement the list type. However, it is necessary to define the cell type and to implement it somewhere; the place where it is defined must be accessible to the place where the list type is defined and to *nowhere* else. If it were globally visible, as in Smalltalk, the older edition of C++, and Eiffel without clusters, it would be possible to see how the list type was constructed. This would violate the principle of encapsulation. Given access to the underlying representation, there is the temptation to provide "backdoor" methods for accessing the internal structure of a type (here, the cells of a list), so that they can be manipulated by "more efficient" methods—experience shows that they are seldom more efficient or more effective, leading, as they do, to more errors and less abstract code (more messy detail, in other words).

It might be thought that the definition of a class within another class would be an adequate solution to the problem of implementation class visibility. It is, however, a poor solution. One reason for this is that it makes the sharing of such internal classes impossible. We have said that the intention is to prohibit access to the types used to implement other types, the other types being required to be visible. Immediately one thinks that such an implementation type would be used in the definition of only one other class. It can be argued that it is never the case that two classes will ever require access to each other's internal representations. However, there might be cases where this is needed even if it is not advisable. When this occurs, the type used for the implementation must still be hidden from all but those special classes which require access. We therefore have the dual requirements of hiding the implementation class while making it accessible to a select few. This, again, suggests that some type-hiding mechanism akin to modules is required. Such sharing is necessary, for example, when different views are required of the same data structure.

In C++, it is possible to define a *friend* class or routine. If one class, F, is marked as a friend of another class, C, instances of C can directly access instances of F; this provides classes with a way of inspecting and updating private and protected data and methods. The *friend* concept is clearly a mechanism for removing visibility barriers and for avoiding encapsulation. It is the "standard" way to construct a list class in that language [91, 59]. The "approved" method for defining a list in C++, at least in those works cited, is to define a class to represent the cell type which is a friend of the list class. The friend mechanism affords the list class access to the internal representation of the cell class in order to update head and tail values (the operation of adding a new cell to the front of a list—*cons*ing in LISP terms— is defined as destructive assignment to the tail slot of the cell). The problem is that the list class needs to operate upon component cells; the direct fashion introduced by friend classes is, presumably, for more "efficient" access, but this clearly costs more than it earns, for every class can be marked as a *friend* and anarchy will once again reign!

A cleaner approach is to define an abstract cell class to be used by the list class and then to specialize the cell type; this requires access to the cell class (or its interface) and we are still exposing details that should be hidden. What we want is for the interface to represent the list type and for all implementation details to be hidden from view. We return again to the idea that either class nesting must be permitted or that a module concept be added.

In more recent versions of C++, the namespace concept has been introduced, thus solving the above problems. Dylan, Java, Ada and CLOS all provide module-like constructs which have visibility restriction operations. The Theta language [57] also has a module construct and adopts an interesting approach to objects and classes.

In Theta, classes are used to represent user-defined types. They use inheritance in their definition, just like classes do in C++ and other class-based languages. Theta treats its classes as types and a subtype relation is implied by the inheritance relation. Instances of a Theta class represent values of a type. Consequently, variables can be declared to be of a user-defined type and can be assigned to instances of that type. Theta does not, at least according to [57], allow classes to be defined on their own. Instead, Theta differs from the other module-supporting languages in the requirement that classes must be defined inside module-like constructs which are used to control visibility. Theta classes (types) can have multiple implementations. Theta uses modules to contain implementations.

7.4 Classes and Type Operations

Classes are commonly equated with types. An instance of a class is a value in a type. There are clear generator functions and relationships between classes that reinforce this view. When we want a value, we instantiate the class as appropriate; instantiation can specify parameter values for complex types so we can distinguish values of a type. In many class-based languages, we are severely restricted in the range of operations that can be employed in the definition of new classes (types). Typically, a new class is defined by specialization of an existing one; some languages allow the definition of a root class for a new subtree (C++ allows this, for example, for it has no fundamental root class, unlike Java, Eiffel and Dylan), thus defining a whole new family of classes. Container classes can be used to construct more complex types: vectors, lists, trees, maps (tables), and so on.

If classes are types, then much of object-oriented programming is concerned with the definition of new types (frequently, this amounts to implementations). Types are included in other types. A program consists of instances of the types it defines. Types must be instantiated and used by some kind of structure. In some languages (Ada, Dylan, CLOS, for example), instances can be created and manipulated inside modules. In these languages, the operations which act upon instances and which are not part of the class-definition mechanism can be grouped independently of classes. This is true of C++, but it lacks a module construct, so there are potential visibility problems (which are usually solved, in none too principled a fashion, by manipulation of *external* and *static* declarations and grouping of routines in files).

In a language like Java, a *pure* object-oriented language ("pure" in the sense that it is only possible to define classes and instances; routines must be defined inside classes and types are exclusively identified with classes), it is not possible to write a collection of routines that perform a set of operations without including them in a class. There is often a tendency to equate classes with some form of grouping or modularizing construct employed solely to keep related routines together. For example, the main loop of a programming language interpreter might be implemented as a class for this reason; a class presents a well-defined interface, as should a module. The tendency to define modules as objects adds more confusion as to the role of the class construct. One reason for this is that modules are very often only instantiated once, while a type has many instantiations. In Java, as in Eiffel or Smalltalk or Sather, the main loop of an interpreter must be written as a method in a class and this fact makes it sensible to put into that class the routines that directly support that loop. Such a class would, of course, instantiate types such as a type representing the runtime stack and some kind of variable storage (assuming a procedural language), as well as tables holding the code to implement language primitives and library routines. Indeed, in a pure language, this code must be represented in terms of instances of classes. If one wants a primitive to write a value to the screen, it can either be implemented in the main loop as a method call or as a primitive in a table (the latter is preferable for it reduces the size of a typically over-long loop); yet, in a pure language, that primitive routine must be implemented as a class whose *single instance* is stored in the primitive table. This technique certainly enforces a well-defined and universal interface for primitives: in the class defining the primitive, there will be a main method that performs the action of the primitive, and this main method will have a name and signature defined in the abstract class representing all primitive operations. The representation is based upon an abstract class that defines the interface presented by the classes implementing primitive operations. If the interface requires a little adjustment to accommodate an additional argument, all primitives must have that same interface; this can be wasteful as well as confusing; we have bought regularity at a non-negligible cost.

What we see here is another example of the use of objects as collectors of routines as well as types. This represents a confusion as to what a class is and what its purpose should be. Unless we are able to talk with some degree of sense about what a collection of routines is in terms of the type that such a collection represents, we had better seek an alternative construction or find the appropriate theoretical backing.

We can consider a class to define a product of types (of classes). This product defines its signature. Specialization extends the product with new components. Restrictions can be placed upon the visibility of components of the product, some can be public, others private, and so on. When there is a branch in the inheritance structure, we can equate it with a disjoint sum over the types; in programming terms, a union of the subtypes is defined by the branch and the join (root) of the sub-tree represents the union of its subtypes. Finally, methods can be defined which accept objects of one type (class) and return objects of another type (class). The information in the input object is used in the creation or modification of the object that is returned. This provides us with an arrow, or function, operation over objects (it is very common in C++ to see this kind of construct). It should be noted that product and sum can be considered static operations; they apply to classes and not to instances, while arrow applies only to instances (to objects). In a class-based language, it is not in general possible to define a function over classes; what we have is a function over instances of a class (or values of a type). This might be seen to be totally correct for classes are usually defined prior to runtime and represent the static structure against which instantiation provides a dynamic collection of objects that represent the changing state of the program; classes provide a framework, in other words.

The reason for introducing products, sums and arrows is that they are the standard mechanisms for defining types mathematically. Certainly, there are other operations such as restriction and complementation that are available mathematically to appropriate structures. What we have in most class-based languages is a much more restricted collection of operations, two of which are conflated under the general name of "specialization" or "subclassing". However, given one class, it is not, in general, possible to map it to another class. This is the case even in languages providing meta classes. Interestingly, such operations are possible in more recent versions of ML which support structures and functors [42, 43].

The argument against arrows is that they require the structure of classes to be present at runtime. This might represent a prohibitive overhead in some cases, for example where the program is very large or when speed is of the essence. In compiled languages, there is the tradition of removing all extraneous information; indeed, the concept of compilation is often expressed as being the mapping between a surface (textual) form and a form which is more readily executed by the hardware. The compilation process completes before the program is executed; the result of the compilation process is a complete program that is ready to run (clearly, this concept also subsumes that of linking to necessary libraries). Under these circumstances, the idea of maintaining the classes that are required by a program is strange.

No matter what the status of arrow types in a particular language, it is important to see that a class-based language is based, *inter alia*, upon the concept of instantiation. There is a fundamental distinction between a class and an instance of a class. When viewed as types, instances of classes represent values. As values, they can be passed around from method to method; they are first-class entities. With the use of container classes such as lists, sets, maps, bags and vectors, collections of instances can be manipulated; this is what makes complex data structuring manageable (we could manage just with integers, but it would be too painful). It is very rare that a method or routine is considered to be an instance of some object. A collection of methods or routines, together with supporting types, is something that does not appear to have a basis in the interpretation of classes as types. One reason for this is that it can be instantiated, but there seems little point. A second reason is that when asked "what type does it represent?" the answer might not be easy to produce.

There might be circumstances under which it does make sense to instantiate something that looks like a collection of routines, for example if simulating parallel processing, one defines a class to represent the interpreter of a language and then instantiates it for each processor in the simulation. Here, we have a distinct concept that is being modelled by the interpreter class; it is a model of a processor. However, if we consider a module from an operating system, say a storage allocation module, it consists of some types (for instance, a type representing virtual store) and operations upon those types. The operations are more complex than those defined for each component type in the sense that they might relate various types, perform composite operations involving operators from many types, perform format conversion and so on. There is a central purpose to the module's operations but they do not define a type, necessarily. We might want to instantiate a storage allocater in various ways, but we would probably not say that a storage allocater is a type.

Some might point out that modules in a language like Modula-2 [99] are very similar to classes in C++, etc. What makes them similar is that they collect related objects and routines and provide a standard interface, just as a C++ or Eiffel class does. Modules cannot, in general, be instantiated or parameterized; they are created by definition, not by calling a constructor. Some languages with module constructs allow initialization code, Ada packages being one example, but it tends to be relatively inflexible in form and nature. Modules in languages like Modula-2 and Ada cannot be treated like types, unlike a Smalltalk class.

In languages like Modula-2 and Ada, modules can be defined and used. They cannot be refined or specialized; consequently, it is impossible to form alternatives in a space of modules. This contrasts strongly with classes where, as noted above, branches can be used to represent sum types. Modules are also rarely associated with polymorphism and do not naturally support it, while, as we have seen many times, polymorphism is at the heart of the conception of object-oriented languages. Modules serve as encapsulating devices *only*. Modules do not naturally support the three properties we said were essential to object-oriented programming: inheritance, encapsulation and polymorphism.

7.5 Containers and Objects

Objects are often called upon to act as containers for arbitrary routines and types. This amounts to the use of some kind of module. These arbitrary collections are often instantiated only once; the examples of the main loop of an interpreter or the primitives that such an interpreter would use are good examples of this. Such a use of a class is very close to that of a module. Modules, as noted above, cannot be instantiated and only one actual copy exists in a program at any time. It is a central property of modules and of the classes forming arbitrary collections that they are instantiated once (or only a very few times). This is, however, a property that can be expressed easily in an object-oriented language.

We have already seen that a module-like construct is of some utility in restricting the visibility of types. Here, we see another use for modules: the collection of routines and types into separate building blocks. This is relatively conventional in its rationale; many languages have been proposed which employ modules, Modula-2, Ada, CLOS and Oberon [72] are well known. What I am suggesting is not even new, for Ada, Dylan, CLOS, Eulisp [69] and Oberon are either class-based languages or contain a class-based sub-language. In each of these cases, classes can be defined and their visibility restricted. By means of import directives, types can be used that are derived in other modules and thus form the basis of types that are defined within a module.

It can be objected that modules are inflexible. They can only be instantiated once and they can be composed only by declaration and by import and export lists; modules are not first-class objects unlike instances. Bracha [16, 17] has proposed a module operation formalism for the manipulation of modules. Bracha defines a module as anything with an interface; that interface specifies a set of services. Modules in their conventional sense are primarily intended to collect elements and provide them with a well-defined interface. The idea of operating on modules is not a new one, as Taivalsaari [93, 94] notes (for example, see [39] or [44]). Taivalsaari employs module operations, as noted in Chapter 3, as the basis for the Kevo prototype-based language. Here, we suggest them as a way of making modules more flexible in a class-based language that interprets types as classes. If we adopt the module operations proposal, we can construct modules by means of various forms of combination as in a language like Kevo. If a copy or cloning operation is included in the set of operations, we have the concept of an instantiable, perhaps parameterized module construct (I have explored this in [29]). These are proposals for research, so I will say no more here.

8. Reflection

8.1 Introduction

The concept of *computational reflection* has been studied for a long time. In the last few years, in particular since the emergence of object-oriented languages, reflection and the associated concept *introspection*, have been studied with some intensity. The reason for this is that the two concepts promise to give us more flexible languages which can be extended to suit an application's needs more closely. They also allow the introduction of new features such as distribution and parallel execution with less disruption than is normal. Furthermore, these two concepts give programmers access to the internals of programs, thus facilitating the construction of debuggers and profilers. Finally, introspection gives access to the execution mechanism itself, thus permitting programs, at least in principle, to adjust the way in which they are executed. It should be noted that the terms reflection and introspection are often used in an interchangeable manner.

Reflection has been adopted in a number of object-oriented languages, in the sense that it has been introduced ("bolted onto" an existing language), for example Beta [54]. The Oberon language [72], which some might argue is only marginally object-oriented, has been equipped with reflective features as well. Java has been equipped with an introspection API and Java Beans are claimed to be introspective (the use of the term "introspective" for Java Beans is questionable). The degree and power of the reflective facilities in these languages is somewhat restricted because of the way in which it was introduced. It is to languages of the Smalltalk and LISP groups, and to some prototype-based languages, that we must look if we want to see examples of a more far-ranging application of these concepts. It might be argued that these languages are insignificant and have too small a user community or are defunct and so are ineligible for study. This is clearly mistaken if we want to see how reflection has been *successfully* used in object-oriented languages. Moreover, many issues of fairly central importance have been tackled in the LISP and Smalltalk group and to ignore them would be to ignore important contributions to object orientation.

When discussing reflection, we must make a distinction between the *object* and the *meta level*. So far, we have considered only object-level programs; these are the programs that we are used to writing and running. *Object-level programs* are programs that are written in a language and which do not manipulate the constructs of the language—they make use of these constructs. *Meta-level programs* are programs that are about a language and which manipulate that language's constructs in various ways. In *reflective* or *introspective* languages, meta-level operations and objects are included in a language, so it becomes possible *within* a language to manipulate the constructs of that *same* language.

Manipulation of a language's constructs often results from *reification*, that is, the operation of representing a language construct (such as the runtime stack, the inheritance structure, procedure continuations, the binding environment or the structure of classes and instances) in the same language. Thus, if we want to reify the local binding environment of a method in Java, we will employ a representation of the binding environment that can be manipulated by Java methods. We would almost certainly implement a binding environment as a class with methods to store and read values and to look up variables within that environment; we would also have methods for adding new bindings and for creating the environment. The representation within the language of an environment is not a separate representation; for reflection and introspection to work, the representation must be connected to the one that is used to implement the language. Therefore, the class representation of environments in our example must be either the very same representation as that used by Java methods or must be inter-convertible with the actual representation. By inter-convertibility, we mean that it must be possible to convert from the representation that is used in the runtime system into the class-based representation, and it must be possible to convert the class-based representation to the one that is used in the runtime system.

Smalltalk is not often thought to be a reflective language. However, many of the constructs it employs at runtime are represented as Smalltalk objects. This means that Smalltalk can manipulate its own runtime structures.

Reflection and introspection are processes that are intimately bound up with representations of programs and how such representations are coupled to behaviour at runtime. In an introspective program, the two must exactly coincide for full introspection implies that a program is implemented in terms of the self representations that it employs. A reflective program can reify its own structures, but does not go as far as to describe its own interpretational mechanisms in ways that it can represent to itself and, thereby, alter using its own operations. The property of being able to reify its components is often called *openness*. We therefore speak of *open implementations* [52] of programs.

In order to engage in reflection, a program must represent itself and it must describe its own behaviour. These two aspects will be repeatedly seen below.

The organization of this chapter is as follows. In the next section, the concept of the meta class and its relation to the class concept is introduced.

An infinite regression is adduced and then resolved. With these preliminaries out of the way, Section 8.3 deals with the use of meta classes in class-based reflection. The section contains many examples of how parts of a class-based language can be redefined using meta classes. The concept of the Meta-Object Protocol or MOP is introduced in Section 8.4 and its advantages are considered. Section 8.5 deals with self representations, abstract syntax and abstract classes; *inter alia*, it describes how abstract classes can be used to represent abstract syntax at runtime, thus permitting program modification. Java's rather rudimentary reflective features are discussed in Section 8.6. Thus far, prototype-based languages have been ignored; Section 8.7 redresses the balance with a discussion of introducing reflection into the message-passing structure of a simple prototype language. The chapter ends with a glimpse at the future.

8.2 Class and Meta Class

The Smalltalk model is a *pure* object-oriented one. Everthing in Smalltalk is an object; integers are objects, booleans are objects, lists are objects, arrays are objects, blocks are objects, methods are objects and even *classes* are objects. For the reason that all entities in Smalltalk are instances of classes, the language provides a root class from which everything else is derived; this class is called *Object*. Hitherto, we have always considered classes to be definitional entities which define instances. Thus far, it has always been stated that instances are the objects in class-based object-oriented languages. Now, classes are objects. The other entities are uncontroversial in the sense that there is a clear sense in which they can be objects and instances of classes.

When classes themselves are considered objects, it is necessary to ask the following question:

What is the class of a class Object?

Before, when classes were just considered defining devices, this question would have no sense. When classes are considered to be objects, they must be instances of some class or other. This question is ignored in languages like Eiffel, Sather, Java, and C++.

It is clear that, for Smalltalk at least, an answer to this question must be given. The answer is that every class is an instance of a class called *Class*. At first, this immediately appears to introduce an infinite regression. If *Class* has a class C, what is C's class, and what is the class of C's class, and so on? Furthermore, what would be the point of defining, far less providing, a class for *Object*, the Smalltalk root class?

The answer to the first question is that we are free to halt the regression at any point we care. Let us therefore agree that the class of *Object* is called *Class*, and that *Class* is its own class. This decision stops the infinite regression and it does so in a fashion that is perfectly acceptable on logical grounds. The effect of such a decision is to introduce what appears to be a loop in the inheritance hierarchy as shown in Figure 8.1.

Fig. 8.1. *The loop in the inheritance hierarchy.*

This loop arises because the class of *Class* refers to itself. The loop (sometimes called the "boring part" of the inheritance hierarchy) is, in fact, an infinite path in the inheritance hierarchy; alternatively, it is the least fixed point of the inheritance relation (which is recursively defined).

Even though there are good reasons for introducing this structure, this approach to defining *Class* in terms of itself is strange. It is strange only if we require all class definitions to be *predicative*; if we permit at least some of them to be *impredicative*, all is well (in essence, predicative constructs rely upon a more fundamental type of structure on which to base a definition; impredicative ones permit the *definiens* and *definiendum* to coincide). The fact that *Class* has itself as its class, does not prevent the specialization of that class to produce effective and useful subclasses; all it means is that *Class* is defined in terms of itself. In practical terms, this loop causes no problems and we can ignore it for most of the time—it only becomes an issue when deciding what to include in *Class* (we will make some suggestions below).

The second question asks what the point is of providing a class for the root class. In C++, there is no such class and all is fine; the same applies to Java, Eiffel, Sather, Beta, Oberon, Dylan, CLOS, Object Pascal, and a whole host of other languages. The reason in favour of such provision is that it allows the language to give access to at least some of the primitive operations of the language in a form that conforms to the syntax and semantics of that same language. It gives programs access to their own primitives in terms of the protocols that are used in ordinary programming. This allows the programmer to adjust or change features of the language that are unsuited or inappropriate for an application or range of applications.

We will see that, *inter alia*, the following primitive operations can be made visible in a meta class, and hence available for redefinition or incorporation (using *super*):

- the instance-creation operation and its associated operation;
- the initialization of instances;
- the operation used in searching the inheritance structure;
- the operation used to invoke a method.

These and other operations will be discussed in detail below. We will also draw out the implications of such exposure of a language's primitives. The above list has been restricted to operations defined for class-based languages for the reason that reflection in class-based languages is more developed than in other approaches to object-oriented programming languages.

Before moving on, it is important to make an observation about prototype-based languages. In a prototype-based language, there is no need to introduce the infinite regression which occurs as a result of defining a class for the root class. One reason for this is, quite simply, that there are no classes. A second reason is connected with the way in which objects are created. Prototypes are made by copying other prototypes and then modifying them. A prototype object representing the system functions that would be encoded in a meta object can serve as the basis for all prototype definitions; this implies that all prototypes can access system functions directly without needing a special meta class. Even when meta objects are introduced into a prototype language, the infinite regression can still be avoided because of the copy and edit approach to creating objects.

8.3 Meta Class and Reflection

8.3.1 Introduction

As noted above, the introduction of the meta class into a class-based language allows programs to access the primitive operations of the language. In this section, we will explore some of the more common applications of an explicit meta class. These applications all depend upon the fact that, in a class-based language, it is possible to create a specialization (subclass) of a class.

The reader will note that, in this section, we will often talk about inheritance as if it were a purely runtime process. This would be the case in a class-based language that was interpreted. We are not restricted necessarily to purely interpreted languages for some compiled languages defer inheritance searches until runtime. An alternative is to perform a search for slots in superclasses when an instance is created; this requires a search through the inheritance structure to find the current values, particularly when a distinction is made between instance and class variables. CLOS collects slots when classes are defined; however it is possible to adjust the slots of a CLOS class at runtime, so a search is still required in order to ensure consistency.

8.3.2 Redefinition of Instance Creation Methods

Instance creation must be performed by any class-based language. Therefore, there must be mechanisms of some kind that are used to implement this process. In a language that supports a meta class, that meta class has ordinary classes as its instances, so we can, if we so choose, introduce the slight complication that instance creation can result in the creation of instances of meta classes as well as ordinary (object-level) classes. In its simplest form, instance creation deals with the creation of instances of object-level (ordinary) classes. We will discuss each in turn and briefly consider cases where a new version of instance creation might be required.

Let us first consider the case of the instantiation of an ordinary class (an object-level class of the kind to which we are accustomed). This process often involves the allocation of storage for the instance and the initialization of the instance's slots. Thus, it is necessary to allocate storage and then call the constructor to initialize slots, including those slots which are inherited. Let us assume that we want to alter the data structure used to hold instances of a class. This might be done if the original choice were too costly or because it is required to perform other operations using the new representation. For example, the standard representation might be in terms of a vector of slots. Although implementation using a vector is reasonable, it does imply that the slots in an instance must be fixed when the instance is created. If it were necessary to add or remove slots at runtime, a vector might not be the representation of choice; a hash table might be better, although more costly.

If such a representation change were required, it would be necessary for the instance creation method supplied as standard to be redefined. This can be done by creating a new meta class for those object-level classes which are to have a variable number of slots. This new meta class, *VariableSlot-MetaClass*, would be defined as a subclass of the standard meta class *Object* and will define a new instance-creation method which employs the hash table representation for instances.

The definition of the new instance creation method must also make provision for the initialization of slots in new instances. In languages related to Smalltalk, this is done by a method that is often called new; in languages of the CLOS variety, the method is called *make*. Both take a variable number of parameters, each representing the initial value of a slot. If we are dealing with another language, there will be a convention that allows the identification of the instance creation method (**make** in Eiffel, a naming convention in C++ and Java). The method for instance creation defined in *VariableSlotMeta-Class* will take a variable number of arguments and will initialize instance slots. The interface provided by *VariableSlotMetaClass*' creation method will be the same as that in the standard meta class *Object*; the method in *Object* is redefined according to the normal rules for method redefinition.

Let us consider another case. It is not usual for a class to keep track of its instances. Normally, when an instance is created, its class does not record the fact, still less retain pointers to its instances. If we wanted to define a new kind of class that kept track of its instances, we can create a new meta class, again a subclass of the standard meta class. The new meta class will extend the standard instance creation method with a piece of code that will store a pointer in a slot in the object that represents the instance's class. Thus, when an instance of this new kind of class is created, the instance creation method will update a slot in the class so that it holds the address of the new instance.

This requires a slight modification to the instance creation method. It is a case where *super* can be used to very good effect. First, the instance is created in the usual way via a call to *super*, say (the method in the standard meta class might have an inner statement to allow such extension). The call to *super* will return a pointer to the new instance (we can arrange for this even when instances are not heap-allocated), and we store the pointer in the class's special slot (say, by *cons*ing it onto a list held in the slot). What else is required depends upon a number of factors, taste and personal preference being one criterion.

Basically, a slot must be provided in the object-level class for which we have defined the new meta class. We need, therefore, to define a new kind of meta-level class, and to extend the class-creation method. This meta class is a subclass of the standard meta class and it differs from it by the fact that the new, counting slot is defined for all instances; that is, for all classes which have this meta class as their meta class. The new method updates the value of this slot when it is called. When we define a new object-level class, we need to set the object-level class's meta class to be the new counting meta class. When object classes that engage in counting are created, they have exactly the same behaviours as all other classes (this is because the new meta class is a subclass of the standard meta class), but increment the counter when new instances are created.

If this example is programmed in CLOS, the new method does not have to be redefined. Instead, it is enough to define the new meta class in the way described above; then, an *after* method can be defined for the make creation method. The *after* method, when called, increments the counter slot. This makes the process considerably simpler than the description above; we opted for the more complex option because it is the approach that must be taken in the absence of CLOS's slot combiners. For a discussion of the CLOS approach, see [53] (pp. 72–4).

The last example shows that the arrangement of classes can become rather complex. In a class-based language, it is necessary to represent mechanisms for instance creation and manipulation, and for the creation and manipulation of classes themselves. The latter requires a specific meta class, perhaps called *MetaClass*. This class will contain methods for manipulating class structures (representations of classes) and will contain the basic methods for manipulating objects. Its instance is *Class*, which provides methods for implementing instances of classes. A system of the kind required for the second example would be bootstrapped from the definition of *MetaClass*. These additional details were not introduced above because they add complexity to the overall picture. The provision of this basic structure is important for full introspection and for the definition of meta-object protocols, topics we will explore below.

8.3.3 Redefinition of Inheritance Methods

In Chapter 4, we saw that multiple inheritance is, to say the least, controversial. Part of the controversy is due to the fact that there is little agreement as to how the inheritance structure should be searched for slots and methods. Of the many techniques, those based on linearization are based upon an algorithm that traverses the inheritance graph in a particular way, collecting classes and then removing duplicates.

If the standard meta class contains an inherit method which is called when it is necessary to inherit a value, it is possible to create a subclass which redefines that method. Thus, it is possible to implement any kind of inheritance algorithm that one wants by performing such a redefinition in a subclass of the standard meta class. Object-level classes that are to be based upon the new meta class must declare it as their meta class.

By redefining the inheritance method, it becomes possible for a single language to emulate the inheritance methods of others. For example, the FLAVORS [21] inheritance algorithm can be implemented in CLOS, as can the LOOPS [15] algorithm; this allows legacy code to be supported with greater ease. It also has the implication that the most appropriate inheritance algorithm can be employed in a program (more than one algorithm can also be supported).

8.3.4 Redefinition of Method Call Protocols

There is no reason why a meta class should not define how methods are called. This was proposed by Maes [63]. There are different ways to approach the process of method call, one being the message-based approach employed in Smalltalk [40] and SELF [25], another is the more familiar procedure call. We will first consider the message-based approach.

In Smalltalk and SELF, methods are accessed by sending messages to the instance for which the method is defined. The message names the object to which it is to be sent and it contains parameter values; the message also has a name called its *selector*. The selector denotes the method to be invoked, and represents the method name. This is an analogue of calling the method as a procedure, for the selector names the method, and the arguments are the parameters to the call. The difference is that the selector must be interpreted by the object which is receiving the message. In the normal course of events, the selector is used to index the desired method in the object's class; the class contains a method dispatch table which relates selectors to the actual methods to be invoked. Methods in Smalltalk are represented in terms of objects, as they are in SELF; messages, too, are represented as objects.

Message selectors introduce a level of indirection between a method and the way in which it is called (the way in which a method is called is referred to as its *call protocol*). Selectors serve to index method objects in the dispatch table and are usually identical to the names given to the methods in the methods section of a Smalltalk class definition (or to the method slot in SELF).

Given a method call protocol defined in terms of selectors, it becomes possible to redefine how selectors are interpreted. This involves the creation of a subclass of the standard meta class. This new class will over-ride the *callMethod* method inherited from the standard meta class. The new method might intercept some selectors and re-direct them to other classes, for example skipping a generation in the inheritance structure. This technique, if generalized, can lead to a form of delegation. Method combination is another technique which can be performed by this means.

8.3.5 Slots as Objects: An Example of Reification

In order to guarantee full reflection or introspection, it is important to represent slots as independent entities; slots should be reified in order to allow their manipulation by reflective methods. This implies that there should be a meta class to represent the class of slots. If this is provided, as it is in the CLOS MOP [82] and in other introspective object-based systems [33], manipulation of slots becomes very easy, requiring the definition of a new slot class and the definition of the standard meta class required to represent instances in order to ensure that any new slot types are included in instances as required.

Normally, a slot holds a single value (vectors count as single values or instances of their type). Sometimes, it is necessary for a slot to hold more than one value. This might be done by storing a vector or list in the slot, but this is a somewhat awkward solution, particularly if the additional value to be stored is an annotation in the form of a string. It would be equally awkward to define a separate slot, by hand, to hold the annotations for the data slots of an object. It is far easier to define a subclass of the slot class which will contain, in addition to the slots it must contain in order to fulfil its role as an instance slot (the slot to hold its "official" value, slots holding accessor functions, type predicates, etc.), it will contain a slot to hold the annotation. A type predicate can be included to ensure that the slot will only contain strings, if desired. This modification to the class representing slots is easy to produce: it is just a simple subclass of the slot class.

The next step is to create a subclass of the meta class representing instances so that, rather than creating instances of the original slot class, it creates instances of the new slot class when initializing a class instance. When the standard meta class for instances, the class often named *Class*, creates an instance using its creation method, it must create a runtime representation for the slots in the instance. In some cases, the slots will just be elements of a simple vector (which might have to hold pointers to types that do not fit into a machine word), but, in others, the instance's representation of slots will be instances of a class, and, hence, will be complex structures. We assumed this second option would be the case in order to re-define the slot type. We require the slots inserted into instances to be of the new kind, i.e., the kind which supports annotations, so we need to create a new subclass of *Class* and redefine the instance-creation method so that it makes slots of the new kind.

Annotations on slots can be extremely useful, so can subslots and linked slots. If a slot has subslots, it can represent complex information in terms of substructures. If a slot is divided into subslots, each subslot can represent a *facet* of the object that is stored in the main subslot (one is usually designated as the *value* or *main* subslot). Classes whose slots are divided into subslots can be defined in a fashion directly analogous to that described in the annotations example. Linked slots are also defined in a similar way. Linked slots are slots that are linked in pairs so that an update to one of the slots is visible to the other slot. This is usually implemented by making the slots point to their value. This, again, requires a modification to the class that defines slots; the details of modification are left to the reader—the previous examples should point the way.

8.3.6 Other Examples

There are many other examples that could be cited. Some examples will, quite naturally, depend upon the features presented by a particular reflective object-oriented language. For example, under appropriate circumstances, it is possible to reflect upon the invocation of methods; one use would be to trace calls to multi-methods in order to determine which is most commonly called. Such an investigation might lead to some optimization. Another example relates to the formation and manipulation of the inheritance structure. This, as noted above, is necessary for finding slots, but, in a language supporting multi-methods, it is of considerable importance when selecting the right method to apply given a set of inputs.

In Smalltalk (see [40]), the class *Class* defines a protocol for accessing meta information about classes. This protocol extends to a great many aspects of the structure and content of classes and instances. It allows the programmer to query objects, particularly classes, and determine their properties. The class *Behavior* is of particular interest here.

Class *Behavior* defines the minimum state required by objects that have instances; it defines, in particular, the state used by the Smalltalk-80 interpreter. Class *Behavior* contains methods that can be seen to fall into one of four categories:

- creating method dictionaries, class instances or class hierarchies;
- accessing the contents of dictionaries, instances and variables;
- testing the contents of dictionaries, the form of instances and the class hierarchy;
- enumerating subclasses and instances.

In Smalltalk, methods are stored in dictionaries that are indexed by the method's *selector*. Access to the method dictionaries is, therefore, in terms of strings denoting selectors. The *Behavior* class's protocol contains methods for storing dictionaries in classes, adding and removing selectors (and associated methods). It also contains methods for compiling and decompiling methods.

The class contains methods for setting the superclass of a class, for making one class a subclass of another and for removing classes from the subclass relationship. It also contains methods for creating instances of classes.

The accessing part of the protocol gives the programmer access to the methods of a class. This includes provision of methods for returning the selectors of a class, and returning compiled methods and source code. It also gives the programmer methods for finding and manipulating the instance and class variables of a class, as well as access to the class hierarchy so that questions can be answered about where a class resides in the class hierarchy.

The class protocol can also be used to alter the structure of classes. In the class *ClassDescription*, there are methods for adding and removing instance variables. There are also methods for assigning and testing the category of the receiving class; Smalltalk classes are organized using a simple classification so that the runtime dictionaries upon which the language relies can be organized. The categories include: magnitudes, numbers, collections, kernel objects, kernel classes and kernel support. Both messages and classes are organized according to the classification and class *ClassDescription* provides methods for organizing them. The categorization has an impact upon the way in which compilation is performed, so class *Behavior* additionally contains methods for printing various information about instances.

The provision of operations like those just described makes the task of writing compilers and runtime environments considerably easier. Much of the routine work is already performed by the meta classes. This was, presumably, the original motivation for including these classes and others. However, the operations described, together with the others in the protocol, give the programmer access to the internals of the runtime system and, of course, provide access to the Smalltalk compiler. This means that operations such as finding classes by the selectors they contain, finding all instances of a subclass of some class, dynamically moving a subtree of the inheritance hierarchy and altering the structure of classes (by addition or removal of class and/or instance variables). Given that strings serve as a standard representation for code and for selectors, so dynamic compilation of methods is also possible. These methods help to begin to bridge the gap between an object-oriented program at runtime and a database of objects. It also gives the programmer considerable power to change the program as it runs, but, unfortunately, it does so in relatively unconstrained ways. In the next section, constrained modification using the concept of the *Meta-Object Protocol* is introduced and discussed.

8.4 Meta-Object Protocols

A Meta-Object Protocol (MOP) [53] is a specification of an object-oriented language in that same language. Thus, the definition of CLOS [82] contains the specification of the CLOS extensions to Common LISP, and extends this specification by defining a MOP for CLOS. The CLOS MOP is a description of CLOS as an extensible CLOS program. In this description, each fundamental element of the CLOS language is represented by first-class objects. Thus, classes, slot definitions, generic functions, methods, specializers and method combiners are all represented by classes in the CLOS MOP. The methods associated with these various objects is what provides CLOS with its behaviour.

For the reason that the classes and methods describe the CLOS language, they can be considered to be meta-level objects. The protocol followed by these objects is what constitutes the MOP. The protocol is the interface described by the various classes: their methods and class interfaces.

From the examples in the last section, it can be seen that such a self-representation is needed if the extensions described there are to be possible. We have assumed that the meta classes have obeyed some well-specified protocol which has allowed us uniformly to access and manipulate specializations of the meta classes we assume. The meta classes that we assume describe the language which we are extending and enriching.

How, then, could the design of a protocol be approached? The following are three points taken from [53] (p. 132):

- Two broad kinds of protocol can be defined: functional and procedural. Functional protocols can be designed in such a way that memoization is made possible while still allowing the user control over what answer is computed. On the other hand, memoization is not an option for procedural protocols where temporal predictability is the central concept. Procedural protocols can be designed so that the user can reliably predict when certain activities will take place in relation to others. Those procedural protocols that permit some activities to be over-ridden are more flexible, but less predictable than those which allow new activities to augment existing ones, but not replace them.
- Layering, or the provision of layers of protocol, makes customization or adjustment of the implementation easier. Lower layers are concerned with smaller changes, while higher layer protocols are used to make more global changes. Higher layer protocols, by their nature, are more complex than

those lower down the hierarchy. Higher-level protocols can, in general, avoid dealing with the details so essential to the lower levels.

- Procedural protocols forming part of the execution critical path can be divided into a functional protocol which computes a procedure. The procedure is called on the critical path; it can be removed from this path by precomputing it. This approach can be taken when optimizing method selection, particularly in generic functions.

These points about protocol design are dependent upon the existence of appropriate representations. For example, when a functional protocol engages in memoization, it is necessary to have some representation appropriate to the storage of intermediate values; this representation can be tailored to suit the needs of the various optimization processes.

8.5 Self Representation, Abstract Syntax and Abstract Classes

As has been stressed, it is essential, when incorporating reflection into a programming language to incorporate constructs which can be used in the representation of that language. We have seen that CLOS requires, *inter alia*, classes, slots, generic functions and methods to be given an explicit, class-based representation. When we consider prototype-based languages below (Section 8.7), we will see that explicit representations are useful although problematic there, and that reification of the message-passing mechanisms is necessary for behavioural reflection.

Much of the work on reflection has been conducted in the context of interpreted languages. In a compiled language, changes to a program are hard to make. Additions are relatively easy to make; dynamically linked libraries can be used to augment or replace behaviour, but this is a relatively coarse method. If the program is to be changed, it is necessary to compile into the language the variations that one wants. Usually, a programming language has a fixed syntax which gets in the way when engaging in reflective processing.

There are ways of obviating this problem. One approach is to equip the language with a pre-processor which permits the programmer to define syntactic constructs in terms of the language's abstract syntax. These constructs are pre-processed to construct valid program components which can be included in the final program. This is a somewhat cleaner version of the age-old LISP technique of representing programs as data, but it does require a pre-processing step (the LISP technique is the second way). The third way is to arrange for the language's compiler to be made available at runtime (as it is in Smalltalk and LISP) and to arrange for the compiler's output to be integrated with the runtime image. Programs can be represented and manipulated as strings, then compiled and integrated with the running program.

Of the three approaches, the first is most in line with the so-called "open" programming approach.

The protocol outlined in [52] defines so-called "open" programs. An open program is one that defines interfaces to its components, allowing components to become part of the main programming interface to a program. Another way of viewing an open program is as a library or toolkit of parts which can be manipulated in controlled ways by means of additional parameters (methods, in an object-oriented context). The toolkit approach also requires that concepts that would otherwise remain hidden become reified, thus affording the programmer access to the internals of the program. A truly open compiled language would allow runtime manipulation and redefinition of structures. These, together with other such operations, require dynamic compilation, a process which is not currently available in C++.

Abstract syntax is all very well, but it only deals with syntactic matters. In [86], Steyaert describes an open implementation of an object-oriented programming language called *Agora*. Here, the syntax and semantics of the language are presented in terms of an object-based description (*Agora* is a prototype-based language that uses mixin-based inheritance). This description naturally includes abstract objects. The reason for this is that it contains concepts which should not be instantiated, but, instead, are factors of concepts which are instantiated. What Steyaert defines in [86] is a framework in the object-oriented sense. By starting with a representation of the language in itself, reflection is naturally facilitated. The framework approach allows the description to be open in the sense that the constructs it contains can be modified by specialization; it also facilitates the use of the description's objects in the processing of the language.

As I noted in [30], it is possible, once a syntax and semantics have been constructed in an object-oriented language, to construct a parser which generates parse trees which can then be used for code generation and for interpretation or both. Dynamic compilation can also be based upon this approach.

The concepts which appear in an object-oriented description of an object-oriented language must be complete. Steyaert in [86] is interested in a prototype-based language with class-based features. However, if we were to be content with a class-based (or an inheritance-based) approach to language design, we could introduce a number of additional features such as the explicit representation of inheritance hierarchies, method definition, representation and call, and, as a side effect, the possibility that method combination in highly flexible ways could be defined. Given the remarks of the previous paragraph, it would appear possible to combine interpretative and compiled techniques in a single language while maintaining a considerable degree of flexibility in the result.

8.6 Reflection in Java

The Java language, from version 1.1, contains a set of interfaces and classes to perform reflection. At the time of writing, Java uses reflection in order to support Java Beans and to support object serialization. Java Beans are software components that allow reflection so that a user can obtain information about their interfaces, the events to which they respond, and so on. Serialization allows arbitrary objects to be converted to and from a stream of bytes; the byte stream can be stored in disk files. Serialization allows objects to be stored on disk, for example, without having to engage in conversions from internal to printable representations. The various constructs used to implement reflection in Java are implemented as classes.

Java does not adopt the approach that is most commonly adopted. It does not define meta classes, nor does it define abstract classes to represent the semantic structures used by the language and its interpretation mechanism; nor, equally, does it allow the user to manipulate an abstract syntactic representation of the application program. Instead, it defines a set of special-purpose classes which are able to inspect other classes; these special-purpose classes have access to the internal runtime representations of other objects.

The reflection classes defined in Java are collected into the reflection package. There are classes to perform the following tasks:

- determine the data slots, methods and constructors of any class;
- create an instance of a class using any available constructor;
- access the variables (or slots) of any object;
- call the methods of any object;
- create an array of objects that are instances of any class.

These reflection operations work even when the class that is being operated upon by them is not represented by any information in the class issuing the requests.

In addition to the operations listed above, the package allows other operations to be performed. For example, the array operations include those which permit elements of arbitrary arrays to be accessed. Type information can be obtained from class constructors and data elements; a class type is provided as part of the API to handle this information (the *Modifiers* class). Using the *Member* class, it is possible to determine the shared constants, variables and methods of a class, and the *InvocationTargetException*, is thrown when a constructor is called through *constructor.newInstance()* or a member through *member.invoke()* throws an exception which is encapsulated in the thrown instance of *InvocationTargetException*.

Unfortunately, all of the classes of the reflection package are marked as *final*. This means that the user is not permitted to specialize the classes; in any case, most methods are marked *native*, indicating that they are machine specific and implemented in the native code of the host, so some specializations would be hard to produce.

8.7 Reflection in Prototype-based Languages

Reflection has been studied to a relatively greater extent in class-based languages than in prototype-based ones. One reason for this, clearly, is that there are far fewer prototype- than class-based languages. As a consequence, prototypes are somewhat less understood than classes and instances and, therefore, the opportunities for reflection are less well known. This is particularly true of structural reflection in which a language provides descriptions for its own structures; in class-based languages, object and meta classes jointly perform this function. In a prototype-based language, there are no classes; it is, thus, necessary to find alternatives to play the roles of classes and, more particularly, meta classes.

At first sight, it might seem that it should be possible to define both prototype and slot in terms of prototype and slot (this description follows [34]). We could define a prototype as a set of named slots and a set of methods. The methods needed must be, minimally, a method to create a new object with a fixed set of slots and to assign values to those slots. This method creates a completely new object. A prototype must also be equipped with a clone method which acts as a second creation method, but operating by copying an existing prototype. We will also need a method that responds to messages, calling the methods associated with an object, delegating to its parents when necessary.

Next, we need to define a prototype slot. Since slots can be divided into constant, mutable and method types, three kinds of slot object will be needed, one for each kind of slot. The definition of slots could be performed as follows. Starting with the constant slot object, we define a method to fetch the value slot's contents and define a value slot in the object. For a mutable slot, the constant slot object is cloned and an update method is added; the reader (value fetch) method is obtained by delegation from constant slot. Finally, the method slot introduces a method for invoking the method stored in the slot. The method slot object could be a clone of constant slot or mutable slot, depending upon how methods are treated.

The next problem is more difficult. When we come to define an object, we need to install slots in it. This is where the representation either becomes totally *ad hoc* or we are forced to give up and seek alternatives. We could, certainly, clone slots and collect them together to form objects. A pre-processor could do this and assemble prototypes for us, ready to execute. This would allow each prototype to gain access to the representation of its slots. However, this has the unfortunate property that if we want to define a new kind of slot, it is necessary to alter the pre-processor (relatively easy if it is an object), but if we want to change the representation of existing slots in some way, we are prevented from doing so; such modifications can be very useful during the process of bootstrapping to a reflective system. The reason for this is that it is usually assumed that prototype objects are immutable (apart from slot fillers) once created; this assumption ensures that the interface presented by an object does not vary. Furthermore, the appropriate pre-processing object needs to be employed; determining which one might prove to be problematic.

We really need to *instantiate* slots in order to compose objects. In a class-based reflective language, slots are instances of classes and, therefore, subject to the constraints imposed by the definition of their class. When instantiated, a name is associated with a structure. We can perform such association, but it is hard to hide the structure in a prototype. If we could instantiate slots in a prototype object, we could be sure that we have the right slots in the right prototype, and the right methods for accessing them. Perhaps, if prototypes were associated with meta objects in the way that Maes [63] associates objects and meta objects, a structural description might be easier; this remains an open question, and Maes does not address it. This is not, in any case, a proposal without its own difficulties.

In [66], it is stated (p. 142) that they have experienced difficulty in providing structural descriptions for prototype-based languages. Instead, they propose an alternative which they call *behavioural reflection*. They point out that the coupling of a prototype with its description seems to go against the spirit of prototypes. The original idea was that a prototype would be a self-sufficient entity that does not require the additional support provided by a class object. A description would serve, in some sense, as a class definition; we have, therefore, a *reductio* argument! In [96], Ungar and Smith explicitly warn *against* reflection and the SELF implementation allows only limited facilities for introspection.

Malenfant *et al.* [66] propose the concept of behavioural reflection as a viable alternative in prototype langauges to the structural reflection found in class-based approaches. This has the advantage that prototypes are simpler than class-based approaches, so behaviours can be more easily revealed. Moreover, prototype languages are founded upon the behavioural concept of message passing, while most class-based languages employ procedure call as the fundamental unit of behaviour.

The emphasis in behavioural reflection is on the behaviour of objects; this is revealed in the way in which they handle messages. In order to account for it, it is necessary to engage in a little structural description, but not as much as would be required in order to implement a fully structural reflection; this description is intended to be just enough to describe which slots are in which object. The description primitives proposed in [66] are:

- *size(o)*: return the size of object o;
- *name(o,i)*: return the name of the ith slot of object o;
- *contentsAt(o,i)*: return the contents of the ith slot of object o;
- *contentsAtPut(o,i,v)*: set the value of the ith slot of object o to be v;
- *isMethod(o,i)*: returns true if the ith slot of object o is a method.

They assume that there is an original object which they call *Root*.

A meta object is associated with each object. The role of the meta object is to describe the associated object's behaviour. In particular, the meta object is charged with deciding the way in which its associated object reacts when it receives a message; this is a common place, in object-oriented languages, to shift to reflective processing. The usual way to describe message execution is to factor it into two operations: method lookup and method application. In the normal way, we represent each of these component operations as a method in the language—the methods *reify* the two operations—so they can be redefined if and when it becomes necessary.

This approach appears to lead to an infinite regression for the reason that meta objects are, themselves, composed of slots and respond to messages; slots are accessed by sending messages and these messages must elicit a response. Thus, when we send a message to a meta object that requests the execution of an object-level message, the meta object must respond to the message; it must apply the two operators, lookup and apply, in order to respond; this suggests an infinite sequence of meta-meta-...meta-objects in order to describe the message-handling behaviour of the level below.

In order to implement the proposed changes to the fundamental prototype structure, a meta object (which can be shared among several objects and act like a local interpreter for them) is provided for each object. The meta objects respond to method lookup messages by returning method objects that are able to respond to messages requesting the application of the method. A basic lookup and a basic apply method must be provided in order to support these proposals. This still suffers from the infinite regression problem. The solution is to provide an object which refers to itself (an infinite loop is therefore represented; or, still a viable alternative, we permit impredication). The basic object is called, in [66], *BasicMetaObject* and which is its own meta object; this allows it to interpret its own messages and it defines the standard message-handling behaviour for the rest of the system.

Because the basic method invocation protocol requires a method slot to be looked up before its method can be applied, *BasicMetaObject* must be able to respond to the lookup message like every meta object in the system. The lookup method with which it responds to lookup messages is the primitive lookup method provided by the language, but in a reified form. The reified form is as another method object, called *BasicLookup*. The result of sending an apply message to *BasicLookup* is another reified method object, *BasicApply*, which reifies the apply primitive defined for the language.

The three objects we have just described form the kernel of the language, together with the *Root* object.

When an object receives a message, it sends a lookup method to its meta object to ask it to look up the object's method. The meta object responds to its method by sending a message to its meta object. Messages are sent to meta objects until the *BasicMetaObject* receives the lookup method. *BasicMetaObject* responds to this message by looking up the lookup method in itself and returns it to the sender of the lookup message. Each time down the chain, the lookup method from the previous meta object is used to lookup the local lookup method. Eventually, the original meta object is reached and its lookup method is retrieved and applied to the original message receiver. A similar chain of apply messages allow the application of the lookup method (applying the *contentsAt* primitive); eventually, the slot in the original request receives an apply method that is applied to the original object, and the result is computed.

One feature of this model that differentiates it from others, particularly the open application approach displayed in Agora [86] and CLOS [82] is that this prototype-based model engages in tower reflection in a way directly analogous to Smith's 3-LISP language [80]. The reflective towers, which are global in 3-LISP and other tower-reflective languages that do not involve objects (e.g., [31, 32]), become local to the methods which engage in reflection. A deeper understanding of reflective towers is required, therefore, before any optimizations can be applied to the reflective process.

8.8 Prospects for the Future

Throughout this chapter, I have mentioned aspects of object-oriented languages that are experimental or are only the results of *gedanken* experiments: my ideas on parsing and interpretation and dynamic compilation is an example. Another example is that reflective processing can, in principle, allow an interpreted program to compile itself by calling compiling and optimization methods (perhaps combined with some kind of linkage mechanism).

Work is also required on reflection in prototype-based languages, and in the so-called *multi-paradigm* languages which combine, e.g., functional or constraint programming with objects. The role of reflection in object-oriented databases appears to be an almost untouched area.

Some people have written reflection off as a well-understood process. We believe, on the contrary, that research has only just scratched the surface of what is possible. Reflection is naturally described in object-oriented languages because of encapsulation, inheritance and polymorphism; it also benefits from the restricted size of most objects. Part objects such as those promoted by Beta [54] also serve to assist the reflective process by permitting flexibility within strictly scoped constraints.

9. C#

9.1 Introduction

In the summer of 2000, Microsoft announced its .NET platform and a new programming language called C#. The .NET platform is based on a Common Language Runtime that is similar to the Java Virtual Machine and on a set of libraries that can be used by a variety of languages that are able to inter-operate by compiling into an intermediate language called IL.

This chapter is concerned with the C# language *only*. Matters such as the scope and organisation of the .NET framework and on the Common Language Runtime fall outside the subject of this book, so they are not described. The Common Base Library defined for C# programs (a large collection of classes similar to the Java class library) is mentioned briefly at the end of the chapter.

This chapter, then, concentrates on the C# language. It contains an exposition of the main structures of the language. Because C# is a relative of both Java and C++, it is natural to compare the three. Such a comparison is conducted throughout the chapter.

The chapter's organisation is modelled on the first few chapters of this book. Classes and instances are considered first. Inheritance is the next subject to be examined. Methods and operators come third in the list, followed by polymorphism. Finally, the Base Class Library is outlined.

The C# conceptions of class and instances, as well as inheritance, are relatively standard. Methods are somewhat more interesting because of the introduction of so-called *properties* and *delegates*. The type system is quite close, at the class level, to that of Java but includes an interesting and extremely powerful type unification that is a consequence of the introduction of *value types* that are also used to represent all primitive types.

The current chapter does not cover issues such as events and the various forms of namespace that can be employed by C# programs. The reason for this is, again, that these issues are not directly related to the concepts that define the semantics of the language.

9.2 Classes and Instances

C# is a class-based language, like C++ and Java. Classes act as templates for the creation of instances. Like the other two languages, C# treats a class semantically as the definition of a new type. Variables are declared as having a type that can be the name of a class (there are also primitive types that are not classes). C# classes are defined as a unit, unlike C++ classes. In C++, a class is typically defined in a header file. The header contains the definition of the interface and an accompanying file contains the implementation. C# follows Java in avoiding this. Classes are defined in a single unit, with the implementation of its methods included in that unit. The data slots of the class (the *data members* in C# terms) are also declared in a manner similar to Java. C# avoids the header concept completely.

C# like both C++ and Java permits the definition of nested or inner classes. The scope of an inner class is restricted to the class in which it is defined.

A simple example of a C# class is the following:

```
class ExampleClass {
    int x  = 0;
    int DoubleX ()
    {
        x++;
        return x;
    } // end method
    class Inner {
        int y;
        void printY ()
        {
            Console.WriteLine (x+y);
        } // end method
    } // end inner class
} // end class -- note no semicolon
```

The class contains three kinds of entity. A *data* member (data slot). At the outer level, x is declared as an integer and initialised to the value zero. Next, a *function member* (a method) is defined. The method DoubleX doubles the value of x and returns that doubled value as its result; it also updates x in the instance of the class whose DoubleX method was called. Finally, there is the definition of an inner class, which represents a *type member*.

The inner class has its own local data member (y) and a method—classes do not define their own local types if there is no requirement. The method printY prints the value of the sum of its local data member (y) with the value of x. Inside a nested class, the members (slots) of its enclosing class are visible. The visibility rule is always outwards, so the following:

```
class ExampleClass {
   int x;
   int SumXY ()
   {
      return x + y;
   } // end method
   class Inner {
      int y;
      ...
   } // end inner class
} // end ExampleClass
```

is not legal C#. The reason for this is that y is not visible outside of its defining class. In the SumXY method, only x is visible; y is not visible.

9.2.1 Class and Instance Variables

C# follows C++ and Java in making a distinction between class and instance variables (members). If a member of a C# class is marked as static, it is shared between all instances of the class. Thus,

```
class ExampleClass {
   static int x = 0;
      ...
   int incX ()
   {
      x++;
   }
   ...
} // end class
```

Data member x is declared as static and there will only be one instance of it created at runtime. The incX method increments the value of x. If there are three instances of this class, each time an instance calls incX, the *same* variable will be incremented.

Methods can also be annotated as static with the same effect. Type members cannot be so annotated for the reason that they cannot, logically, be shared, since they are private to the class in which they are defined.

9.2.2 Access Levels

Classes and their type members can be annotated in order to declare their level of accessibilty. The following access modifiers are defined in C#:

- public;
- protected;

- `private`;
- `internal`;
- `protected internal`.

The first three have a similar interpretation to the corresponding Java or C++ concepts. The remaining modifiers are particular to C# and are discussed below when considering namespaces. Like Java, but unlike C++, data and function members are individually annotated, while C++ divides the class definition into sections.

Classes can be marked as `sealed`. This annotation has the same interpretation as Java's `final`. That is, it is not possible to derive subclasses from a `sealed` class.

There is a constraint on type access modification. A type or type member must not be declared to be more accessible than any of the types it uses in its declaration. Moreover, modifiers cannot be used when they conflict with the purpose of inheritance modifiers.

9.2.3 Data and Method Access Modifiers

Data and function members of a C# class can be annotated with an access modifier. Furthermore, a data member can be marked as either `const` or `readonly`. Thus, a data member can be declared as:

```
const int x  = 0;
```

The expression on the right of the assigment symbol must be such that it can be *completely* evaluated at compile time; `const` denotes a compile-time constant. On the other hand, a data member declared as `readonly`, such as:

```
readonly int x = e;
```

is evaluated at runtime. This implies that the expression appearing on the right-hand side of a `readonly` declaration can contain references to variables and to methods.

9.2.4 Instance Creation

Class instances in C# are constructed in a way that will be familiar to Java programmers. It is also similar to the constructor for heap-allocated instances in C++. The general form is:

ariable = `new` *classname (optional parameters);*

The `new` operator calls the appropriate constructor defined in the class named *classname.* The appropriate constructor is the one that has a signature that corresponds to the optional parameters. The appropriate constructor is the one that defines the same number of parameters as appear in the call and, for each parameter, the type of the actual parameter corresponds (modulo the

C# well-typing rules) to the type of the formal parameter. This definition has to be slightly relaxed because a constructor might have a **params** parameter (see Section 4.3, below), so the number of actual parameters can be greater than that of the constructor.

A constructor is defined in a way similar to Java or C++. It is a function member whose name is the same as the class in which it is defined. Thus, for class **ExampleClass**, the constructor will be named **ExampleClass**. Constructors can be overloaded, so different signatures can be employed. For example:

```
class ExampleClass {
    private int    x = 0;
    private float  f = 0.0;
    private string s = ''null'';
    public ExampleClass ()
    {
        // null body
    } // end constructor
    public ExampleClass (int xv)
    {
        x = xv;
    } // end constructor
    public ExampleClass (float fv)
    {
        f = fv;
    } // end constructor
    public ExampleClass (string sv)
    {
        s = sv;
    } // end constructor
} // end class
```

The first constructor has no parameters. It leaves the values of the data members unchanged. The second constructor takes an integer argument and sets x. Similarly, the other two constructors modify only one of the data members. All of the above constructors are **public**; other access modifiers are legal.

To create an instance of **ExampleClass**, one of the following statements can be used, depending upon which data members (if any) are to be set to a value other than the default:

```
ec = new ExampleClass();
ec = new ExampleClass(2);
ec = new ExampleClass(2.14159);
ec = new ExampleClass(''new string'');
```

(It is assumed that **ec** is a variable of type **ExampleClass**.)

A class may call one of its overloaded constructors before executing the body of its method using the `this` keyword, as is shown in the following example:

```
class ExampleClass {
    private int x;
    public ExampleClass () : this (99) { ... }
    public ExampleClass (int y)
    {
        x = y;
    } // end constructor
} // end class
```

Assume the following call:

```
ExampleClass ec = new ExampleClass();
```

The instance, `ec`, that is created will have its `x` member set to the value 99. The reason for this is that its parameterless constructor calls the overloaded constructor with an integer argument prior to executing its own body. The call to the constructor with an integer argument is given the value 99, which is then passed to the body of that constructor. The body sets `x` to the value of its argument.

If a constructor is not defined, the C# language states that a parameterless constructor will be automatically created.

9.2.5 Static Constructors

C# allows constructors to be marked as `static`. This allows initialisation code to be executed before the first instance of the class is created. At the same time, it allows initialisation code to be executed before any static member of the class is accessed. A class can have only one static constructor. Static constructors must have no parameters and must have the same name as the class in which they are defined.

9.2.6 Finalization and Destruction

In C#, as in Java, all instances are created in the heap. C# provides a garbage collector to manage the heap. C# defines a *destructor* member function. Java defines a *finalization* operation but the `finalize` method is rarely used in Java classes. C#'s destructor is syntactically similar to the C++ destructor but its semantics are completely different.

In C#, the destructor for class *classname* has the following syntax:

optional attributes classname() body

It is a method with the same name as the class in which it is defined; that name has a mandatory tilde (" ˜ ") prefix. Destructors take no arguments.

Destructors are just a syntactic mechanism for declaring a `Finalize` method (called a *finalizer*). A destructor is expanded by the compiler into the following:

```
protected override void Finalize ()
{
   // user-supplied code
   base.Finalize();
} // end method
```

The code provided by the programmer in their destructor method body is inserted into the `Finalize` method. The last line calls the finalizer defined in the class's super class (the `base` keyword will be explained below in Section 4.2 when considering inheritance).

Finalization code is typically called by the garbage collector to provide class-specific clean-up operations. Rather than rely upon the compiler to generate an appropriate finalizer, it is best explicitly to define a `Finalize` method. This is also a good idea because the finalizer semantics of C# differs so radically from the destructor semantics in C++, the crucial difference being the interaction with the garbage collector. In C++, destructors actually manipulate memory and perform deallocation; in C# they do things like tidy the instance before deallocation by the storage manager. This is a big difference.

It only makes sense for there to be one finalization method for each class, where such a method is defined.

9.2.7 Dot Notation and Member Access

The last code example shows the use of the dot (".") to refer to members of a class. This is the same as in Java and is the same as the syntax for stack-allocated C++ instances. C++ uses the symbol -> to denote access to visible members of a heap-allocated class.

9.2.8 Abstract Classes

It is possible to define abstract classes in C#. An abstract class can contain abstract methods. In order to declare an abstract class, the keyword `abstract` is employed. It is also employed to declare a method `abstract`. Abstract methods have no implementation and they are implicitly declared `virtual` (for more discussion of `virtual` methods, see Section 4 on methods, below). An example of an abstract class is:

```
public abstract class ExampleClass {
   public abstract int foo ();
} // end class
```

This is an abstract class because it is marked with **abstract**, just as it would be in Java. The method **foo** is abstract and has no implementation (it has no body, only a signature).

As in other languages, C# abstract classes cannot be directly instantiated.

9.2.9 Indexers

The concept of an *indexer* is novel in C#. It is not a concept of either C++ or Java. An indexer provides a way to index elements in a class that encapsulates a collection. Indexers use array syntax (square brackets). The following example comes from [5] (p. 42):

```
public class ScoreList {
    int[] scores = new int[5];
    // indexer:
    public int this[int index]
    {
       get {
              return scores[index];
           }
       set {
              if (value >= 0 && value < 100)
                 scores[index] = value;
           }
    } // end indexer
    public int Average ()
    {
       int sum = 0;
       foreach (int score in scores) sum += score;
          return sum / scores.length;
    } // end Average
} // end class
```

The class can be used as follows:

```
public class IndexerTest {
  static void Main ()
  {
     ScoreList sl = new ScoreList();
     sl[0] = 9;
     sl[1] = 8;
     sl[2] = 7;
     sl[3] = sl[4] = sl[1];
     System.Console.WriteLine(sl.Average());
     } // end main
  } // end class
```

In this example, the collection is an array of int. The collection could be
a hash table, an array list, a bit array, a queue, a stack, a sorted list or
a string collection. The collection could involve the implementation of an
interface. The indexer is declared with identifier this and arguments inside
array-reference brackets. The internals of the indexer resemble properties (see
below, Section 4.4): there is a *setter* and a *getter* routine. The setter is used
to set the value of elements of the collection, while the getter is needed to
retrieve values.

Inside the indexer and the Average method, the scores array is treated
just as a local array. However, in the IndexerTest class, the use of the indexer
can be seen. Here, it is composed of the name of the instance (sl) and array
brackets around indices. In effect, the sl[x] notation is giving controlled
access to the scores data member, which is private to class ScoreList and
should, therefore, be invisible to Main.

9.2.10 Self Reference

The non-static members of a C# class may refer to the instance in which
they appear using the this keyword. The use of this is identical to that in
Java and C++. The this pseudo-variable can also be used in constructors
(as seen above) or to declare or access indexers. The most common use for
this is to disambiguate variables, for example:

```
class ExampleClass {
    string name;
    public ExampleClass (string name)
    {
        this.name = name
    } // end constructor
} // end class
```

The qualification this.name on the left-hand side of the assignment in the
constructor makes it refer to the name that is declared as a data member in
the class. On the right-hand side, the unqualified name refers to the parameter
to the constructor. This is a common idiom in Java and in C++.

9.3 Inheritance

C#, like Java, is a language based on single inheritance. It achieves the effect
of multiple inheritance by means of multiple interface inclusion, a feature it
shares with Java. The complexities of C++ multiple inheritance are avoided
and a considerably simpler semantics results.

When one class, A say, is derived by inheritance from its super class (its
"base" class, in C# terms), the declaration of A is written:

```
class A : B {
   ...
} // end class A
```

This syntax is similar to that employed in C++. Unlike Java, there is no keyword denoting inheritance (Java uses **extends**). After the colon, there can be *exactly one* classname, the name of the base class (super class) from which this one is inheriting.

The C# class system has a root class, called object. If a class is defined without a super class (as have all examples in this chapter so far), class object is assumed to be its parent. The existence of a single root class has been discussed elsewhere (Chapter 6, Section 6), and will be mentioned again when considering polymorphism.

The rules for converting between class types in C# are the familiar ones. If class A is derived from class B, A may be *implicitly* upcast to B, and B may be *explicitly* downcast to A. C# adds an operator called **as** that returns null if the downcast fails. The language also defines an operator, is, that performs type tests.

9.3.1 Calling Base-Class Constructors

When a constructor of a derived class is called, it must call its base class' constructor. If the base class' constructor has no parameters, this is performed implicilty by the C# compiler. If the base class constructor takes one or more parameters, there must be an explicitly programmed call on that constructor so that the appropriate arguments can be passed. `

The basic form of a call to a base class constructor in C# is identical to that in C++. It consists of the constructor's header (name and parameters) followed by a colon, followed by the keyword **base** and the required arguments inside parentheses. For example, assuming that MyClass has a constructor that expects an integer argument, the following is a legal constructor:

```
class ExampleClass : MyClass {
   public ExampleClass (int x, int y) : base(x)
   {
      // body of constructor
   } // end constructor
} // end class
```

If a class has a parameterless constructor that calls an overloaded constructor, the following is a legal declaration of a call to a base class constructor:

```
class ExampleClass : MyClass {
   public ExampleClass () : this(99) {}
   public ExampleClass (int x) : base(x)
   {
```

```
    // body of constructor
  } // end constructor
} // end class
```

Again, it is assumed that the base class has a constructor that expects an integer argument. The first constructor expects no arguments but it calls one that takes an integer parameter, which is called before the body of the zero-adic constructor. The unary constructor, when called, will call the base class (MyClass) in order to ensure base-class (superclass) initialisation.

The order in which classes are constructed and finalized is as standard. Constructors are called in a way that respects the inheritance chain in C#. Therefore, the order is least to most specific. The constructor for object is therefore always called first and the constructor of the most specific class is called last. Thus, if a constructor in class MyClass is called, the constructor for object is first called, then, in descending order, all the constructors for the intermediate classes until the constructor for MyClass is reached. The constructor for MyClass is called last. The same rule is followed by static constructors.

The finalization rule works in the reverse order to the constructor rule. That is, it works by finalizing the most specific class and works up that class' inheritance chain until it reaches object. This means that local slots are finalized before inherited ones. It should be remembered that finalization depends upon the garbage collector, so the exact time at which finalization occurs cannot be predicted. That is, there is some non-determinism in the operation of the storage manager, so C# software should not make any assumptions about when finalization code will be run.

Initialisations of data are always performed by C# before the constructor for the class in which they appear is called. This makes all locally declared slots (data members) available to the constructor. Data members that are marked as static (class variables, in other words) are initialised before any static constructors are called.

It is worth noting that, in C#, it is not possible to determine exactly when a static constructor is to be called. For this reason, code should not be written that relies upon a particular ordering of calls to these constructors. The order in which static constructors are called is non-deterministic in C#.

Classes in C#, as in Java, rely upon interfaces to provide multiple inheritance. C++ uses multiple inheritance and a fairly complicated system of superclass annotations to control what is inherited and how.

9.3.2 Interfaces

Interfaces are common to C# and to Java. Like Java interfaces, C# interfaces are akin to classes but only provides a specification not an implementation. As such, an interface is closely related to a purely abstract class (an abstract class that contains no implementations). Classes in C# can implement more than one interface but can inherit from only one class—this is identical to the rule in Java.

An interface consists of one or more method specifications, properties and indexers (and events, although the latter are not considered because they are implemented in the library). All the members of an interface are implicitly public and implicitly abstract; they are, therefore, virtual and non-static.

The syntax for using an interface is similar to that employed in Java. An example of this is:

```
public class C : Interface1, Interface2 ...
{
    // Body of class C
} // end class C
```

Class C implements Interface1, Interface2, etc.

If a class inherits from a superclass (base class in C# terms), the superclass name must appear before any interface names. Thus:

```
public class C : Superclass, Interface1, Interface2
{
    // Body of C
} // end class C
```

Here, class C inherits from superclass Superclass and implements interfaces Interface1 and Interface2.

Interfaces can extend other interfaces in Java (after version 1.2) and in C#. For instance:

```
interface I2 {
    int Bar ( ... );
} // end interface
interface I1 : I2 {
    bool Foo ( ... );
} // end interface
```

This is an interface called I1 that extends the interface I2. The combined interface specifies two methods: Foo and Bar, one method is inherited from each parent.

If there is a name clash between two interfaces, whether produced by interface extension or by interface inclusion in a class header, or because of the presence of a class member with the same name, C# allows the programmer to implement explicitly an interface member to resolve the conflict. Consider the following case:

```
public interface I1 {
    string Foo ( object o );
} // end interface I1
public interface I2 {
```

```
   object Foo ( string s );
} // end interface I2
public class C1 : I1, I2 {
   string I1.Foo ( object o );
} // end class C1
```

Note that the explicit definition contains the name of the interface. Explicit implementations require a *fully qualified* identifier for the entities with clashing names.

Unlike implicit interface implementations, explicit ones cannot be declared as `abstract`, `virtual`, `override` or `new` modifiers. In addition, they are implicitly public; an implicit definition requires the `public` modifier. To access a method that is defined in this way, it is necessary to cast to the appropriate interface type first, as in:

```
C1 c = new C1 ( ... );
I1 i1 = (I1)c;
I2 i2 = (I2)c;
... = i1.Foo( ... );
... = i2.Foo(''...'');
```

This hints that interfaces are *type definitions*, just like classes.

If a base class implements an interface member with the `virtual` or abstract modifier, a derived class can override it. If not, the derived class must contain a reimplementation of the interface in order to override that member. Consider the example (taken from [5], p. 57):

```
public interface IDesignTimeControl {
   ...
   object Delete ();
} // end interface
public interface IDelete {
   void Delete ();
} // end interface
public class TextBox : IDelete, IDesignTimeControl {
   void IDelete.Delete () { ... }
   object IDesignTImeControl.Delete () { ... }
} // end class
public class RichTextBox : TextBox, IDelete {
   public void Delete (){ ... }
} // end class RichTextBox
```

This example allows the programmer to use a `RichTextBox` as an `IDelete` object. This makes it possible to call `RichTextBox`'s version of `Delete`.

In C# a class can be implicitly cast to an interface that the class implements. If interface X inherits from interface Y, X can be implicitly cast to Y. An interface can also be cast to any other interface or non-sealed class.

An explicit cast from interface I to a sealed class S is permitted *only if S* can implement I.

9.4 Methods and Operators

Methods have a syntax that is similar to Java and C++. Examples of methods have already been given, so no time will be spent on the fine details. Instead, attention is paid to binding and some of the language-specific details of methods.

9.4.1 Dispatch

Unlike Java, C# uses early binding as default. This is the same as C++. In C#, if the programmer wants late binding, it must be explicitly requested. The request for a dynamic dispatch takes the form of the virtual annotation, as in C++.

The corresponding method declaration in C# takes the following form:

```
public virtual int v_method (char c, int y)
{
    // body of v_method
} // end method
```

Note that v_method has a body or implementation. The implementation can be overridden in a subclass of the class in which a virtual method is declared. The implementation is required just in case the method is called in an instance of the class in which it is defined.

In C++, the definition of a method that overrides a dynamically-dispatched method consists simply of the declaration of the prototype (signature) plus an implementation. In C#, the overriding definition is legal only when the override keyword is present, as in:

```
public override int v_method (char c, int y)
{
    // overriding body
} // end overriding definition
```

The override keyword *must* be present to make the overriding definition legal. Furthemore, the overriding method *must* have a signature that is *identical* to the one that is being overridden.

Once this protocol has been observed, dynamic dispatch works as in other late-bound languages.

The C# approach to late-bound methods is different from that in Java and other languages that employ dynamic dispatch as default. Because C# is early bound by default, it is necessary to tell the compiler that a dynamic dispatch is required.

The C# approach cleans up a potential cause of errors in C++. It is very easy to confuse dynamically-dispatched methods with so-called "pure virtual functions." The latter are abstract methods and it makes no sense to supply a body for them. The = 0 notation in C++ is a warning that an abstract method is required and denotes the fact that no body is supplied in the defining class. It is easy to miss or omit the = 0 or to write an abstract method when a late-bound one is required.

C# imposes the constraint that abstract and late-bound methods can never be marked as `private`. This makes sense because `private` methods are only visible in their defining class, thus making it impossible to implement or override them in any derived class.

Related to the specification of dynamic dispatch is the hiding of methods. C# allows the hiding (redefinition) of data, function and type members of a base (super) class. The following is an example of redefinition of a dynamically-dispatched method:

```
public class A {
   ...
   public virtual void foo () { ... }
   ...
} // end class A
public class B : A {
   ...
   public override void foo () { ... }
   ...
} // end class B
public class C : B {
   ...
   public new void foo () { ... }
   ...
} // end class C
```

Here, method `foo` in class C hides the definition in class B. It should be noted that the keyword `new` is used to denote the overriding. The signature of the hiding method must be identical to that of the hidden method. The C# language requires the `new` keyword whenever a non-virtual method hides the corresponding method in the base class. This is intended to catch errors whereby a method unintentionally hides a method in one of its super classes. It is, therefore, possible to hide early- as well as late-bound methods.

9.4.2 The Base Keyword

It is also often necessary to call methods in the super class or base class. The C# device for this involves the use of the `base` keyword. In this case, as in constructor definition, `base` refers to the super or base class. The standard method access operator is used to reference the component of the base class that is being accessed. Consider a class, C1, that is a subclass of class C and assume that class C defines a method m, inside the methods of C1, the following is a call to the method m in C:

```
base.m( ... );
```

A more extended example will make matters clearer:

```
class C {
    ...
    public int m (int x) {}
    ...
} // end class C
class C1 : C{
    ...
    public int m1 (int y, int z)
    {
        int xx = 0;
        ...
        xx = base.m(y);
    } // end method m1
    ...
} // end class C1
```

This example shows that the **base** call can return values as well as take parameters. The call is the same as a call to an instance but the instance name is replaced by **base**.

The C# rule for accessing class members via **base** states that data, type and function members can be so accessed (depending upon their access annotations). The process of finding the corresponding member begins with the immediate superclass of the instance making the call and proceeds until a matching entity has been found. Should there be no matching entity, the compiler will signal an error.

9.4.3 Parameter Annotations

C#, like Java and C++, uses call-by-value as its standard parameter-passing method. As in C++, however, it is possible in C# to change the method. To effect this, C# provides two parameter modifiers, **ref** and out that modify the formal parameters of a method.

The **ref** modifier states that the parameter it modifies must be passed *by reference*. An example will help explain this. Consider a class defining the following method:

```
public class C {
    ...
    public void m (ref int p)
```

```
{
    p++;
} // end method m
} // end class C
```

What happens is that, with a **ref** parameter, a reference to the actual parameter is passed instead of the value of that parameter. Thus, the address of the actual argument is passed to the method. In order to make this work, C# requires that the **ref** qualifier be used for each actual parameter that is to be substituted for a reference parameter.

For each **ref** parameter, the compiler plants code to pass the address of that parameter to the called method. The effect is as if the actual and formal parameter shared the same store. This is the same as the & parameters in C++ and **var** parameters in Pascal.

To see how this is used, consider a client class that calls m in a method. It is assumed that the class that defines m is instantiated and the instance is called **inst**:

```
public void clientMeth ()
{
int v = 99;
C inst = new C(...);
    inst.m(ref v);
} // end method clientMeth
```

After the call to **inst.m(v)**, the local variable v will have 100 as its value. Note that at the point of call, the **ref** keyword qualifies the variable v. The **ref** v instructs the compiler to pass the address of v instead of the value of v to the call of **inst.m**.

The **out** annotation is the converse of the **ref** annotation. An **out** annotation states that the qualified parameter must be a variable and that it will be bound to a value on return from the method. It is like the **ref** parameter in that the address of the actual parameter is passed into the method so that the formal and actual parameters share storage. (In fact, in both cases, the pointer is *constant* within the method body.)

The following is an example of an out parameter:

```
private void m (out int x) { x = 99; }
private void user ()
{
    int y;
    this.m(out y);
} // end method user
```

When m is called, a constant pointer to the actual parameter y is passed. The out annotation must precede the actual parameter in the list of actual parameters. Inside the body of m, the formal parameter x is treated as a pointer to a region of storage of the appropriate type. Inside m, it is necessary to assign a value to x or an error will be signalled by the compiler.

The out parameter is a natural consequence of the C# rule that all variables must be initialised before their first use. Among other things, it allows private and protected methods to be defined that perform variable initialisations.

The params is used in C# to allow an arbitrary number of parameters *of the same type* to be passed to a method. The params modifier can only be used as the *last* parameter. A simple example shows its use.

```
class Sums {
    ...
    public int addVec (params int[] nums)
    {
        int total = 0;
        foreach (int i in nums) total += i;
        return total;
    } // end method addVec
    ...
    public static Main ()
    {
        int sum7 = 0;
        int sum3 = 0;
        ...
        sum7 = addVec(1,2,3,4,5,6,7);
        sum3 = addVec(5,7,11);
        ...
    } // end Main
} // end class Sums
```

9.4.4 Properties

In Java, it is frequently necessary to write something akin to the following:

```
foo.getBar(foo.setBar(''message'', false);
```

This is sometimes called the use of a *property*. Properties are a formalisation of *getter-setter* method combinations. This is an extremely frequently encountered pattern, so its formalisation and regularisation is a reasonable idea. The following exemplifies the use of a property in C#:

```
public class OceanLiner {
    XYCoord loc = null;
    public XYCoord Location {
        get{ return loc; } // end getter
        set{
            loc = value;
```

```
        } // end setter
      } // end property
   } // end class OceanLiner
```

This property, `Location`, is defined to represent the location of an ocean liner. The property has type `XYCoord`, which is assumed to be defined and to represent a co-ordinate pair in Cartesian co-ordinates. Its getter is denoted by the keyword `get`. The getter, here, simply returns the value of the private data member `loc`. The setter assigns a value to `loc`.

The value that is assigned is first bound the implicit parameter `value`. In the definition of `value`, C# introduces a little polymorphism, for `value` must always be of the correct type in order that the property be well-typed. Thus, for each property, `value` is implicitly declared with the appropriate type. The type must be inferred from the type of the variable to which it is assigned.

Finally, note that the getter and setter are enclosed within brackets that group them into the property.

The above might be used as follows.

```
private OceanLiner l = new OceanLiner( ... );
   // create an instance of C
private XYCoord position = new XYCoord( ... ) ;
   // create an initial coordinate
qe2.Location = position; // set a value into X
...
loc = qe2.Location; // get a value from X
```

Note that the basic syntax is the same as for public slots (data members). Assignment consists of a reference to the slot on the left-hand side of the assignment, while access consists of a reference on the left-hand side of assignment or in an inner expression. This removes the need to define explicit setter and getter functions.

It is possible, in C#, to define an abstract property. In this case, the setter and getter methods are defined without a body—a semicolon replaces the body statement. Properties can also be `virtual`, `static` or `unsafe` (the `unsafe` keyword introduces methods and blocks within which pointers can be defined, set and dereferenced and in which pointer arithmetic operations are permitted). Properties can override and be overridden. Properties can also have access modifiers—they do not have to be public—they are, in all respects apart from the definition of setter and getter methods, identical to data or function members of a class.

Properties are related to so-called *virtual* slots in some knowledge representation and object-oriented languages. In this sense, a *virtual* slot is one whose value is computed from the values stored in other slots (perhaps in instances of other objects), rather than being directly stored in the slot. This is a concept that is of considerable utility, even though it can be somewhat obscure on the page.

9.4.5 Delegates

C# introduces the concept of the *delegate* into the C++ family of languages. A delegate is a type that defines a method signature. A delegate instance can, therefore, represent and invoke a method or list of methods that match the delegate's signature. The declaration of a delegate consists of a name and a method signature, The signature of a delegate includes the return type and can also contain parameter modifiers in its parameter list. The actual name of any matching method is irrelevant to the delegate.

An example delegate is:

```
delegate int ExampleDelegate (ref int x, bool b);
```

This definition allows the programmer to create instances of the delegate that contain and invoke methods that return an int when supplied with a reference to an integer and a boolean value. This delegate might be instantiated as follows:

```
ExampleDelegate foo = new ExampleDelegate(RealMethod);
public int RealMethod (ref int x, bool flg)
{
    // body of RealMethod
} // end method RealMethod
```

If a delegate has a void return type, it is a *multicast delegate*. Multicast delegates can contain and invoke more than one method.

The operator += is used to add methods to a multicast delegate. The following code fragment shows this in a fairly abstract setting:

```
class ExampleClass {
    delegate void MultiCaller ();
    private void TestDelegates ()
    {
        MultiCaller m = null;
        m += new MultiCaller(Alpha);
        m += new MultiCaller(Beta);
        m();
    } // end TestDelegates
} // end class ExampleClass
```

In this example, MultiCaller is defined as a multicast delegate. Inside TestDelegates, two methods, Alpha and Beta are added to m, an instance of MultiCaller, which is executed via the call m().

A delegate can be removed from a list using the -= operator.

It is possible, though somewhat low-level, to think of a delegate as a pointer to a method or list of methods with the same signature.

Delegates solve problems that must be handled in C++ with function pointers or in Java by interfaces.

Methods can be overloaded in C# in a fashion similar to Java and C++. The process of overloading is the same as in these other languages. However, the existence of ref, out and params parameters makes for slightly richer signatures and, hence, more possible combinations available for overloading.

9.4.6 Operator Overloading

C# allows the programmer to overload operators, provided the operator is from a restricted set. This is similar to C++, but not identical for the reason that C# tightens the semantics of overloading slightly and restricts what can be overloaded.

The operators C# allows to be overloaded are:

```
+           -          !     ~                   ++    --
|           ^          <<    >>                  !=    >    <
>=          <=
true        false
* (binary only)    /    %    & (binary only)
```

It should be noted that the assignment operator cannot be overloaded (unlike in C++) and also that true and false are defined as operators. Attention will be paid to this convention after more general properties of operators have been discussed.

An operator is a static method with the keyword operator preceding the operator to be overloaded and its parameters. For example:

```
public static bool operator == (T x, T y);
```

The most frequently overloaded operators are == and !=, value equality and its negation. The value of the argument expressions are compared. When overloading the == operator in C#, it is necessary to overload the Equals method. This makes newly defined classes consistent with other classes in Microsoft's .NET framework, and it also allows classes the perform equality overloading to act transparently as base classes. The following is an example:

```
public class XYCoord {
    double x = 0.0;
    double y = 0.0;
    public static bool operator == (XYCoord c1, XYCoord c2)
    {
        return (c1.x == c2.x && c1.y == c2.y);
    } // end operator ==
    public static bool operator != (XYCoord c1, XYCoord c2)
    {
```

```
        return (c1.x != c2.x || c1.y != c2.y);
    } // end operator !=
    public override bool Equals (object o)
    {
        if (o is XYCoord)
            return this.==(XYCoord o);
        else return false;
    } // end method Equals
} // end class
```

Note how the overridden definition of Equals redirects control to the locally defined equality operator.

C# divides operators into logical pairs. Equality and its negation form one pair; less than and greater than form another pair, and so on. It is a requirement in C# that, if one of a logical pair of operators is overloaded, the other operator should also be overloaded. In the example above, the == operator was overloaded; in order to comply with the C# requirement, != was overloaded as well.

The keywords true and false are used as operators when defining types with *three-state* (or *three-valued*) logic (this is used by the C strcmp function). The use of true and false is to allow three-state logic operations to be integrated with the more standard two-valued ones. The following is intended to show how this overriding might be used:

```
public class C {
    private int x = 0;
    ...
    public static bool operator true (C c)
    {
        return c.x == 1;
    } // end operator true
    public static bool operator false (C c)
    {
        return c.x == -1;
    } // end operator false
    public bool undefined (C c)
    {
        return c.x == 0;
    } // end method undefined
} // end class C
```

In this example, the value of x is used to determine the truth value. If x is one, it is taken to be true; if it is minus one, it is assumed to be false. This will allow the class C to be integrated with conditionals and loops because the value of x is now interpreted, thanks to the above definition, as a boolean value. The problem remains that there is the possibility that x will take the value zero. This is taken into account above by defining a method `undefined` that tests for this case.

The operators `&&` and `||` are defined in terms of their bitwise counterparts in C#. This has the implication that neither need be overloaded. The array indexing operation `[]` can be overloaded using indexers. Assignment, as noted above, cannot be overloaded in C#, but the combinations such as `+=` are automatically evaluated from their corresponding binary operators, thus permitting type-specific behaviours in the presence of overloading.

9.5 Polymorphism and Types

C# has an interesting approach to types. In this section, the opportunities for polymorphism afforded by C# are reviewed. Then the concept of the `struct` is described and its use in the language is discussed. The use of `struct`s is of some interest because it unifies the type system and offers the programmer considerable flexibility in representation.

Like all object-oriented languages, C# supports polymorphism. Some examples have already been encountered in this chapter:

- the implicit polymorphism introduced by the inheritance chain with its concomitant operations of up- and downcasting;
- the polymorphism introduced by constructor, method and operator overloading.

These forms of polymorphism are common to all object-oriented languages and have been extensively discussed in previous chapters. C#, in this respect, is a conservative language.

9.5.1 Structs

Instances of C# classes are created in the heap. This implies that all access to instances is by means of a pointer. Classes can be considered to be *reference types*. It is often desirable to allocate instances on the stack. C++ permits this, as does Eiffel [67]. In Eiffel, there is a conceptual distinction between *reference types* and *value types*. Eiffel value types are allocated on the runtime stack and their lifetime is restricted to that of the block in which they are declared (C++ imposes the same restriction for stack-allocated instances). The syntax of value and reference types in Eiffel is the same. Eiffel makes semantic distinctions between the two kinds of type.

C# makes a distinction similar to that of Eiffel but re-introduces the concept of the `struct`. In C++, structures can be defined as well as classes. In some of the C++ references, for example [92], the keyword `struct` is used as a synonym for `class`.

Syntactically, a C# `struct` is similar to a `class` but is semantically different and there are properties of classes that are not shared by structs. Within a C# `struct`, it is possible to define data and function members (data slots and methods), as well as type members.

Although related, the C# conceptions of `struct` and `class` are distinct and there are differences that are enforced semantically.

A `class` defines a reference type while a `struct` is a value type. As a consequence, `structs` usually define simple types for which value semantics is more appropriate. For example, value types employ a bitwise copy model for assignment and reference types implement assignment as a pointer or reference copy. When an object of a value type is assigned to a variable, the contents of the object are copied to the variable. This copy is performed byte-by-byte (by extension, bit-by-bit). When assigning a reference to a variable, only the pointer is copied.

Next, C# classes require full inheritance for their definition. A `struct`, on the other hand, inherits from the root class, `object`, and is implicitly `sealed`. Both classes and `structs` can implement interfaces, however, so `structs` can engage in a limited form of inheritance.

It is permitted to define a parameterless constructor in C# classes. It is also possible to initialise data members within a class. In a `struct`, these operations are not permitted. The default parameterless constructor for a `struct` initialises each slot with a default value (zero for most types). If a `struct` defines a constructor, all of its slots must be assigned by the constructor. This constraint applies to all constructors that a `struct` defines.

Classes in C# are permitted to have destructors. As mentioned above, a destructor is a method that calls a finalization method. This method is used to tidy an instance up before the storage it occupies is collected as garbage by the storage manager (garbage collector). Because value types are stack-allocated and have a lifetime that is controlled by the scope at which they reside, destructor methods make no sense for them. When a `struct` goes out of scope, the storage it occupies is returned to the stack and recycled in the usual manner when entering and leaving a scope.

There are rules relating to polymorphism that `structs` obey. These rules are similar to those for classes. For example, a `struct` can be implicitly cast to an interface that a class implements. (The interface defined by a class is, in effect, the definition of the class without its data and type members and with no implementations). In addition, a cast from an interface I to a sealed struct S is permitted *only if* S can implement I.

9.5.2 Type Unification

The existence of value types allows C# to provide a unifying mechanism for types. This facility is absent in Java and C++ and is, to my knowledge, quite novel for there is no other language I know of that can do this.

In most languages, there is a sharp distinction between primitive types like `int`, `char` and `bool` and user-defined types. C# is designed from the viewpoint that *all* primitive types should be defined as `structs`. The name of each C# primitive type is just an alias for a system-defined type that is defined as a **struct**. For example, **int** is an alias for the type **System.Int32** and **long** is an alias for **System.Int64**. This, in itself, seems of little interest until it is remembered that a **struct** can define methods, which has the implication that primitive types can be defined as **structs** that define the methods that operate on that type. Thus, the **System.Int32** struct defines arithmetic operations as well as methods like **ToString**, an operation that converts the value to a string for printing. Because C# operators can be overloaded, the operations defined for primitive types can be applied to any class or **struct** type. This has the implication that +, for example, can be extended from an integer operation to an operation, say, over polar coordinates.

It is possible to define new primitive types by defining the appropriate **struct**. This is a powerful feature.

C# reference types can be handled generically because it is possible for multiple reference types to share the properties of a common ancestor type. For example, a method that takes a reference to type T can be applied to any type that is derived from, or implements, T. To perform the same operations on value as well as reference types, every value type has a corresponding hidden reference type. Instances of this hidden type are created when the value type is cast to a reference type. The C# term for this is *boxing*.

Boxing avoids a problem with Java. In Java, the primitive types are accompanied by a set of wrapper types. Thus, the Java primitive type **int** is accompanied by a class type **Integer**. The **Integer** type wraps an object of type **int** and allows it to be treated like any other reference type. Unfortunately, it is necessary, in Java, to perform the wrapping and unwrapping manually. C# performs these operations automatically.

The following is an example of boxing and unboxing.

```
class Queue {
  ...
  public void Enqueue (object o) { ... }
  public object Dequeue () { ... return ... }
} // end class Queue

Queue q = new Queue();
q.Enqueue(99); // box the int value 99
int val = (int) q.Dequeue(); // unbox the int value
```

In the example (taken from [5], p. 17), a class implementing a FIFO queue is defined. The class has a method for enqueueing objects and a method for dequeueing them. To make the methods completely general, the type **object** is used for their parameter and return types, respectively. Next, a queue object is created by instantiation and an **int** value (99) is enqueued. In Java, this would require the programmer to write:

```
q.Enqueue( new Integer(99) );
```

The C# compiler, however, detects the fact that a primitive type is being implicitly cast to a reference type and boxes the int value. On the next line, a dequeue operation is performed. Here, there is an explicit cast to a primitive type, so the compiler inserts code to unbox the object to an int. In Java, this would require the programmer to write an explicit unwrapping by calling a method defined in Integer:

```
Integer ival = (Integer)q.Dequeue();
int val = ival.intValue();
```

(This could be written on one line but the above is considered clearer for expository purposes.)

Boxing and unboxing are consequences of the unified approach to types adopted for C#. This principle implies that all types should be treated identically.

Finally, C# restores the enum from C++ that was omitted from Java. Enumerations were removed from Java because its guiding principle was to maximise the benefit of classes. Since an enumeration can be written as a sequence of static manifest constants that constitute the body of a class, the enumeration was considered redundant. This was unfortunate because of the notational convenience represented by the enum. C# enums are represented by default as non-negative integer constants. It is possible to change the representation and to provide explicit values for the elements (the latter is possible for the default representation), for example:

```
public enum Colour : byte {
    Red=1, Green=3, Blue=5, Yellow=7
}
```

The operations that can be applied to enums form a fairly extensive set. Comparison, addidition and subtraction, assignment (including += and -=), increment, decrement and the size operation are all permitted. In addition, enums can be converted to and from numeric types. A special case is the literal constant zero ("0"), which can be implicitly converted to an enum.

9.6 Base Class Library

Independent of the .NET framework is the C# *Base Class Library*. This is a large library of useful classes, similar in scope and content to the Java class libraries. The Base Class Library is used to construct working C# programs. The entities it defines are all C# classes.

The Base Class Library contains classes to implement the following:

- core Types;
- text;
- collections;

- streams and I/O;
- networking;
- threads;
- security;
- reflection;
- serialization;
- remoting (remote method calls);
- web services;
- data access;
- XML;
- graphics;
- rich client applications support;
- Web-based applications;
- globalisation;
- configuration;
- advanced component services;
- assemblies;
- diagnostics and debugging;
- interoperation with unmanaged code;
- component and tool support;
- runtime support;
- native OS facilities.

The Base Class Library is provided to support programming. It does not extend the language but makes extensive use of its facilities. Because it does not extend the language, it will not be considered in any more detail.

A. BeCecil

BeCecil stands for **Block-structured** extensible **Cecil**. It is a theoretical core
language with multimethods. The aims of BeCecil were to be as simple as
possible and to be an orthogonal version of languages like Cecil, CLOS and
Dylan. BeCecil is able, within the confines of a small language, to express a
wide variety of programming patterns including Abstract Data Types, procedural patterns and, of course, object-oriented ones. BeCecil, like Cecil, is a
prototype-based language. It is possible for BeCecil programs to be defined
that display other kinds of behaviour.

BeCecil supports the following programming idioms:

- BeCecil supports a *prototype-based object model* that unifies classes and
  instances into a single *object* concept. It supports inheritance between objects; multiple inheritance is supported;
- BeCecil supports mutable state and object identity;
- BeCecil supports *multi-methods*. They are collected as generic function objects that have first-class status. Each multi-method case of a generic function can be a nested, lexically-scoped closure. Unlike Dylan or CLOS, Be-
  Cecil's multi-methods are not linearised in terms of specificity. Specificity-
  based linearisation permits ambiguous definitions;
- instance variables are modelled as a special kind of multi-method implementation. This integrates them into the method dispatch mechanism;
- BeCecil has a static type system that separates types from objects and
  subtyping from code inheritance. It also guarantees that all dynamically-
  dispatched messages reach the most specific matching multi-method case
  at runtime;
- extensible, customisable objects are supported. Generic functions, superclasses and supertypes can be added to existing objects or types by external
  clients of those types;
- BeCecil supports scoping and encapsulation of all declarations, including
  object, type, inheritance, subtyping and multi-method declarations. This
  limits their static visibility and dynamic effect to a restricted region of
  program text. This feature allows clients to extend existing objects in a
  nested scope, thus hiding extensions from other, unrelated clients. It also
  supports the traditional encapsulation of an object's hidden state;

- BeCecil supports a notion of *separate typechecking*. Modules (named collections of declarations) can be statically typechecked in isolation from clients, unrelated modules, and any extending modules. Multi-Methods cause problems for modular typechecking; ambiguities can arise between different additions of multi-method cases to a common generic function.

BeCecil is intended to be a core subset of Cecil. It does not model all of Cecil directly, however. It does not model non-local returns, predicate classes and parameterised types.

The remainder of this Appendix is intended only to give a flavour of what can be done in BeCecil. The source for these examples is [23]. The interested reader is recommended to browse the Web site at `www.cs.washington.edu` for more information on Cecil and related topics.

For reasons of space, it is not possible to cover all aspects of BeCecil. Instead, the aim, in this Appendix, is to show how a core language can be used to express many common idioms. More examples can be found in [23]. I hope that the reader will find study of BeCecil (and Cecil) as rewarding and stimulating as I have.

A.1 Programming Standard OO Mechanisms

An object can only be created by an object declaration. Objects in a program can act as classes or instances in other object-oriented languages. Each object has a unique identity. The following is the declaration of a class `Point_rep`. (Following Chambers and Leavens, [23], the suffix `_rep` (standing for "representation") is used to distinguish classes from types in examples.)

```
object Point_rep
```

An object can be declared to inherit from another object by an inheritance declaration. More than one inheritance declaration can be used with the same object, in which case multiple inheritance is used. The following states that the object called `Points_rep` inherits from an object called **any** and declares another object `CP_rep` (representation of coloured points) that inherits from `Points_rep` and an object called `Colour_rep`. The **any** object is the root object.

```
Point_rep inherits any
object CP_rep
CP_rep inherits Point_rep
CP_rep inherits Color_rep
```

In BeCecil, there is no distinction between inheritance and the "instance of" relationships. BeCecil therefore resembles a prototype-based language. For the reason that an instance of a class is merely an object that inherits from that class, instances of a class are created in exactly the same way as are subclasses. The following declares an instance of `Point_rep` called `my_point`:

```
object my_point
my_point inherits Point_rep
```

BeCecil objects can also be generic functions. A BeCecil generic function is similar to a collection of multi-methods in CLOS. Unlike CLOS or Dylan, the methods in a BeCecil generic function need not all have the same arity. To define the generic function **equal**, the following would be needed:

```
object equal
equal inherits GenericFun_rep
```

The generic function **equal** can be extended by means of a **has** declaration. This adds a method to a generic function. For the following example, it is necessary to assume that the generic functions x and y are implemented for points. The following is a generic function that is specialised to two **Point_rep** arguments:

```
equal has method (p1@Point_rep, p2@Point_rep) {
    and(equal(x(p1),x(p2)),equal(y(p1),y(p2)))
}
```

Note the unusual syntax: $F@CN$, where F is a formal parameter name and CN is the name of a class or type. The symbol denotes a typing, so p1Point_rep states that p1 must be of the type of **Point_rep**. In Cecil and BeCecil, the CN component is called the *specializer* object.

The instance variables of an object are modelled in BeCecil; they do not form an integral part of an object. The construct that models instance variables is called a *storage table*. Storage tables relate *keys* to *values*. Keys consist of a tuple of object identities and values are single objects. BeCecil's generic functions can contain both storage tables and methods. The reading of a storage table is similar to applying a generic function. If no value is currently stored in a storage table, a default value is returned.

Consider the following example in which x and y are objects that act as instance variables. Each instance variable is modelled as a generic function that has a **storage** (storage table) attribute. The storage table can be thought of as mappings from points to integers. The := 0 in each storage table declaration provides the default value (here, 0).

```
object x
x inherits GenericFun_rep
x has storage (p@Point_rep) := 0
object y
y inherits GenericFun_rep
y has storage (p@Point_rep) := 0
```

Storage tables can be modified using an assignment expression. In assignments, the expression on the left-hand side of the := provides the key, while that on the right-hand side provides the value that is to be associated with the key. Thus, the x co-ordinate of **myPoint** can be set to 3 by:

```
x(myPoint) := 3
```

Storage tables can also be used to represent program variables. The following shows this:

```
object my_var
my_var has storage() := 0
my_var() := 255
plus(my_var(), 1)
```

The result of the last expression will be 256.

BeCecil has *acceptors*. Acceptors are like methods and can process an argument. Acceptors allow any storage table to be replaced by an acceptor and a method. They also permit the equivalent of "write-only" fields (slots). When used in an assignment, the key is bound to the formal parameters and the value is bound to the identifier that is to be found on the right-hand side of the := in the acceptor's declaration. The following example shows the use of acceptors:

```
object xy
xy inherits GenericFun_rep
xy has acceptor (p@Point_rep) := v {
   x(p) := v
   y(p) := v
}
```

The following expression will, therefore, return 28:

```
xy(myPoint) := 14
plus(x(myPoint), y(myPoint))
```

Dispatch in assignments is dynamic (like method dispatch). However, in assignments, only the specializers of the generic function's acceptors and storage tables are considered. A generic function's methods are ignored when dispatching an assignment. Similarly, when dispatching an application, only the methods and storage tables of a generic function are considered.

To achieve information hiding, BeCecil has the capability to hide a recursive declaration sequence. This was chosen because it affords the ability to hide generic functions. This is implemented as BeCecil's hide declaration. It is similar to the local declaration in Standard ML [42, 43] in that declarations in its declaration sequence are visible only in the sequence that follows the in keyword. The following example (from [23], p. 8, spellings mine) demonstrates the use of hide construct:

```
object Greyscale_rep
Greyscale_rep inherits Colour_rep
hide
   object scale
   scale inherits GenericFun_rep
```

```
        scale has storage (c@Greyscale_rep) := 0
   in
       initialize has
             method (c@Greyscale_rep,intensity@float_rep)
       {
          scale(c) :=
           truncate(multiply(min(max(0.0, intensity), 1.0),
                   255.0));
          c
       }
       intensity has method (c@Greyscale_rep) {
          divide(mkFloat(scale(c)), 255.0)
       }
       paint has method (c@Greyscale_rep, r@Region_rep {
          ...
       }
   end
   intensity has acceptor (c@Greyscale_rep) := f {
       initialize(c,f)
   }
```

There is a great deal to say about this example.

The above constitutes an implementation of a greyscale model of colours. The interface presented to clients allows them to create a colour that is based on grey intensities expressed as a floating-point number between 0.0 and 1.0. The hardware uses a 0 to 255 representation, however. Since the hardware might change, it is required to enforce the invariant that every instance has all its intensities represented by integers in the 0 to 255 range. This enforcement is performed by hiding the storage table for instances of this class. The code resembles a C++ class declaration with a private and a public part (the private part coming before the public one).

It is, of course, possible to over-ride methods inherited from a superclass. In BeCecil, it is possible to use a directed form of actual arguments. In this form, the expression is written followed by the symbol and a list of class names. The method selected must be one that has both the object that is the value of the expression and at least one of the named classes inherited from the corresponding formal parameter's specializer. The following example shows how the GreyPoint_rep class would be written as a subclass of Point_rep and Greyscale_rep:

```
object GreyPoint_rep
GreyPoint_rep inherits Point_rep
GreyPoint_rep inherits Greyscale_rep
initialize has method (gsp@GreyPoint_rep, i@int_rep,
     j@int_rep, intensity@float_rep)
   {
```

```
        initialize(gsp@Greyscale_rep, intensity);
        initialize(gsp@Point_rep, i, j);
        gsp
    }
object mkGSP
mkGSP inherits GenericFun_rep
mkGSP has method (i@int_rep, j@int_rep, intensity@float_rep)
{
    object res
    res inherits GreyPoint_rep
    initialize (res, i, j, intensity)
}
equal has method (gsp1@GreyPoint_rep, gsp2@GreyPoint_rep)
{
    and(equal(intensity(gsp1), intensity(gsp2)),
        equal(gsp1@Point_rep, gsp2@Point_rep))
}
```

Notice how the equal and initialize methods uses directed arguments to call the methods specialised on Point_rep and Greyscale_rep.

Generic functions are objects. This has the consequence that they can be used as first-class procedures. The following generic function can act as a *while*-loop.

The generic function while has a method that takes two generic function arguments. These are a condition (c) and a statement (s). These generic functions are expected to have zero-argument methods that can be executed in order to perform parts of the loop. The implementation depends upon the existence of another higher-order generic function, ifTrue; it takes a boolean and a generic function as arguments. The ifTrue function calls the generic function with zero arguments if the boolean evaluates to true. The generic function loop, passed as the second argument to ifTrue is declared within the method for while. Because the standard static closures are constructed for methods, c and s within loop refer to the formal parameters of the while method (hence, at runtime, are bound to while's actual parameters).

```
object while
while inherits GenericFun_rep
while has method (c@GenericFun_rep, s@GenericFun_rep)
{
    object loop
    loop inherits GenericFun_rep
    loop has method (){ s(); while(c, s)}
      ifTrue( c(), loop)
    }
```

A.2 Syntactic Sugar

As can be seen from the above examples, BeCecil provides a number of syntactic sugars for the declaration of variables, inheritance, instantiation, generic function declaration, formal arguments, expressions and so on. This makes the core language somewhat easier to write than would otherwise be the case.

A.3 A Small Example

In this section, the sugared BeCecil code will be given that implements a list in terms of abstract classes. The reader should have no problems in relating the following code to the core language presented above.

The example exploits abstraction in BeCecil. Two abstract classes are used, list_rep and nonempty_rep, a concrete object, nil, and a concrete class cons_rep. The abstract class list_rep defines the protocol for accessing the elements of a list and provides a general implementation of do that can be inherited by concrete objects.

```
object list_rep inherits any
gf isEmpty -- to be implemented by subclasses
gf do      -- to be implemented by subclasses
fun length (c@collection_rep) {
   var res := 0
   do (c,
       anon method (x) {res() := plus(res(), 1); nothing})
}
```

For the reason that BeCecil does not distinguish between classes and objects, the empty list can be represented as a concrete object that inherits from list_rep.

```
object nil inherits list_rep
isEmpty has method (n@nil) { nil }
head has method (n@nil) { head(n) } -- loop forever!
```

There now follows the code for nonempty_rep and cons_rep. These two classes are used so that one can inherit isEmpty from nonemtpy_rep more easily. The slots of cons_rep are hidden; this makes them similar to instance variables in a more traditional language (it is unclear how the protected annotation of C++, Java and C# can be supported). An initialisation method is used to allow subclasses of cons_rep to initialise the hidden fields.

```
object nonempty\_rep inherits list_rep
isEmpty has method (l@nonempty\_rep) { false }
object default_list_elem inherits any
```

```
object cons_rep inherits nonempty_rep
gf initialize -- generic initialiation function
hide
   field hd of cons_rep := default_list_elem
   field tl of cons_rep := nil
in
   initialize has method (c@cons_rep, x, l@list_rep) {
      hd(c) := x;
      tl(c) := l;
      c
   }
   tail has method (l@cons_rep) { tl(l) }
   head has method (l@cons_rep) { hd(l) }
   tail has acceptor (l@cons_rep) := new_tail
      { tl(l) := new_tail }
   head has acceptor (l@cons_rep) := new_head
      { hd(l) := new_head }
end
fun cons (x, l@list_rep){ initialize(new cons_rep, x, l) }
```

The implementation of equal is broken into three cases and uses multi-method dispatch:

```
equal has method (x@list_rep, y@list_rep) { false }
equal has method (x@nil, y@nil) { true }
equal has method (x@nonempty_rep, y@nonempty_rep) {
   and (equal( hd(x), hd(y)), [equal( tl(x), tl(y))])
}
```

A.4 Concluding Remarks

There is a considerable amount more that could be said about BeCecil (and, indeed, about Cecil). The temptation to make this Appendix very much longer has been resisted for the reason that these languages might not be to everyone's taste. For my own part, I find them fascinating and believe that they point towards the future of object-oriented programming, both in terms of language and in terms of methods. The aim of this Appendix was to whet the appetite for these languages; I hope I have done that and I urge readers to discover more for themselves.

B. Mixed-Paradigm Languages

B.1 Introduction

Mixed-paradigm languages are those languages which combine different approaches to programming. The most common approaches encountered today are:

- object-oriented programming;
- logic programming;
- functional programming;
- constraint programming;
- rule-based programming.

Each paradigm has its own strengths and weaknesses.

In AI and Knowledge Engineering, some so-called knowledge representation systems combine paradigms. Thus, in AI, a combination of rules, objects and procedures can often be found. LOOPS [15] was an early and relatively successful attempt to combine these paradigms. In the object-oriented community, there is also interest (see, for example, [64]) in combining object-oriented programming with one of the other paradigms.

The combination of declarative programming of all kinds has appealed to those interested in combining paradigms. Declarative programs specify *what* the program is to do, not *how* to do it. *Imperative* programs, those written in languages like Ada, Pascal or C, specify how to perform the computation. *Declarative* programs are most immediately different from conventional, imperative programs in that they do not contain loops or assignments. Instead, declarative languages provide binding mechanisms of various kinds and iteration is handled by recursion. Declarative programs are often said to be "side-effect free" because it is not possible to update variables once they have been initialized (variables tend to be copied rather than updated).

McCabe [62] has produced a combination of logic programming and objects. In this combination, called *Logic and Objects*, methods are expressed as Prolog clauses which are attached to objects in the usual way. Objects are fully supported by system-defined predicates. Logic does not, however, seem to sit well with objects. The objects used in logical theories tend to be treated as simple entities whose properties are defined by axioms; it is theories that are combined to produce more complex ones. Wegner [98] argues that logic is about specification while objects are concerned with models.

The *Claire* language is a combination of rules and objects. Objects take their usual form and methods are composed of collections of rules. Rules take the familiar `if...then` form. Their condition parts can contain calls to iterators as well as to slot access and other side-effect free operations. The action parts contain calls to operations that update slots, construct objects and so on. Problems with this approach include the following. It is often hard to relate rules to objects. Often, rules are implemented as special objects, but this is an implementation matter. In certain circumstances, it is useful to have higher-order procedures; it is hard, given the usual organization of rule-based systems, to see how this can be supported. However, users very often find rules easy to write and easy to understand.

The functional approach has received a little attention. The greatest attention has probably been paid by workers building objects on top of Scheme or another LISP dialect (Scheme and other LISPs have side-effects, even though functional programming is the preferred method for programming in them). Functional programming is an approach in which programs are written only in terms of functions and their application to arguments. A program is typically the composition of a number of functions. Modern functional programming is based upon strongly typed, higher-order functions. Strong typing makes correctness easier to show and also detects many errors at compile time. Higher-order functions are functions that can be passed as inputs or returned as results from other functions. Higher-order functions allow functions to be treated on the same basis as integers or characters—they are "first-class citizens". The combination of functions and objects resembles Category Theory in many respects and it allows the transformation of objects.

Constraint programming is based upon the idea that a computation need not be specified in detail. Instead, the solution to a problem is expressed in terms of what it should "look" like. Solutions are expressed in terms of the constraints which they should satisfy. Thus, in a constraint language, the solution is expressed as a collection of conditions; together, these conditions describe what the solution should be, not how it is to be derived. Borning has developed two generations of an object-oriented constraint-based system called *ThingLab* and *ThingLab-II*. Consultation of the literature shows, however, that there are many constraint satisfaction algorithms and that algorithms typically work in limited, frequently finite, domains. This suggests that the general-purpose algorithms needed by a general-purpose programming language might turn out to be elusive; it might be the case that the programmer has to specify the satisfaction algorithms, an undesirable situation.

Of the approaches described above, it is only the logic programming approach which makes orthogonal persistence a natural concept. The combination of databases with programming languages appears a highly desirable one for a number of reasons.

Because functions have been so infrequently combined with objects, and being more knowledgeable in the areas of logic, rule-based and functional programming than in the area of constraints, the remainder of this chapter will focus on functional programming. The aim of the chapter is to explore the issues raised by the combination of a strongly-typed higher-order functional programming language with an object-based core.

In the next section, I present the fundamentals of functional programming which include:

- referential transparency and substitution;
- functions;
- conditionals and recursion equations;
- higher-order functions;
- type inference

Evaluation strategies, including lazy evaluation, is considered in Section 9.2.2. Thereafter, I present a class-based functional language (Section 9.3). The first subsection (Section 9.3.1) outlines the class-based component, while Section 9.3.2 considers how functional languages must be modified to handle integration with classes. Finally, the design is reviewed.

B.2 Functional Programming: An Overview

Functional languages might be somewhat unfamiliar to many readers. For this reason, this section introduces the primary concepts in functional programming and the next section presents an example language based upon these ideas. There are many functional languages in use at present and, consequently, there are slight differences in syntax and in emphasis. Here, when specifics are required, the model adopted for the Haskell language [49] will be employed; Haskell is a functional language that was designed as an internationally agreed language against which others could be compared.

Functional languages constitute one kind of *declarative* programming language in that they specify *what* is to be computed, not *how*. Declarative languages in general, and functional languages in particular, have the property of being *referential transparency*. This term means that an expression evaluates to the same value in every context. More specifically, it has the implication that an expression can always be substituted for its value everywhere that it occurs. For example, if we have:

$$e_1 = 2 + 2$$

and:

$$e_2 = 3 + e_1$$

then we can immediately find the value of e_2 by substituting the right-hand side of e_1 for its occurrence in e_2:

$$e_2 = 3 + 2 + 2$$

Referential transparency guarantees that substitutions like this can be performed in *all* cases. Another example is the familiar one from school mathematics books:

> "Let x be the number of apples and y be the number of oranges in a bath of water; let z be the number of toy (sic!) battleships. Let t be the total number of things in the bath. Write down an expression for t. If there are an equal number of apples and oranges and there are two battleships, how many apples and oranges are there if the bath contains twenty-six items."

So, we write:

$$t = x + y + z$$
$$z = 2$$
$$26 = 2 + (x + y)$$

Therefore:

$$
\begin{aligned}
24 &= (x + y) \\
&= (x + x) \quad \text{(say)} \\
&= 2x \\
&= 2 \times 12
\end{aligned}
$$

The problem is solved by substitution of values for variables. Once the value of the variable is known, it can be substituted into all the other expressions in which it appears.

The most significant implication of referential transparency is the following:

> *A functional program can be evaluated by substituting expressions for the values they denote.*

In the case of functions, the expression which defines the function is substituted for the function symbol. The arguments to the function are evaluated and substituted in a similar fashion. The time at which evaluation of arguments takes place can vary, as will be discussed below. However, the general principle (the one which applies in abstract cases without reference to computers) is the above.

The substitution principle stated above has profound implications for functional programs. It implies that there is no need to maintain a state for a functional program. Procedural programs have variables which can be updated at any time; they use iterative constructs in the form of loops. In procedural languages, there must be a *state* (often represented by the contents of the store during execution) which is updated by the operations of the program (variable assignments). The state of the program changes through time because of thcsc updates. Functional programs contain variables which cannot be updated once they are bound to a value. This implies that variables are *placeholders* for values, just as the substitution principle suggests.

The substitution principle and, more generally, referential transparency, imply that the functional programs have a simpler semantics than do procedural ones. In particular, the semantics does not have to deal with the program's state. The proof rules for a functional language are also simpler for that reason; indeed, the proof rules are just the program's text plus a few mathematical principles such as substitution and various forms of induction. The programmer can argue that a program meets its specification by means of simpler processes than the "mental execution" [7] of loops and assignments (when arguing about procedural code, the programmer has to follow loops around, verifying that variables hold the expected values, and so on—these are operations that impose considerable "cognitive load" and are, therefore, mentally taxing and subject to error). Indeed, substitution and various forms of induction are typically employed in informal reasoning about functional programs.

Sometimes, substitution is interpreted as a *reduction* process. This is because the complexity of an expression is reduced by each substitution. Because functional programs rest upon recursion, not iteration, substitution becomes a little more complex. In effect, substitutions must be delayed until the recursion comes to an end (one can think of the substitutions being placed on a stack until the base case is encountered and its substitution performed).

A modern functional program is based on the idea that a computation can be expressed as a set of *recursion equations*, each equation defining a relationship between inputs and outputs. A *recursion equation* is an equation that can define a recursive function. Functional languages employ variable binding constructs, function calling and recursion.

The general form for a function definition is one or more equations of the form:

$$f(x) = e$$

where f is the name of the function, x is the argument to the function, and e is an arbitrary expression. In the case of recursive function, the cases are divided, thus:

$$f(x_1) = e_1$$
$$f(x_2) = e_2$$

where the expression evaluated is either e_1 or e_2 depending upon the form (or value) of the argument to f. If the argument to f has the form or value x_1, e_1 is evaluated to produce the result; if it has the form or value x_2, e_2 is evaluated. The precise sense in which "the form or value" of an argument is to be interpreted is explained below.

In order for the definition of f to be recursive, one of the e_i must contain a call to f. Thus, the following is a recursive call:

$$f(x) = \ldots f(v) \ldots$$

The development of recursive functions is often based upon *induction principles* which frequently take the form of a base case and an induction step. The factorial function can be written as:

$$f(n) = 1, n = 1$$
$$f(n) = n * (n - 1), n > 1$$

The expressions to the right of the comma are conditionals (side-conditions). If the expression to the right of the comma evaluates to *true*, the expression to the left of the comma is evaluated as the value of the function body. If the expression to the right of the comma evaluates to *false*, the following equation is evaluated. If there is no following equation, an error should result. The above pair of equations is therefore equivalent to:

```
f(n) = if n = 1 then 1 else n * (n - 1) endif
```

This alternative style, one in which equations are replaced by conditionals is also relatively common. In this style, there is one conditional branch for each equation in a set of recursion equations.

The recursive style is standard for functional programming (for more examples, see [19] or [45].

Functional programming is directly based upon the typed λ-calculus. All functional programs can be directly re-written as expressions in the λ-calculus. Functional programs inherit the concept of *free* and *bound* variables from the λ-calculus.

Let := be a new symbol in the λ-calculus to define functions. A simple recursion equation:

$$f(x) = e$$

can be written as:

$$f := \lambda x.e$$

A conditional expression can be introduced into the λ-calculus as a new primitive written as:

$$c \rightarrow e_1, e_2$$

where c is the conditional expression (evaluating to a truth value or Boolean), e_1 is the expression which is evaluated if c evaluates to *true*, and e_2 is evaluated if c evaluates to *false*.

With this λ-calculus conditional, a set of recursion equations of the form:

$$f(x_1) = e_1$$
$$f(x_2) = e_2$$

can be written in our enriched λ-calculus as:

$$f := \lambda x.x = x_1 \to e_1,$$
$$x = x_2 \to e_2$$

B.2.1 Control Structures and Semantics

Functional programs are based upon the concepts of *application* and *composition*. Both of these concepts are also the foundation of the λ-calculus.

Application is the process of supplying a function with its actual parameters. Given a function, *add1*, say, the expression:

$$add1(2)$$

is called the *application of the function to its arguments*. The application of a function to its arguments causes the evaluation of the function using those arguments (application is similar to function call in procedural languages). In order to evaluate a functional program, values must be supplied to the program's functions.

Composition is an operation which applies to functions. Given two functions, f and g, the composition, h, is written:

$$h = g \circ f$$

which can be defined in terms of application as:

$$h(x) = g(f(x))$$

This can be interpreted as follows. First, f is applied to x to yield a result to which g is then applied. Thus, if $f(x) = a$, for some arbitary a, then $h(x) = g(a)$. Composition is a way of constructing more complex functions from simpler ones.

Given that it rests upon the simpler operation of application, it can easily be introduced into a functional language. In a functional language, the composition of two functions is often expressed by application as in the last equation. However, it is also possible to define a new function which is the composition of two other functions in one of a number of ways. In a functional language explicitly providing *lambda* expressions, it is possible to write:

```
h = lambda x => g(f(x))
```

In languages lacking this expression, it is written as:

```
h = gf
```

In each case, the function is considered to be *higher-order*. In the case of explicit *lambda* expression, the evaluation of h returns the *lambda* expression which can then be applied to an argument of its own. In the second case, the combined function **gf** is returned when h is evaluated; the combined function is still a function and can be applied to an argument of its own to compute a value. This is the first use of higher-order functions that will be encountered.

There are constraints upon both composition and on application. In particular, the expressions formed by composition and application must be well-typed (i.e., have correct type assignments). Similarly, if a function is of type $A \rightarrow B$, it can only be applied to objects of type A. It will produce values of type B. For composition, the following holds. If f is a function from type A to type B, written as $f : A \rightarrow B$, and $g : B \rightarrow C$, the composition gf is well-typed and has the type $A \rightarrow C$. If f had a type $A \rightarrow B'$, where $B \neq B'$, the composition cannot be formed because it would be ill-typed.

The λ-calculus provides recursion as a control structure (usually this is expressed in terms of the **Y** combinator, see [48]). Let f be a recursive function defined as follows:

$$f(x) = \ldots f(x') \ldots$$

The following λ-expression is one possible form of the previous one:

$$f := \lambda x.\mathbf{Y}(\ldots f(x') \ldots)$$

where the **Y** combinator takes a λ expression as its argument and converts it into a recursive call. The transformation involves converting the expression within brackets into a form based on *self-application* (i.e., the application of a function to itself).

B.2.2 Evaluation Strategies

The relationship between the λ-calculus and functional programming is fundamental. The λ-calculus has two ways of converting expressions, both of which are based upon a mechanism resembling simplification.

The first of the conversion methods is identical to *call by value*: the arguments to a function are evaluated before they are passed to the function's body. Call by value is called *applicative-order* evaluation. Thus, given the following function application:

$$f(2 + 3)(4 + 5)$$

call by value will first evaluate $(2 + 3)$ to 5 and then $(4 + 5)$ to give 9. Once evaluted, the above expression becomes:

$$f\,5\,9$$

and the evaluation of f can proceed.

The other form is called *normal-order evaluation*. It works as follows. Assume a function f such that:

$$f := \lambda x.\lambda y.e(\ldots x \ldots y)$$

So, f is a function which uses the values represented by x and y in its body (presumably as arguments to the expression e). Under normal-order evaluation, the argument expressions are passed *unevaluated* into the function. Given the application of f to arguments $(2+3)$ and $(4+5)$, the above λ-expression therefore becomes:

$$e(\ldots (2+3) \ldots (4+5))$$

Normal-order evaluation does not suffer from some of the problems from which applicative-order evaluation (call by value) suffers. Under call by value, the function f will not be evaluated if one of its arguments causes an error or if the evaluation of one of its arguments fails to terminate. Thus, if f is called:

$$f(1+2)(2/0)$$

the division by zero will cause an error, so f will not be evaluated. Similarly, if g is defined by:

$$g(x) = g(x+1)$$

the call:

$$f\,1\,(g(2))$$

will fail to terminate and f will not be evaluated. The reasons for these problems is that applicative-order evaluation evaluates its arguments.

One interpretation of normal-order evaluation is that it delays the evaluation of the arguments to a function until they are required. This means that argument expressions should not be evaluated prior to being passed into the body of a function. The point at which the expression is evaluated depends upon the body.

Some functions require their arguments to be fully evaluated before they can be applied. The arithmetic and logical functions are in this class. Thus:

$$x+y$$

requires both x and y to be fully evaluated to some form of number before $+$ can be applied to them to produce a result. Similarly,

$$b_1 \wedge b_2$$

requires both b_1 and b_2 to be fully evaluated to Boolean values before $\wedge$ can be applied; an identical constraint is imposed by $<$, $\leq$, and the other relational operations.

There are, however, contexts in which a function does not require all of its arguments to be fully evaluated. Consider the conditional expression defined above. Given:

$$c \rightarrow a_1, a_2$$

it should be clear that c must be fully evaluated because a Boolean value is required before the appropriate expression can be chosen for evaluation. If c evaluates to *true*, a_1 will be evaluated; if c evaluates to *false*, a_2 will be evaluated. However, it is the case that *only one* of the a_i is evaluated once c has been evaluated. This immediately suggests that if the a_i contain references to arguments passed to the function in which the conditional appears, those arguments need only be evaluated *after* the condition expression c has been evaluated.

A further example permits the introduction of list notation. Many functional languages have lists as a primitive data type. Literal lists (i.e., lists written as literal values) are written as:

$$[e_1, e_2, e_3, \ldots]$$

where the e_i are elements of the list; the elements must be of the same type, unlike list elements in LISP and Prolog. The empty list is written as: []. Every list has the empty list as its final element (this property permits inductive proofs).

Lists can be constructed by use of the *cons* (or *constructor*) function. This function takes an element as its first argument and a list (possibly the empty list) as its second argument. The *cons* function is written as '::' as follows:

$$1 :: []$$

(Note that *cons* is an infix function like the arithmetics). This function application returns a list of one element of the form:

$$[1]$$

The application of *cons* to its arguments is commonly referred to as "consing". The application of *cons* to a non-empty list:

$$1 :: [2, 3]$$

produces the following list:

$$[1, 2, 3]$$

Most languages provide built-in functions to operate on lists. In particular, *null*, which tests for the empty list.

Now, assume an expression, e, and a list, l. If it is desired to *cons* e onto l, as in:

$$e :: l$$

It is not necessary to evaluate e until the first element of the list represented by $e :: l$ is required. The reason for this is that the list can be passed as the unevaluated form represented by $e :: l$ until the value represented by e is required. Many other data constructing operations are similar to *cons* in this respect.

Functions which do not require the evaluation of all of their arguments are said to be *lazy*. A more general term covering evaluation schemes in which evaluation is not performed until values are required is *delayed* evaluation. Functions requiring the evaluation of all of their arguments are said to be *eager*.

Lazy evaluation is one way to implement normal-order reduction. An early attempt to implement normal-order reduction was *call by name* in Algol-60. When an argument was passed by call by name, a procedure was created of no arguments and whose body was formed from the argument; if the argument's value was needed, the procedure was evaluated to yield that value, otherwise the procedure was passed into other procedures using call by name. The procedures of no arguments were called "thunks". There are problems with call by name. It requires the construction of new procedures and it is not always possible to determine which expression will constitute an argument until runtime.

The concept of the thunk was re-introduced in Scheme [26]. In Scheme, there are two functions called `force` and `delay` which implement a delayed evaluation scheme. The programmer has to apply these functions by hand for the Scheme compiler is only able to perform call by value parameter passing. If the programmer wishes to delay the evaluation of an expression e, they write:

```
(delay e)
```

and to force the evaluation of the delayed expression, it is necessary to write:

```
(force e)
```

The result of (delay e) is often called a *promise*; as far as the Scheme evaluator is concerned, promises are ordinary data types, so can be passed and returned like any other data type. When the value of the delayed expression is not required, the promise is just passed to other expressions.

Lazy evaluation is the standard method for evaluating functional programs. There are many ways to implement lazy evaluation:

- lazy template instantiation;
- combinator reduction;
- supercombinator reduction.

The first is a form of direct implementation of the λ-calculus in which each construct is represented by a direct analogue. The reduction process attempts to imitate the reduction operations of the λ-calculus. Combinators, on the other hand, are an algebraic representation of computable functions that is equivalent to the λ-calculus; the primary difference between combinators and λ-calculus is that the latter has variables whereas the former does not. The original attempt at an algebra of combinators was undertaken by Curry (see [48] for a more recent account) who showed that all functions can be reduced to four basic combinators: **S** (distribution), **K** (head), **I** (identity) and **Y** (self-reference)—the last, the so-called "paradoxical" combinator, is needed to represent recursion. Supercombinators were introduced by Hughes [50] as a representation of computer functions without reducing them completely to combinatory logic. Supercombinators can be derived from any λ-expression by appropriately defining the free variables it contains. Much work has been done on supercombinators as an implementation method (see [70] for more details).

All of these evaluation methods handle higher-order functions properly. Unfortunately, the details of these evaluation methods cannot be covered here. The reader is advised to consult one of the standard references, for example [70, 71, 37]. For the remainder of this chapter, lazy evaluation will be assumed. Lazy evaluation is important because it *delays the evaluation of some of the arguments to functions*. This can have profound consequences for object-oriented languages.

B.2.3 Higher-Order Functions

Higher-order functions have been encountered when considering the composition operation, defined by:

$$f \circ g := \lambda x.g(fx)$$

This is a higher-order function and can be applied to any pair of functions which satisfy the type constraint defined above. Higher-order functions are extremely useful and somewhat complex; as will be seen, they are of considerable utility to the mixed language that will be described below.

A higher-order function is a function which either takes a function as its input or produces a function as its output. Composition is just one such function. Composition takes two functions as input and returns (evaluates to) a function which is their composition. The composition function can be generalized so that it takes a third argument, the extra argument being a function which is the method by which the functions are to be composed. This generalized function is still higher-order; indeed, it takes *three* functions (one of which might itself be a higher-order function) as arguments and evaluates to a function which is their composition with respect to the third argument:

$$\circ_m(f, g, m) := \lambda x.(m(f, g))(x)$$

Some might argue that higher-order functions can always be replaced by first-order functions with recursion; it is also argued that higher-order functions cause programs to slow even further. The first argument is undoubtedly true, but higher-order functions afford a welcome increase in expressive power and they permit recursion to be removed to a considerable extent. A fuller treatment of higher-order functions has been relegated to this point in the chapter because of these negative arguments.

Here, some useful higher-order functions will be defined and explained. The aim of this subsection is to familiarize the reader with an aspect of functional programming that is often considered hard or obscure.

A classic example of a higher-order function, is the *twice* function which applies its functional argument twice. If the function *add1* is defined as the function which adds one to its argument, *twice(add1,x)* will call *add1* twice on *x*. The *twice* function can be defined as:

$$twice(f, x) = f(f(x))$$

This is an example of a higher-order function which just takes a function as its input. If the *add1* function is substituted for f and 2 is substituted for x, the following is obtained:

$$add1(add1(2))$$

Substituting the definition of *add1* gives:

$$add1((\lambda x.(x + 1))2)$$

followed by:

$$add1(2 + 1) \Rightarrow add1(3)$$

Again, substituting:

$$(\lambda x.(x + 1))(3) \Rightarrow 3 + 1 \Rightarrow 4$$

(where $\Rightarrow$ is the evaluation function). This sequence shows how *twice* works and also shows its correctness.

Higher-order functions can be used in highly effective ways with lists. The standard way to operate on a list is to write recursive functions that iterate over each element of the list. Writing such functions can be extremely tedious.

If higher-order functions are available, the function which returns the list composed of the results of applying a function to every element of a list can easily be defined:

$$map(f, []) = [] \quad map(f, (h :: t)) = f(h) :: map(f, t)$$

Here, the notation based upon cases has been employed, the choice as to which equation to evaluate is based upon the form that the second argument takes. If the second argument, the list, takes the form of the second argument in line one ([] or the empty list), the empty list is returned. If the second argument takes the form of $(h :: t)$, a list whose first element (or *head*) is h and whose *tail* (the rest of the list) is t, the second equation is evaluated (it is possible that t can be empty). The evaluation of the second equation consists of applying the first argument to *map*, f, to the head of the list ($f(h)$) and consing that onto a *recursive* call to *map*. The recursive call applies *map* to f and the rest of the list (the tail represented by t). If the input list, l, (the second argument to *map*) is:

$$[v_1, v_2, \ldots]$$

The result list computed by $map(f, l)$ will be:

$$[f(v_1), f(v_2), \ldots]$$

The termination of this function is easy to show. If the input list is empty, the first equation is selected and the function terminates. If the input list has a length greater than zero, the second equation will be chosen for each successive element. With each selection of the second equation, the length of the list is reduced by one and t is bound to the rest of the list (the tail). Each time the second equation is chosen for evaluation, the length of the tail decreases by one. Eventually, the length of the tail will be zero and the first equation will be chosen. Thus, the function terminates.

Many other useful higher-order functions can be defined over lists, for example:

- the function which tests that every element of the list satisfies some property;
- the function that tests that some element of the list satisfies some property;
- the function that applies a binary operator to a list reducing it to a single value (there is another version which applies the operator from the end of the list to the front).

These functions and the others which can be defined have the effect of removing recursion from programs. Instead of reasoning about the application of a function to every element of a list, for example, one need only reason about the input function and the input and output lists. The other functions that can be defined similarly relieve the programmer of the need to engage in large amounts of induction.

Functional programs, like the λ-calculus, are *lexically* scoped. Free variables in a function take the values which are defined for them at the lexical point of definition of that function. This is exactly the same rule as in Pascal, C and Scheme. When functions are passed as arguments or returned as values, they are converted into *closures* in many implementations. A closure is a reference to the function plus an *environment* which records the values of all of the free variables in the function. The manipulation of closures ensures that all free variables have the correct interpretation. (When functional programs are compiled into supercombinators or **SK** combinators, free variables can be eliminated, thus eliminating the need for closures; under these schemes, functions are passed and returned as references.)

Higher-order functions also have an additional use. They can be used to create *partial* applications of functions. A partial application is an application of a function to a subset of its arguments; the result is a function. For example, the *addn* function can be defined as:

$$addn(x, n) := x + n$$

To obtain the same effect as *add1*, the following could be written:

$$addn(x, 1)$$

This will add 1 to x. However, writing the above is somewhat less convenient than calling *add1*. The *add1* function can be derived from *addn* in the following way:

$$add1 := \lambda x.addn(x, 1)$$

This is a function which returns a function. The returned function has a body in which the first argument to *addn* remains variable, but the second is fixed as 1.

Partial application is a way of specializing general functions. It works by fixing one or more of the arguments to the general function while keeping the remaining ones as variable. Partial application can be used in many contexts; they also have application in mixed-paradigm languages.

B.2.4 Hindley-Milner Type Inference

Functional programming languages are typically strongly typed, just as Pascal, Ada, C++ and many other languages are. Most modern functional languages are also polymorphic in a sense not encountered in object-oriented languages. Furthermore, most functional programs do not contain—need not contain, indeed—type declarations. These two properties are a consequence of the type inference system that is employed.

The Hindley-Milner inference type system is able to infer the types of functions and variables from the context in which they appear. The type inference system works by forming sets of equations about the types concerned and then solving those equations. The details of the inference system can be found in many books on functional programming, for example [70]. The most important aspect of this for present purposes is that, in many cases, it obviates the need for type associations because they are automatically inferred.

A second consequence is that polymorphism is introduced. It is possible to write functions whose input types are not specified but are considered to be polymorphic in the sense that *any* type will be satisfactory. For example, many list operations deal with the structure of lists, not with the elements that form the lists. The function which computes the length of a list is one such function. It can be defined by:

$$len := \lambda l.l = [] \rightarrow 0, 1 + len(tl(l))$$

Here, the contents of the list are not relevant. Thus, lists that are composed of any type are admissible as an argument. Many functions operating on the *structure* of data and which do not transform the values contained by those structures are polymorphic; any type which admits the operations applied by the function is admissible as an argument to such a function.

The higher-order function *map* introduced above is polymorphic. It accepts lists composed of any type as inputs; this then constrains the type of function admissible as the first argument. If the polymorphic list type is denoted by $list(\alpha)$, where α denotes any type, the function appearing as the first argument must have type $\alpha \rightarrow \beta$, where β denotes any type—β *can* be the same type as α. So if α is the integer type, if f doubles the value of its argument, α and β will be the same type; if α is the character type and f converts lower case to upper case, leaving all other characters unaffected, α and β will be the same type. If, on the other hand, α is the integer type and f computes the square root of the absolute value of its argument, β will denote the real type. (These examples, incidentally, indicate how type inference operates.)

B.2.5 Syntactic Sugar

This section ends with the introduction of three constructs which are aimed at making λ-expressions easier to write. Each construct introduces local variables into functions; one introduces local recursive functions. Two of the constructs are top-down in nature, while the third, which is introduced last, is bottom-up.

The first construct is the *let* construct. It has the form:

```
let  < binds > in <exp>endlet
```

where *binds* takes the form of a sequence of variable bindings, each of which has the form:

$$var \;=\; exp;$$

where *var* is the name of a variable and *exp* is any expression. There is a restriction on *exp* however, for it cannot define a recursive function. The reason for this will become clear when a more formal account of the semantics of *let* expressions is given.

A *let* expression is evaluated as follows. The expressions in the bindings (*binds*) are evaluated to produce values which are then bound to the variables (*vars*). Then the expression between the *in* and the *endlet* (the *body* of the *let*) is evaluated to produce a result. Thus, given:

```
let v1 = 1;
    v2 = 2;
in
  v1 + v2
endlet
```

the expressions 1 and 2 are evaluated. Then they are bound to their respective variables, so v1 is bound to 1 and v2 is bound to 2. Then the body (v1 + v2) is evaluated yielding 3. This process is exactly the same as if:

$$(\lambda v_1.(\lambda v_2.v_1 + v_2))(1)(2)$$

had been written. Indeed, this is the correct translation of the *let* expression.

The equivalence between *let* and λ-expressions also shows why recursive functions cannot be defined using *let*. The reason is that the name of a recursive function must be known during the evaluation of its body so that a call can be made to itself. In *let* expressions, the name is unavailable. A *let* expression can define local functions *provided* that they are *not* recursive.

This constraint leads to the *letrec* construct. It has the same form as *let*:

letrec <*binds*> in <*exp*> endlet

where *binds* is as above. Here, the local bindings (*binds*) can define recursive functions.

Both *let* and *letrec* are both bottom-up constructs requiring local variables to be known prior to the writing of the expression in which they occur. The *where* expression is a top-down construct:

<*exp*> where <*binds*>

where *binds* is as above. Here, the main expression appears first and the auxilliary definitions come after. A concrete example is:

```
v1 + v2
where v1 = 1;
      v2 = 2;
```

It is clear that the main expression is defined first and the auxilliaries come after.

The *where* expression permits the definition of local functions of any kind, including recursive ones. Thus, it is possible to write:

```
map(f,l)
where f([]) = []
      f(h :: t) = f1(h) :: f(t);
```

The *where* expression is identical in semantics to the *letrec* expression. The semantics can be defined in terms of a two-stage mapping involving rewriting into *let* expressions. The expansion for *letrec* is given (the reader can supply the corresponding *where* expansion). One version of this is as follows. Given:

```
letrec v1 = e1;
       v2 = e2;
in
  v1 + v2;
endlet
```

```
let v1 = **a1**;
    v2 = **a2**;
 in
 v1 := e1;
 v2 := e2;
 v1 + v2
endlet
```

The transformation continues by transforming the *lets* just derived into a *lambda* expression as given above.

The transformation of *letrec* into *let* just given has as its aim the declaration of the variables bound by the *letrec*. These variables can refer to recursive functions and, thus, must be in scope when the body of the function is defined. However, if a simple *let* is employed, the variable name is not in scope because the function body is evaluated before it is bound to the variable (recall the transformation to a *lambda* expression). The above scheme first binds arbitrary expressions (ideally, expressions which have no meaning and which would cause an error if they were ever to be involved in "proper" expression) to the local variables. Then, the programmer-defined expressions (the e_i) are *assigned* to the v_i. This is, therefore, a transformation which a user cannot perform.

There are transformations which are entirely declarative. Paton-Jones [70] describes some declarative transformations in detail. Apart from the fact that the above transformation employs side effects, the difference between his approach and ours is that his description is couched in terms of pattern expressions.

B.3 An Impure Language

In this section, we describe a mixed-paradigm language based upon functional and class-based programming. The language is *im*pure, so it will be possible to write functional programs and ignore the object-oriented component if the programmer so desires.

The aim here is to present a simple language based upon class-based programming. The reason for being simple is that there will be fewer concepts and, therefore, a better opportunity to explore the alternatives. In some ways, the language is conservative because this will allow us to employ relatively well-understood constructs.

We do not pretend that the language design presented in this section is anything more than an example. There will be issues that we cannot treat in detail for lack of space and time. There will be aspects of the language that are inelegant and there will certainly be constructs which are missing (e.g., exceptions). The decisions as to what to include and what to exclude are open to revision in any case (mixed-paradigm languages are, in a sense, experimental). I do hope, however, that the design which is presented below has some measure of consistency and that it can be used as a programming language.

It is instructive to begin with an impure language because it will allow us to compare the result with functional programming and with such popular object-oriented languages as C++. Furthermore, should the combined language prove deficient in some respects, it will still remain possible to produce solutions to problems using a more functional/object-oriented than purely object-oriented fashion. Furthermore, given the novelty of mixed-paradigm languages, they might be viewed, in some quarters, as competition for the equally novel functional language concept.

I will first outline the object-oriented component of the language and then move on to the functional part. The functional component is relatively straightforward and conventional. In the object-oriented part, I will identify classes with types. This will assist the definition of the functional part and help in addressing some painful issues.

B.3.1 The Object-Oriented Component

My intention is to keep the object-oriented component relatively simple; I intend to use the better understood constructs.

First, I have decided to make the language class based. The reason for this is that class-based languages are relatively well understood while prototype-based ones are less so. In addition, it will be easier to compare the strengths and weaknesses of our language with a larger body of languages than would be the case if we had chosen prototypes as a basis for the language. When we compare the impure and pure versions of the language, we will consider the prototypes versus classes issue again. For the meanwhile, we concentrate on classes.

A class is defined by a class structure which is composed of a set of slot definitions plus an inheritance specification. In some languages, the $Te\Lambda o\Sigma$ object-oriented component of Eulisp [69] contains slots for specifying the meta class, the constructor function for the class and a predicate for testing whether objects are instances of the type defined by the class. We will restrict ourselves to the more conventional form; class definitions consist of inheritance and slot specifications. We will consider them in that order.

As has been shown above, multiple inheritance is problematic. It is extremely hard to find an account of it which is suitable for all cases; the concept of multiple inheritance is essentially difficult and imposes an additional overhead when attempting to decide how to define a class and decide what is inherited. As a consequence, it has been decided to employ simple inheritance *only*. Simple (or single) inheritance has a simple semantics and simple verification conditions. Each class only has one superclass and there is a simple ancestor sequence through which to search when looking for slots and methods.

The choice of simple inheritance raises questions, as has been seen, about how multiple views of an object can be represented or how an object can be classified in many different ways. These are part of the rationale for multiple inheritance, but, as has been argued above, multiple inheritance does not, in reality, provide good responses to these challenges. I will consider these issues again at the end of this chapter when I review both mixed-paradigm languages.

The specification of the slots in a class also impacts upon the way in which they are accessed. In particular, there is a distinction between slots which are directly accessible and those which can be accessed *only* via reader and writer functions (accessor functions or accessor methods, in general terms). If a language provides accessor functions, the slots upon which they operate can all be made private to the class in which they are defined. This pushes the visibility problem back one stage for it now reduces the visibility question to that of the visibility of the accessor functions. If accessor functions are adopted, the way in which they interact with inheritance must be considered.

The concept of decoupling slots from the ways in which they are accessed appears to be a useful concept. In languages which employ accessor functions, it is possible to define one set of names for internal use and another for external use. Thus, slots can be given names that are meaningful within the context of the class and its methods, but can be accessed using functions that do not have the same name. The Dylan language, for example, allows the internal name to be the default for the external name. Under such a scheme, a slot named `foo` inside a class has a default reader function called `foo` and a default writer function called `set-foo!`. Accessor functions are best considered as system-defined methods so that they can be handled in exactly the same way.

An example of a slot definition together with its accessor methods is:

```
slot s : int, reader: read-s, writer: set-s!
```

Even if slots are manipulated using accessor methods, the question still remains as to whether a distinction between levels of visibility is provided. Given that encapsulation is a primary aspect of object-oriented programming, it appears to make very good sense to distinguish between those slots which are private to a class and those which are visible. Such a distinction is valid for a class when considered in isolation but it can lead to problems when considered in the context of an inheritance structure. Public slots are visible to *all*, no matter what they are. C++ and Java recognize the need to restrict visibility to the subclasses of a class. The advantages are clear; the converse is that the relationship between classes is more complex. Ideally, there should be a distinction between interface and implementation. For this reason, we will only make a distinction between public and private slot access methods.

Slots will be considered entirely private and their access methods will have their visibility controlled. As far as the programmer is concerned, there will be no distinction because slots will be marked as *private* or *public*. Initially, we will not introduce a *protected* restriction. Methods will be divided into private and public as well. The default will be for slots to be *private*.

An example public slot definition is:

```
public slot s : int, reader: read-s;
```

A private slot might be defined as:

```
private slot sc : char, reader: read-sc, writer: set-sc!;
```

The access methods in an impure language can be considered to be ordinary functions. If we were to adopt the *multi-method* approach as in Dylan, Cecil and CLOS, we would need to have global variables to hold the method dispatch tables. If we have a pure language, we would need to store the access methods in the method tables associated with objects because there are no global variables in a pure language, nor are there functions which are not associated with a class.

For the remainder of this chapter, an *ordinary* function is one that is not defined as a method in a class. Ordinary functions are global in the sense that they are not defined within the scope of a class. Functions which are also methods, which we will simply call *methods* or sometimes *method functions*, are also distinguished from ordinary functions by the automatic insertion of an extra formal parameter in their parameter list; the new parameter will always appear first in the parameter list and will refer to the object on which the method is called. The first parameter of every method is the *self* reference which allows the method to access the objects of the class in which it is defined.

An important issue is that we do not want access methods to clash with any other functions (this can happen if the name of an access method is the same as an ordinary function). Furthermore, it would be extremely unfortunate to define an access method and then, by error, define an ordinary function with the same name, thus over-riding the access function. If we adopt something like the method tables encountered in Smalltalk, many of these problems are removed because the name of an access method becomes localized to the class in which it is defined. If methods are localized, it matters not whether another access method with the same name is defined in another class.

Many languages like Smalltalk, CLOS and Dylan introduce an explicit distinction between class and instance variables (data slots). In CLOS and Dylan, this is handled by a slot parameter specifying the allocation of the slot; slots can be allocated on a per-class or per-instance basis. Smalltalk makes a syntactic separation between class and instance variables—they are defined in different sections of the class definition (an identical approach is taken in LOOPS). Java and C++ allow a once per class allocation by declaring a slot to be *static*. The question which faces us is whether to include class variables into our language (it is assumed that instance variables will, as a matter of course, be included).

There are arguments for and against class variables. One argument against them is that they complicate the allocation of classes. Another is that they introduce communication between classes and their instances because class variables can be updated by special methods. Furthermore, they also open the way to a distinction between class and instance methods, a distinction that is found only in Smalltalk, a distinction that introduces new complexities in the runtime organization of the program. The first argument in favour of class variables is that they can be used to represent properties that hold of all instances. The example of motor vehicles is a case in point. The number of wheels of an arbitrary motor vehicle cannot be known until the kind of vehicle is known, but the number of wheels of a motor cycle or a motor tricycle is defined *a priori*. For the two latter cases, a class variable can be used to represent the number of wheels. However, given *write-once* (see below) or *constant* slots, the number of wheels can be set in the class definition without resorting to class variables. For the time being, and until the real need for class variables can be established, they will be omitted from the design of the mixed-paradigm language.

A distinction will be made between constant and mutable slots. Mutable slots are those which can be updated while constant slots can only be initialized. Slots which are declared to be constant are permitted only to have a reader method; should an attempt be made to define a writer method, an error will be raised. The name of the accessor methods will default to that given to the slot but with modification as appropriate. Therefore, following the Dylan convention mentioned above, if a slot is defined with the name foo, its reader method will be called foo and its writer method will be given the name set-foo!. The programmer will be permitted to give a more appropriate name to the reader and writer methods. The default is for slots to be *constant*.

A constant slot might be defined as follows:

```
constant slot ss : int = 2, reader: read-ss;
```

(Note that the declaration of a constant slot together with a writer method is an error—constant slots cannot have writer methods!) Whereas a mutable slot might be defined as:

```
slot s : char, writer: set-s!, reader: read-s;
```

The distinction between constant and mutable slots is extremely useful. It is not, however, the full story. For example, it is often extremely useful to define slots which are given a value when the object is created but which cannot thereafter be updated. One example of this is a slot which holds the size of an array. If the array is to be re-sized during the life of the object, a conventional mutable slot can be employed to hold the size. However, if the length of the array is to remain constant, there is an inherent risk if the length is held in a mutable slot. Clearly, the length of the array cannot always be determined at the time when the class is defined, so the programmer usually has to resort to the use of a mutable slot, making sure never to update it. The size slot must, of course, be private to the class in which it and the array are defined.

This argument leads us to introduce a new kind of constant slot. This new kind will be called a *write-once* slot. Only one value can be assigned to a write-once slot. There are no constraints on the time at which a write-once slot can be assigned a value. The only constraint is that once given a value, a write-once cannot be updated. In the array example, the array's size would be held in a write-once slot. When the object holding the array and its size are created, the size is assigned to the slot; the slot remains constant thereafter.

It might be desirable to alter a slot's read-write status. Most languages require a slot to maintain its status over time. However, what might be variable across an ancestor class might need to be fixed for a subclass. For example, a *MotorVehicle* class might have a slot to specify the number of wheels, but a *MotorCycle* class needs to fix that number at 2 (assuming that motor cycles are differentiated from combinations of motor cycle and side-car, if such combinations are encountered these days). This issue relates to the *redefinition* of slots and methods, and the allowable modifications that can override existing slots and methods.

Slot initialization is an aspect of class definition and instantiation. C++ provides no facilities for doing this and it is missed; Java, on the other hand, provides such facilities—indeed, some Java compilers demand variable initialization. The language being designed here would benefit from slot initialization. CLOS and Dylan allow slots to be initialized by literal expressions as well as functions that are called when an object is created (when the class is instantiated). We could write the two forms as $s := e$ and $s := f$ where s is the name of the slot, e is some expression that can be immediately evaluated (a literal value), and where f is some function which can be called to yield a value with which to initialize the slot s.

Initialisation of a slot with a literal expression is useful, but initialization using a function is more flexible; it allows arbitrary computation to be performed when instantiating the class. However, limitations are sometimes imposed on the functions used in slot initialization; in particular, it can be difficult to supply the right kind of parameter to an initialization function for there can be restrictions imposed on the form of the instance creation particularly if the instantiation function is automatically generated when the class is defined. When such restrictions are imposed, slots which *ought* to be constant must be represented by mutable slots so that a method can be called to set the slot to the correct value, not the value actually given by its initialization expression. The method used to perform this task is typically only called once and represents an unwanted addition to the namespace. Furthermore, this scheme forces a constant slot to be mutable. We therefore have a choice as to whether the instance creation function is allowed to be flexible in form, or alternative mechanisms for slot initialization are to be provided.

If constructor functions are defined by the user, as in C++ and Java, it is possible for the programmer to determine what the arguments are. The convention in these languages is that the constructor has the same name as the class. The alternative used in Dylan and CLOS is to use a general-purpose instantiation function called make. The make function can have any arguments the programmer chooses, so it is polyadic as well as being polymorphic. Of the two schemes, the author prefers the one adopted in C++ and Java, but with some extensions. In particular, the constructor function should be permitted to be higher-order; it should accept, at the very least, functions as arguments.

The burden of type definition falls upon the definer of an application's classes. It is necessary, however, to specify the built-in types for the language; some types are value types, while others will be containers. The choice of built-in type is not particularly important for the semantics of the language, but a well-chosen set makes programming easier. While considering types, it is also necessary to consider the issue of polymorphism and the role of generic types in the language.

The choice of built-in types (value types) is relatively easy because it is roughly the same as in other languages: boolean, character, integer, floating point (in some form), and string. I will permit two string types: fixed length and variable length. I will also introduce an empty type which corresponds to void in the C family and to unit in the ML family [42, 43]. This will be the type used to represent a parameter list of length zero and to represent the type of a function which returns only a useless value. This empty type will be called *unit*. Each of the value types will be represented by a class, so a value of the appropriate type will be considered an instance of its class (this is the approach adopted by CLOS, Dylan, Eulisp and Java) because it introduces the basic types into the inheritance structure.

Enumeration and subrange types are not included at this point. It is unclear as to how they relate to the main class-based representation of types. The subrange type appears to fit better into a class-based type system because it is based upon the idea of constraining a supertype. Enumeration types are based upon enumerating instances of a type; the enumerated instances might bear no relation to each other apart from being arbitrarily associated in the enumeration. Constants representing the minimum and maximum integer values will be included, as will mapping functions between character and integer types.

In addition to these simple types, some container types are required. Functional languages often introduce pair and list types. Lists are polymorphic and can be instantiated so that they contain elements of a particular, often monomorphic, type. Pairs are permitted to contain pairs as elements, so can represent triples, 4-tuples, and so on—they are also polymorphic. Pairs are often written as comma separated values within parentheses, as in:

$$(x, y)$$

It is permitted for a pair to contain other pairs, as in:

$$(x, (y, (z_1, z_2)))$$

or in:

$$(((x, y), z_1), z_2)$$

It is necessary to remind the reader that:

$$(x, (y, (z_1, z_2))) \neq (((x, y), z_1), z_2)$$

Pairs and lists are frequently encountered in functional languages. However, vectors and arrays are also extremely useful, but they represent structures which support side-effects, and this does not fit into the functional paradigm very well. Mapping functions between strings and lists will be provided as standard.

Arrays and vectors (vectors are one-dimensional arrays) are polymorphic in the sense that they contain elements of any type, but, once the element type is fixed, the elements must all be of the same type. There is no problem with reading the contents of an array or vector, nor is there any problem with iterating over the elements. The problem comes when such a structure needs to be updated. Associative tables are also an extremely useful type. Again, they are polymorphic in the same sense as vectors and arrays. The problem which they present is exactly the same as that presented by vectors and arrays; they require update operations.

It is possible to implement these classes using system primitives. We can implement them using an assignment operation which is then represented by an accessor method. It is necessary, here as in the case of slot writer methods, to determine what should be returned from such a method. This is necessary because all functions must return a value of some type, even if it is the unit (empty) type.

The definition of the vector, array and table types, as well as the definition of the list and pair types, requires the language to support generics and, therefore, type parameters must be supported for classes. This, we believe, improves the flexibility of the language. The programmer will be permitted to write generic classes and to instantiate them to form concrete types. If generic types are part of the language, the container classes which have just been discussed become ordinary classes with few special properties. This allows them to form the nucleus of a set of container classes, each of which can be generic.

The general form of a generic type declaration is:

```
defclass FOO[Tyvar] =
```

where FOO is the name of the new class and Tyvar is a formal type parameter; if there is more than one formal type parameter, they are separated by commas, as in:

```
defclass FOO1[Tvar1,Tvar2,...] =
```

Note that these class definitions do not have supertypes. Supertypes, in this language, are specified by the identifier following a colon and before the equality sign in the definition, as in:

```
defclass foo : bar =
```

which defines class foo to have a superclass bar.

Consideration of generic classes leads to consideration of polymorphism in the language. Functional languages very often permit polymorphism; it has been seen that polymorphism is essential in object-oriented programming. As noted above, the inclusion of a root class in a language is something of an advantage. Following Smalltalk, Eiffel, CLOS, Dylan and Java, we will include a root class and call it *Object*. Thus, it will be possible to declare formal parameters, return types and slots as being of type *Object*. Inclusion of the root class also reduces the work that must be done by generics because classes can use *Object* instead of a type parameter; type instantiation will be used when size or speed is an issue and where classes must be tied down to a particular representation. Declarations in terms of *Object* allow a kind of "don't care" polymorphism because any class in the system can be substituted for *Object* for the reason that *Object* is their ultimate ancestor.

Functional languages are usually very strongly typed. Strong typing eliminates a class of error from programs, and there seems to be no good reason to remove the strong typing discipline from this language. Therefore, method and function parameter types and return types will be required. The type of each slot must be declared when defining the class in which it resides. When there is insufficient information for a programmer to decide upon the actual type of a parameter, return type or slot type, the *Object* class can be specified. This scheme has the advantage that type checking can be performed and can be reasonably strict while still permitting the programmer to leave room for doubt. To make class definition easier, a forward declaration construct will be provided so that the compiler can be notified of the name, and, hence, existence, of a class, before it is defined.

Methods are represented by functions. Methods have formal parameters denoting their inputs and have a return type. The return type of a method can be any valid type. Methods can be general or they can perform access operations on slots. When a method is a slot reader function, it returns the type of the slot. When, on the other hand, a method is a slot writer function, it must be decided as to what its return type should be. There are two main cases:

- slot writer methods return the type of the slot;
- slot writer methods return unit type (no useful value).

Of the two, the first appears, *prima facie*, the better because it can be arranged for the writer method to return the value which it is storing in the slot. This can make for simpler code within methods and ordinary functions. This proposal is also consistent with the expression discipline. If a writer method returns the unit type, little useful computation can be performed on the value that it returns, so slot updates must be performed in ways that do not fall within the generally applicative structure of methods and ordinary functions.

Normally, it *can* appear:

- in declarations of variables within methods;
- as return types of messages; and
- as a class identifier.

It *cannot* be employed as:

- the type of an instance variable;
- the type of a formal parameter to a method;
- the actual parameter of a generic class.

Thus, *Same* provides a kind of "self-adjusting" covariance (Blaschek, private communication).

There is a need, even within a functionally based object-oriented language, for a construct which invokes methods higher in the inheritance structure. The two choices are the *inner* and *next-method* constructs. Of the two, the *inner* approach is based on the replacement of a special statement with a composition of statements. This amounts to the replacement of one element of a sequence by a new sequence. This approach seems, initially, to be more closely related to a statement-based approach. The *inner* statement takes the form:

$$S_1; S_2; \mathbf{inner}\ ; S_3;$$

If **inner** is bound to $S'_{21}; S'_{22}$, the overall result is:

$$S_1; S_2; S'_{21}; S'_{22}; S_3;$$

A sequence of which appears perfectly fine for a statement-based approach. Clearly, it is possible to define a pseudo-function called **inner** which can be inserted into a sequence of function applications. Such a definition poses problems. The function must be polymorphic (clearly), but it must also be a function of one argument. Thus, a considerable amount of input must be squeezed into a single argument—tupling and list operations immediately come to mind. These restrictions would appear overly constraining.

The methods are based on *next-method*, although a bottom-up approach appears to fit better with a functional approach. This is because it stands for a complete call to a higher method and is not constrained to appear as a component of a sequence of function applications. The *next-method* pseudo-function appears in CLOS and Dylan, both of which have a significant functional component. When *next-method* is employed, it can be called at any point within the body of the lower method. Thus, it can be called to bind a local variable within a *let* or *where*; it can be called at any point where its results can be consumed or bound for subsequent processing. This appears a more natural approach to calling higher methods. This language, therefore, adopts the *next-method* approach to calling methods higher in the inheritance structure.

Abstract classes will be included in the language. As noted above, abstract classes can serve as interfaces which can be inherited separately from implementations. Abstract methods will also be permitted; they will consist of the annotation *abstract* as a prefix to the definition of the method's header (name plus argument list). If a class contains at least one abstract method, it will be considered to be abstract and thus not amenable to instantiation. Abstract classes will normally be flagged with an annotation declaring them to be abstract; concrete classes have no annotations.

We will not permit the definition of nested or anonymous classes until we become convinced of their utility. As will be seen below, the functional component of the language is enriched with a construct which allows the local definition of classes akin to that used to define local constants, variables and functions. Nested functions have been discussed in previous chapters and, although they can be used to good effect, the visibility problems they incurr appear an over-complication at present. Similarly, anonymous classes serve merely as transient binding contexts; alternative constructs will be provided when the functional component is described.

Constants, variables and write-once constants can be defined outside of any class definition. Constants, variables and write-once constants can be of any type that is in scope at the point of definition.

Are functions types? This is an extremely interesting question. In functional languages, functional types are permitted. If functions are types, lists and sets, for example, can hold functions. When the type is explicitly introduced, function types are defined by relating domain and range (input and output) types. The following is a function type from τ to π:

$$\tau \to \pi$$

Following the convention employed in algebra and category theory, this will be referred to as an *arrow* type. In the current language, it is possible to define functions that map classes to classes, Thus, given that C_0 and C_1 are two (not necessarily distinct) classes, the following is the type of a valid function:

$$C_0 \to C_1$$

Methods can have much more complex signatures than this.

It is possible to answer the question in more than one way. First, functional types can be included in the language. They can be considered either to be similar to the built-in types and considered outside of the class system. Alternatively, they can be represented as classes, having an attribute which contains the functional (arrow) type. The problem with the second approach is that there is no clear sense in which functions can be classified. With the arrow type definition, there are clear relationships between arrow types. This suggests that the type system be divided into two main components:

- a class-based component dealing with objects, and
- a function-based component dealing with arrow types.

This, of course, divides the world into two parts.

On a pragmatic basis, it is extremely useful to have arrow types and to be able to store functions in object slots, and collect functions into tables and lists. On the other hand, there is the problem of the purity of the language, particularly when the language supports only single inheritance. The type variables required by Hindley-Milner type checking can be avoided because of the presence of the root class, so arrow types can be constrained to be monomorphic. Given that the language is impure, and given that this constraint can be imposed (thus simplifying the type checking process), arrow types will be included.

The next question to address is whether iterators are present in the language. The encapsulation facilities provided by object-oriented programming is something that should be prized and not thrown away without good cause. Iterators are an essential technique for performing operations while maintaining encapsulation. My proposal is to introduce a new method kind, one called an *iterator*. Iterator methods specify how to iterate over the elements of a container type. The approach to iterator methods adopted in Sather will be adopted here; iterator methods will be converted automatically into classes which can be instantiated on an independent basis. Thus, although strictly speaking encapsulation is violated by this, the compiler ensures that the programmer is not able to interfere with it in any way. This contrasts with the *friend* mechanism in C++ which we have already discussed and rejected above.

Finally, there is the question of how instances of classes are represented at runtime. For ease and uniformity of processing, they will be allocated in the heap and accessed via pointers. This is very much in line with the representations used in functional languages and the LISP family. The other approach is to permit allocation on the runtime stack as well as in the heap, as in C++ and Eiffel. In functional languages, variable references are almost invariably implemented in terms of heap pointers.

B.3.2 The Functional Component

Initially, the functional component will be defined in terms of those features we intend to include. I deal with issues such as type discipline and evaluation strategy when I have discussed the integration of the functional component with the object-oriented part.

The constructs which are to be included in the functional component are:

- function application;

- function composition;
- let, where and letrec expressions;
- explicit lambda expressions;
- conditional expressions;
- higher-order functions.

Variables and constants are also included. Constructor functions such as the ':: ' function used to construct lists are not yet included because we have not yet considered which types and which forms of type are included in the language as standard and which are included in libraries.

Of the above, the *conditional expression* might need a little explanation. This is an expression of the form:

$$if\ c\ then\ e_t\ else\ e_f$$

This expression is equivalent to the full conditional found in most programming languages, but returns a result. The result returned is the result of evaluating e_t if c evaluates to *true*, or the result of evaluating e_f if c evaluates to *false*. The *else* part must always be present when a conditional expression is written.

Conditional expressions are used instead of the comma-based notation used in Haskell and discussed above. The reason for including the conditional expression in the *if*-based form is that it is easier to read than the comma-based form. Furthermore, and thinking ahead to the definition of methods in objects, *if*-based conditional expressions will make the definition of methods easier to read.

Recursion equations are not retained. We are unsure as to whether definition of methods is best expressed in terms of sets of equations or a single function definition based upon conditional expressions.

We also introduce a *typecase* expression. As noted above, the *typecase* requires less apparatus than do other options, particularly type predicates. The *typecase* has a required default case. Each arm of the *typecase* contains a function call; the result of the entire expression is the result of evaluating the arm tagged with the appropriate type or evaluating the default case. For example:

```
typecase x of
  T1 ==> f1(g1(x));
  T2 ==> f2(g2(h2(x,y)));
  C  ==> f3(g3(h3(x,y,z)));
  otherwise let xx = f1(x)
              in
                 foo(xx,y)
            endlet
end
```

The form of the above expression is similar to that employed when the concept of the *typecase* was first introduced. The symbol to the left of the arrow (==>) is the name of a type (class or built-in type). The expression to the right of the arrow is evaluated if the argument, x, is of the type named on the left. So, if x is of type C, the branch labelled with C will be chosen, and the expression $f_3(g_3(h_3(x, y, z)))$ is evaluated and returns the result of the entire *typecase* expression. If x had a type which did not match any of those mentioned to the left of the arrows, the *otherwise* is evaluated. In the above example, we have put a *let* into the *otherwise* branch; this is just to show that *any* expression can be present. It is worth noting that the functions in the right-hand side in the *typecase* can refer to *any* variables which are currently in scope. Thus, not only is x present as an argument, but so, too, are y and z; xx is introduced as a local variable.

There is a problem with the *typecase* expression when function types are concerned. The existence of the *typecase* implies that type tags are held in the runtime representation of objects; the type tags are small numbers representing the identity of the class to which the object (instance) belongs. Functions, unless they are represented as objects, cannot have tags. Since we do not permit functions to be represented as objects (at least not yet and not here), we cannot apply *typecase* expressions to functions.

Before discussing evaluation, it is important to consider two issues:

- type structure, and
- free variables.

As part of the discussion of the type structure, we include a discussion of the scope of classes.

The first question to ask is whether explicit types are supplied for formal parameters and for return types, or should type inference be employed? For simplicity, explicit types will be employed. This decision is made because of the existence of the root class, *Object*. With this type in existence, the solution to many polymorphic type assignments will involve *Object*; the ways in which *Object* appear in type expressions might cause the Hindley-Milner type inference system to fail to assign types correctly (we suspect that what appear to be circular type definitions will occur because we are explicitly representing a fixed point—this needs further investigation).

The next question concerns the scope of class definitions. In C++, it is possible to define classes within classes; Java permits this and extends it with the concept of the anonymous class. I have above investigated some of the pros and cons of nested classes. Here, we need to decide whether nested classes are a good idea or whether there is an alternative. The idea behind nested and anonymous classes is that they have restricted scope. Since anonymous classes have no name, it is not possible to refer to them in any free sense— Java introduces the construct in a highly constraining context. My attention will, therefore, focus on class scope.

Immediately, it is necessary to consider a possibility that is absent in many languages. Thus, the question arises as to what is the effect of binding a class definition in a construct that looks something like the following:

```
let+ c = defclass C: S = ..... endclass
in
 defclass C1:T =
   ...
   let x = C(p1,p2)
   in
     ...
   endclass
 ...
endlet+
```

In the first case, the variable c is bound to the definition of the class C. Class C has a superclass S and some slots. The class is defined and its definition is bound to a local variable, c, whose scope is the entire let+ construct. Inside the let+, another class, C_1, is defined. Inside class C_1, the constructor of class C is called. Class C is in scope inside the let+ construct, but not outside. Using this construct, it would appear that the scope of a class definition can be restricted to a limited region of program text.

In addition to this use of the construct, the following is immediately suggested. It is necessary to ask what might the result of the following be:

```
let++ c = G[int]
in
 ...
endlet++
```

Here, the variable c is bound to an instance of a generic class, G. The first line represents an instantiation of G with *int* as the actual parameter. The local variable, c, is used to name this instantiation. In the body of the let++ expression, c, can be used to refer to this instantiation of class G. This use is akin to uses of *typedef* in C++ to associate a name with an instantiation of a template class; the construct just employed restricts the scope of that instantiation.

Given these constructs, it is clear that we need to ask about what the local variables are intended to denote in the body of the binding expression. In the first case, c must refer to the definition of a class; in the second, it must refer to an instantiation of a class definition. Class definitions are not, in this language, denotable values, so the constructs can only be employed by a compiler. This has the consequence that the bound variable is an *alias* for the class definition; both cases bind a class definition of one form or another to a variable. A slight change of syntax might make matters slightly easier, so rather than using a construct reminiscent of value binding, we will replace let+ and let++ with letclass. This is justifiable, in any case, because type in Pascal and Ada, and typedef in C and C++ are, in essence, compiler directives which bind synonyms for type names. Our *letclass* acts in a similar fashion and at a similar time.

The *letclass* construct allows classes to be defined and restricted in scope. It also provides a way of instantiating a generic type and restricting the scope within which it can be employed. Classes do not need to be defined within a *letclass* binder; they can be defined at the top level. The purpose of *letclass* is to restrict the scope of class definitions and instances of generics. (All top-level classes are assumed to be defined within a global letclass; this is similar to the top-level structure of functional programs which can be considered to be a *letrec* which binds all function definitions, including those in the library.)

The *letclass* construct is useful in defining things like lists. It will be remembered that the class representing list elements needs to be available within the main list class, but should not be visible at all outside of the definition of the container class. Such hiding is the aim of the *letclass* construct. If the element class is totally hidden, there is no need to employ constructs like C++'s *friend* which gives one class direct access to another. In this language, we can write something like:

```
letclass elt[T] = defclass E[T] with
                    slot data : T;
                    slot next : E[T];
        method next() = ... ;
                  endclass
    in
      defclass List[T] with
        slot head : elt[T];
        method cons(x: T): List[T] = ... ;
        method hd(): T = ... ;
        method tl(): List[T] = ... ;
        ...
      endclass;
    endletclass;
```

It is necessary to point out that, strictly speaking, *letclass* and type parameters are not required if a root type (such as *Object* in other languages) is defined. However, it does serve some use as a little syntactic sugar. The ability to make local definitions in this way, in any case, makes the program easier to read. For these reasons and to stimulate thought, this construct has been included.

What if we want the same class to be local to a number of classes, each of which is to be exported from the *letclass* body. A similar problem occurs in some languages, particularly ML [43]. I adopt a similar solution and introduce a connecting form: the word *and* is introduced between instances of *defclass*, as in:

```
defclass C0 = ...
and
defclass C1 = ...
and
    ...
```

This linking mechanism will also be used to define top-level functions, as in:

```
defclass C0 = ...
and
def f(...) = ...
and
    ...
```

In each case, the entities are defined simultaneously. This means that they are at the same scope level and they can mutually refer to each other.

The last example requires a syntax for top-level functions and for methods. Top-level functions and methods are not expressed as recursion equations so that the syntax can be simplified—equations can be converted to the condition-based form relatively easily.

A function definition has the form:

```
def f(x:T, y:T1): X = ... ;
```

where f is the function's name, x and y are its formal parameters and X is its return type (which can be higher-order). The body of the function will typically consist of a conditional or some kind of binding construct. The following defines a function which returns the empty type:

```
def g( ... ) : () = ... ;
```

and a function of no arguments can be defined by:

```
def h() : X = ... ;
```

Method definitions take the form:

```
defmethod m( ... ) : X = ... ;
```

The difference between the form of the two definitions is that the keyword def is used to define functions and method is used to define methods. Methods *can only* be defined inside class definitions.

Top-level constants are defined by:

```
defconst c:T = ... ;
```

(This is just a notational variant for functions defining constants—the name of a function is a constant.)

It is also possible to define *write-once* variables.

The introduction of functions and initialized expressions immediately introduces the question of free variables. Functions and methods can contain

references to free variables. The value of a free variable is obtained by con-
sulting the environment that is in force where the function (or method) is
defined; the language is, naturally, statically scoped (like the λ-calculus).

If we had defined a *pure* language, free variables would not be present
in their most general form. The reason for this is that, in a pure language,
all definitions are contained within classes. There are no top-level function
definitions in pure languages, for the only possible definition of a functional
element is the method, and methods are defined *inside* classes. Where free
variables occur is in the definition of nested functions; variables defined in
outer functions are in scope in all functions that are defined inside their scope.
So, in:

```
def foo (x : T) : X =
  let xx = ...
  in
    letrec bar(y : T1) : X1 = ...
      ... xx ...
    in
    endlet;
  endlet;
```

the variable xx is defined in the function foo and is free inside the body of
the defining *let*. Within function bar, xx is referenced; the reference is to a
free variable.

The restrictions on free variables make the compiler somewhat easier to
construct, but there would appear to be restrictions on the expressiveness of
the language that results from this restriction.

Sometimes it is necessary to introduce a class before defining it. This
happens when two classes are mutually recursive in their definition. In the
current language, top-level definitions of mutually recursive class definitions
can be performed using the *and* connector, as in:

```
defclass C1 = ... slot s1 : C2 ...
and
defclass C2 = ... slot s2 : C1 ...
```

This defines both classes at the same level. In fact, the top-level definitions
connected by *and* are *simultaneously* defined, so the question of which name
is introduced first does not occur. This fact can have consequences for the
organization of a compiler.

Finally, we need to consider evaluation. The majority of contemporary
functional languages assume lazy evaluation. There appears to be no *a priori*
reason why lazy evaluation cannot be employed as the evaluation strategy of
a mixed-paradigm language.

Having completed the specification, we can now consider this design in a
wider context.

B.4 Review

In this section, I will review some of the decisions made in the last section. The first question to be addressed is: why select a mixed object-oriented/functional paradigm?

The absence of side effects in functional programming is one positive reason for selecting them as a basis upon which to mix paradigms. The side effects which are required are entirely localized within objects. This has the implication that the functional and object-oriented components can co-exist without too much difficulty. The approach adopted above assumes that updates can be performed on objects and can be performed in an eager fashion (i.e., are not delayed arbitrarily by laziness). An alternative approach would be to apply changes to objects only when those changes are required. A further alternative which we did not follow was to *copy* objects between function calls; instead, we assumed heap allocation and access to objects in terms of shared pointers. My approach was deliberately designed to be relatively fast while making object update as simple as possible; furthermore, the approach adopted above was intended to localize the effects of object updates, just as we have discussed.

The second reason is that functional languages typically support higher-order functions. This is an important point for functional programming methodology as well as for mixed-paradigm working. The benefits of the extensive use of higher-order functions, particularly in connection with linear data structures is widely known to functional programmers. Higher-order functions, as will be seen, play an important part in object-oriented functional programming.

We have already seen an example of *partial* application with the *addn* function which is defined as a function of two arguments:

$$\lambda x.\lambda n.x + n$$

This can be partially applied to one argument (x) to yield a new function, as in:

$$(\lambda x.\lambda n.x + n)3$$

which reduces to:

$$\lambda n.x + 3$$

the function which adds 3 to its argument. One crucial fact about partial application is that the resulting function has fewer arguments than the input functions. This means that it carries things around in its closure; these things can be employed in the computation performed by the function.

Using partial application, functions can be defined which operate on particular objects. The object can be bound to one of the function's arguments via application. That object will always be present in the computation represented by the function. The object upon which such an operation acts can be one that is especially created for the function or it can be any object that is of interest.

Partial application is not restricted to the case of partially applying a function to an object or simple value. A higher-order function can also be partially applied to another operation. One example of this is that an object and slot accessor pair (reader and writer methods) might be the inputs to a function. The function performs some computation and updates the slot. In addition, the function might take another parameter which represents the operation that generates the value to be stored in the slot. We might write it as:

$$m(\mathit{self}, s_r, s_w, x, y, f) := \ldots s_w(f(x, y, s_r(\mathit{self})))$$

where s_r is the slot reader, s_w the slot writer, x and y are arbitrary values and f represents an operation to be performed upon x, y and the contents of slot s. This definition can be partially applied in various ways. For example, *self* could be bound, or s_r and s_w could be bound (being careful to ensure that the objects to which the new function are applied have the right slots); x or y or f could be bound to a value. By fixing the reader and writer methods, the location of any operation can be fixed; by fixing *self*, the object to which updates are to be imparted is fixed. If x or y (or both) is fixed, the data upon which the operation depends is fixed.

If f is bound, it fixes the operation which can be performed on the slot. If the other arguments are left unbound, the resulting function performs the same operation on the objects to which it is applied.

If the order of a function such as f is sufficiently high, it can perform computation as to what it should do. This is an intriguing thought which cannot be followed up here for reasons of space.

Another example is that a method might be partially applied to a class other than the one for which it was defined. In particular, the method might be partially applied to an instance of a class that is derived from the method's defining class. This, in essence, provides a kind of specialized method, but one that is separate from the method hierarchy provided by the program's classes.

The next concept is that higher-order functions compose functions of lower order. This implies that simple functions can be defined and then enriched by means of composition so that they can produce the operations required in a more complex situation. This is the fundamental intuition behind *next-method*. The kinds of behaviour exhibited by the *before* and *after* methods in CLOS [82] could be modelled by means of composition. This kind of operation can also provide mechanisms for performing stylized computations on slots.

Factory objects can be encapsulated and extended conceptually by the addition of higher-order functions. Higher-order functions can be defined so that they input parameters which can be used to construct instances of different classes, each of which is parameterized in a particular fashion. By moving to higher-order, it becomes possible to define methods or functions that can construct functions that, when called, will perform factory operations.

The creation of iterator methods could be performed by the construction of higher-order functions. This scheme might work, for example, by returning a pair whose first element is the iterator function for the next element, and whose second element is the current element in the data collection object. The first element becomes unit or nil ([]) when the collection is exhausted.

The full power of higher-order functions might only be revealed when the mixed-paradigm language contains facilities for reflective processing.

Finally, there is the fact to be dealt with that object-oriented programming is extremely dynamic, while functional programming is extremely static. Nevertheless, the two combine in various ways that are extremely encouraging, at least on a theoretical level. One reason for this is that the combination of functions and objects already has a long pedigree in mathematics; they combine to form algebras (one extremely important model for types is as complex algebras) and algebras can be put into a more general setting called *category theory* (see [61] for a wonderful introduction). Category theory is a language for doing mathematics; it studies the actions of functions upon objects. Objects represent entire types of mathematical object, for example Sets, Groups or Semi-groups (monoïds). This corresponds, therefore, to an extremely abstract approach to handling these various kinds of entity; indeed, it relies to a fair extent upon the concept of a higher-order function. Thus, the combination of objects and functions is perfectly natural (if category theorists will pardon the pun!)

We must now turn to other questions. In particular, the following need to be addressed:

- pure languages;
- prototype-based languages;
- the advantages or disadvantages of this approach.

We also need to ask whether the language is one in which programs are easy to define.

In pure languages, the programmer can only define objects. In a pure class-based language, they can only define classes. In a pure functional class-based language, the programmer defines classes whose methods are functions. In a pure functional class-based language, all definitions must be within the scope of a class and are, therefore, scope-restricted. This contrasts with a pure functional or impure mixed-paradigm language such as the one described above in that global variables are permitted; top-level *let*, etc., bindings are also permitted. In a pure language, these constructs cannot appear at top level, so all free variables must, necessarily, occur within method definitions. We adopted an impure language because there appear, at first sight, to be more problems in implementing impure languages than pure ones (in pariticular, problems relating to free variables).

Next, we need to address prototype languages. We gave some initial reasons for preferring not to examine a mixture of functions and prototypes above. Here, we can add some other reasons:

- The implemented prototype languages have all been pure in form.
- The interaction between functions and prototypes appears simpler than in class-based programming. This is a reason for a separate study, particularly one which supports program transformation.
- The relationship between prototypes and functions is not as clear as that between classes and functions. In particular, class-based programming supports finite collections of entities which are classified by a fixed rule, while prototypes are related by a similarity measure. The similarity measure is not fixed.

Finally, we come to two related matters:

- What are the advantages of this language?
- What are the disadvantages of this language?
- How easy is it to program in this language?

These questions are extremely difficult to answer. The reason, clearly, being that there is no implementation upon which to base any comments. In addition, I have a particular perspective which will be different from that of others. More importantly, there have been so few mixed-paradigm languages of the kind discussed above for there to be any significant data on the problem. More work is needed on the evaluation of functional object-oriented languages. The comments on advantages are, therefore, speculative and indicate potential research topics as well as reminding the reader of some points made above.

The primary advantages, as far as can be seen, of this way of approaching object-oriented programming is that restricted scope declarations are possible and higher-order functions can be used to transform programs and compose methods. Higher-order functions and methods can also be used to encapsulate objects and to abstract from them, possibly providing alternative classification methods; the comments about factory objects and higher-order functions are intended to be a start along these lines.

Higher-order functions permit the definition of functions which create other functions; this is a property whose interaction with object operations should be studied further. For example, methods could be defined in this way if classes were not statically defined. If objects were constructed dynamically, it would be possible to define new methods out of old by means of higher-order functions that transform the older ones; such a process would be under the programmer's control, of course. Furthermore, the concept of the factory object could be generalized in various ways.

The localization of side effects, as well as uniform representation, is a goal of pure object-oriented programming. The language described above contains no explicit pointers, so related objects are not connected via complex pointer nests at the mercy of the programmer; relationships are controlled by the runtime system (or the virtual machine). This appears to be an approach which suits persistence better than one that depends upon pointer manipulation. Class-based programming requires the class to be stored as well as those instances which are to be maintained; this appears to be something of an overhead. Mixed-paradigm languages might help here, but the overhead remains, unless a prototype-based approach is adopted.

The disadvantages of the approach adopted above rest upon the relative unfamiliarity of functional programming and the abstract nature of higher-order functions. Functional programs can be expressed as sets of rules, and people find rules relatively easy to understand, so a translation from rules to functions might improve the user's model of the language. Performance, should a language such as the above ever be implemented might also be a significant factor; if it turns out to be too slow, users will employ something else.

In addition, there is the competition from established languages, in particular from Java. The comparison with Java also introduces questions about mobility of code and incorporation in Internet applications. Dylan is a language with many desirable and elegant features. It initially had a LISP-like syntax; the syntax was changed to resemble Pascal mainly because it was thought that it would lead to greater acceptance. When Java was released, the inability of the Dylan implementations to support Internet applications was considered a major disadvantage. There is no reason in principle why Dylan could not be used to implement Internet applications, but, at the time it was released, it did not. Java had these facilities, graphics and it had a close resemblance to C++; retraining for C++ programmers is relatively easy.

Before closing, it is essential to make a few observations about what has *not* been considered in the above design. In particular, it might be argued that my approach to the mixing of classes and functions is somewhat cavalier. I permit localized side-effects by allowing writer methods to be defined for slots. This has the implication that any instance passed as an argument to a function (of any kind) can be directly updated. Usually, what happens in a functional language is that an input structure is transformed by construction of a *new* version which copies the old one into new heap space, transforming components as required. For example:

$$f(T(x, b)) := \ldots T(a, b)$$

where a new (sum or union) structure of type T is constructed and returned by function f. The copy that is input to the function will remain in the heap as long as there are references to it; the new copy will be propagated down the call tree until it, too, becomes garbage.

Clearly, the above preserves referential transparency while our treatment of instances often does not. The alternative is to make updater functions return copies of the instances upon which they operate; this preserves referential transparency, but it also introduces a raft of new problems which we did not have space to discuss. First, it can introduce additional problems for the memory management software, in particular a higher overhead because instances can be large relative to other structures.

It also introduces the question as to how objects are passed to functions and how evaluation strategies affect updates and instance creation. If updates are performed in a lazy fashion, they will be performed only when the value of the updated slot is required, thus producing a new copy of the instance. This has the implication that updates are not performed when an object is passed to a function (method) but is delayed until the new value is required. However, this can lead to a chain of waiting updates, particularly when the instance contains many slots (instances in real applications very often contain many slots, so there might be many updates in waiting). If updater functions are eager, they cause more garbage collections for the reason that the instance must be copied to new cells when the update is performed.

Lazy creation of instances can also cause problems. Under this scheme, instantiation only occurs when access to a slot is required. Thus, if an instance is created and immediately updated, there will be a considerable penalty because the instance that is forced into existence is immediately discarded as a result of the update operation.

We have not investigated these questions to any great degree. Even if we had, they would have required discussion that would have taken us far from the topic of interpretation; it would have required a discussion of implementation.

Any new language, even if it has other aims, will be compared, by some, with Java, at least for the time being—for some people, Java *is* object-oriented programming. My design has ignored the issues raised by Java because I was concerned with how to integrate classes and functions in one particular way. I have concentrated on language design and have ignored such issues as concurrency or distributed programming. Further work is required on mixed-paradigm languages of all kinds and with the needs imposed upon such languages by concurrent and distributed evaluation.

References

1. Agha, G. and Hewitt, C., Actors: Conceptual Foundation for Concurrent Object-Oriented Programming, in Wegner, P. and Shriver, B. eds., *Research Directions in Object-Oriented Programming*, MIT Press, Cambridge, MA, pp. 49–74, 1987.
2. Agha, G., *Actors: A Model of Concurrent Computation in Distributed Systems*, MIT Press, Cambridge, MA, 1986.
3. Agha, G., Mason, I. A., Smith, S. F. and Talcott, C. L., A Foundation for Actor Computation, *Functional Programming*, Vol. 1, No. 1, pp. 1-68, 1993.
4. Aho, A.V., Sethi, R. and Ullman, J.D., *Compilers: Principles, Techniques, and Tools*, Addison-Wesley, Reading, MA, 1986.
5. Albahari, B., Drayton, P. and Merrill, B., *C# Essentials*, O'Reilly and Associates Inc., 2001.
6. Apple Computer Inc., *Dylan Interim Reference Manual*, Apple Cambridge, Cambridge, MA, Web site, 1985.
7. Backus, J., Can programming be liberated from the von Neumann Style? A Functional Style and its Algebra of Programs, *Communications of the ACM*, Vol. 21, No. 8, pp. 613–41, 1978.
8. Bakker, J., *Object-oriented Modelling of Object-oriented Information Systems*, PhD Dissertation, Department of Computer Science, Maastricht University, 1992.
9. Barnes, John., *Programming in Ada95*, Addison-Wesley, Wokingham, England, 1996.
10. Birtwistle, G., Dahl, O-J., Myhrhaug, B. and Nygaard, K., *Simula Begin*, Petrocelli/Charter, New York, 1973.
11. Blaschek, G., *Object-oriented Programming, Programming with Prototypes*, Springer-Verlag, Heidelberg, 1994.
12. Booch, G., *Software Components using ADA*, Addison-Wesley, Reading, MA, 1988.
13. Booch, G., *Software Engineering with Ada*, Benjamin/Cummings, Menlo Park, CA, 1983.
14. Briot, Jean-Pierre, Actalk: A Testbed for Classifying and Designing Actor Languages in the Smalltalk-80 Environment, in *Proc. ECOOOP-89*, pp. 109-129, Cambridge University Press, 1989.
15. Bobrow, D.G. and Stefik, M.J., *The LOOPS Manual*, Tech. Report No. KB-VLSI-81-13, and subsequent revisions, Xerox Palo Alto Research Center, Palo Alto, CA, 1983.
16. Bracha, G. and Lindstrom, G., Modularity meets inheritance, in Meyrowitz, N. (ed.), *Proc. OOPSLA/ECOOP'90*, pp. 303-311, IEEE Computer Society Press, 1991.

17. Bracha, G., *The programming Language Jigsaw: Mixins, Modularity and Multiple inheritance*, PhD Dissertation, University of Utah, March, 1992. ALSO: bra92 on p. 11 of chap 7

18. Bracha, G. and Cook, W., Mixin-based Inheritance, in *Proc. IEEE Computer Society International Conference on Computer Languages*, pp. 303–311, 1990.

19. Burge, W., *Recursive Programming Techniques*, Addison-Wesley, Reading, MA, 1975.

20. Burstall R.M., Sanella, D.B. and Sanella, D.T., *Hope: An Experimental Applicative Language*, Technical Report CSR-62-80, Department of Computer Science, Edinburgh University, 1980.

21. Canon, H., *Flavors, A Non-Hierarchical Approach to Object-Oriented Programming*, Draft, 1982.

22. Cardelli, L., *Obliq: A Language with Distributed Scope*, from Digital Equipment Corp., Systems Research Center Web site.

23. Chambers, C. and Leavens, G. T., *BeCecil, A Core Object-Oriented Language with Block Structure and Multimethods: Semantics and Typing*, Technical Report UW-CSE-96-12-02, December, 1996.

24. Chambers, C., *The Cecil Language: Specification and Rationale*, Technical Report No. 93-03-05, Computer Science Dept., University of Washington, 1993.

25. Chambers, Craig, *The Design and Implementation of the SELF Compiler, an Optimizing Compiler for Object-Oriented Programming Languages*, Department of Computer Science, Stanford University, 1992.

26. Clinger, W. and Rees, J., (eds.), *Revised^4 Report on the Algorithmic Language Scheme*, Artificial Intelligence Laboratory, MIT, Cambridge, MA, 1991.

27. Codenie, W., Steyaert, P. and Lucas, C., Nested Mixins in AGORA, Position paper to ECOOP '92 *Workshop on Multiple Inheritance and Multiple Subtyping*, pp. 29-31, 1992.

28. Cook, W., *A Denotational Semantics of Inheritance*, PhD Dissertation, Department of Computer Science, Brown University, Providence, RI, 1989.

29. Craig, I.D., *A Computable Transformation System for Objects*, Research Report, *in prep.*

30. Craig, I.D., *Writing Compilers using Objects*, Research Report, *in prep.*

31. Craig, I.D., A Reflective Production System, *Kybernetes*, Vol. 23, No. 3, pp. 20-35, 1994.

32. Craig, I.D., Rule Interpreters in Elektra, *Kybernetes*, Vol. 24, No. 3, pp. 41-53, 1995.

33. Craig, I.D., *BBSR*, Research Report No. 94, Department of Computer Science, Warwick University, 1987.

34. Craig, I.D., *Reflection in Prototype Languages*, Research Report, *in prep.*

35. Craig, I.D., *The Dylan Programming Language*, Springer-Verlag, London, 1995.

36. Dahl, O-J., Myrhaug, B. and Nygaard, K., *SIMULA 67 Common Base Language*, Norwegian Computing Center, Oslo, 1968, 1970, 1972, 1984.

37. Field, A.J. and Harrison, P.G., *Functional Programming*, Addison-Wesley, Wokingham, England, 1988.

38. Flanagan, D., *JavaScript—The Definitive Guide*, O'Reilly, Sebastopol, CA, 1998.

39. Fraser, A. G., On the Meaning of Names in Programming Systems, *Communications of the ACM*, Vol. 14, No. 6, pp. 409–416, 1971.

40. Goldberg, A. and Robson, D, *Smalltalk-80: The Language and Its Implementation*, Addison-Wesley, Reading, MA, 1983.

41. Halstead, R., Multilisp: A Language for Concurrent Symbolic Computation, *TOPLAS*, Vol. 7, No. 4, pp. 501-538, 1985.

42. Milner, R., Tofte, M. and Harper, R., *The Definition of Standard ML*, MIT Press, Cambridge, MA, 1990.
43. Harper, R. and Mitchell, K., *Introduction to Standard ML*, Laboratory for Foundations of Computer Science, Dept of Computer Science, Edinburgh University, 1986.
44. Harper, R. and Pierce B., A Record Calculus based on Symmetric Concatenation, *Proc. ACM Eighteenth Annual ACM Symposium on Principles of Programming Languages*, pp. 131-142, 1991.
45. Henderson, P., *Functional Programming*, Prentice-Hall, Hemel Hempstead, 1980.
46. Hense, A.V., Denotational Semantics of an Object-oriented Programming Language with Explicit Wrappers, *Formal Aspects of Computing*, Vol. 3, 1992.
47. Hewitt, Carl, Viewing Control Structures as Patterns of Passing Messages, *Artificial Intelligence Journal*, Vol. 8, pp. 323-364, 1977.
48. Hindley, J. and Seldin, J., *Introduction to Combinators and Lambda-calculus*, Cambridge University Press, 1986.
49. Hudak, P., Peyton-Jones, S. and Wadler, P., Report on the programming language Haskell, a Non-strict, Purely Functional Language, version 1.2, *SIGPLAN Notices*, Vol. 25, No. 5, 1992.
50. Hughes, R.J.M., *The Design and Implementation of Programming Languages*, D. Phil. dissertation, PRG, University of Oxford, 1984.
51. Kikczales, G. and Rodriguez, L., *Efficient Method Dispatch in PCL*, Xerox Palo Alto Research Center, Web page.
52. Kikczales, G. and Murphy, Gail, *Open Implementation Guidelines*, Xerox Palo Alto Research Center, Web page.
53. Kikczales, G., des Rivières, J. and Bobrow, D. G., *The Art of the Metaobject Protocol*, MIT Press, Cambridge, MA, 1992.
54. Kristensen, B.B., Madsen, O.L., Moller-Pedersen, B. and Nygaard, K., The Beta Programming Language, in Wegner, P. and Shriver, B. eds., *Research Directions in Object-Oriented Programming*, MIT Press, Cambridge, MA, pp. 7-48, 1987.
55. Lieberman, H., Using Prototypical Objects to Implement Shared Behavior in Object Oriented Systems, *Proc. OOPSLA-86*, pp. 214-223, ACM Press, 1986.
56. Lieberman, H, in *Object-Oriented Concurrent Programming*, Yonezawa, A. and Tokoro, M., (eds.), pp. 55-89, MIT Press, Cambridge, MA, 1987.
57. Liskov, B, *et al.*, *Theta Reference Manual*, Computation Structures Group, Memo No. 88, Computer Science Lab., MIT, 1995.
58. van der Linden, P., *Just JAVA*, 3rd edn., Sun Microsystems/Prentice-Hall, 1998.
59. Lipmann, S.B., *C++ Primer*, 2nd edition, Addison-Wesley, Reading, MA, 1991.
60. Liskov, B., Data Abstraction and Hierarchy, *Proc. OOPSLA-87* (addendum to proceedings), Sigplan Notices Special Issue, Vol. 23, No. 5, pp. 17-34, 1988.
61. MacLean, S, *Categories for the Working Mathematician*, Springer-Verlag, Heidelberg, 1972.
62. McCabe, F.G., *Logic and Objects*, PhD Dissertation, Dept. of Computing, Imperial College, London, 1988.
63. Maes, P., *Computational Reflection* PhD dissertation, AI Laboratory, Vrije University Brussels, 1987.
64. Madsen, O.L., Issues in Object-Oriented Programming, *Computing Surveys*, Vol. 29A, No. 4, December, 1996.
65. Madsen, O.L., Block-Structure and Object-Oriented Languages, in Wegner, P. and Shriver, B. eds. *Research Directions in Object-Oriented Programming*, MIT Press, Cambridge, MA, pp. 113-128, 1987.

66. Malenfant, J., Dony, C. and Cointe, P., Behavioral Reflection in a Prototype-Based Language, *Proc. International Workshop on Reflection and Meta-Level Architecture*, pp. 143-152, Tokyo, 1992.
67. Meyer, B., *Eiffel The Language*, Prentice-Hall, Hemel Hempstead, England, 1992.
68. FAQ for Eiffel, available from various sources, including the World-Wide Web and Comp.lang.eiffel.
69. Padgett, J.A., *Eulisp Definition*, School of Mathematics, University of Bath, 1991.
70. Paton Jones, S.L., *The Implementation of Functional Languages*, Prentice-Hall, Hemel Hempstead, 1987.
71. Paton Jones, S.L., *Implementing Functional Languages: A Tutorial*, Prentice-Hall, Hemel Hempstead, 1992.
72. Reiser, M., *The Oberon System: User Guide and Programmer's Reference Manual*, Addison-Wesley, Wokingham, 1991.
73. Roberts, R. B. and Goldstein, I. P., *The FRL Manual*, Memo 409, AI Laboratory, MIT, Cambridge, MA, 1977.
74. Rosch, E., Principles of categorization, in Rosch, E. and Lloyd, B.B., (eds.), *Cognition and Categorization*, Lawrence Erlbaum, Hillsdale, NJ, 1978.
75. Sakkinen, M., Disciplined Inheritance, *Proc. ECOOP'89*, CUP, 1989.
76. Sather language definition from International Computer Science Institute Web Site, Berkeley, CA, 1994.
77. Philippsen, M., *Sather 1.0 Tutorial*, International Computer Science Institute, Berkeley, CA, 1994.
78. Schaffert, C., *et al.*, An Introduction to Trellis/Owl, *Proc. ACM Conference on Object-oriented Systems, Languages and Applications*, SIGPLAN Notices, ACM Press, pp. 1-8, 1986.
79. Siegel, J. and Frantz, D., *CORBA Fundamentals and Programming*, Wiley, New York, 1996.
80. Smith, B. C., , *Reflection and Semantics in Programming Languages*, Ph.D dissertation, Technical Report No. 272, Computer Science Laboratory, MIT, Cambridge, MA, 1982.
81. Snyder, A., Inheritance and the Development of Encapsulated Software Systems, in Wegner, P. and Shriver, B. eds *Research Directions in Object-Oriented Programming*, MIT Press, Cambridge, MA, pp. 165–188, 1987.
82. Steele, G.L., ed., *Common LISP The Language*, 2nd edition, Digital Press, Maynard, MA, 1990.
83. Stein, L., Lieberman, H. and Ungar, D., A Shared View of Sharing, in Kim, W. and Lochovsky, F.H. eds., *Object-Oriented Concepts, Databases and Applications*, pp. 31-48, ACM Press, 1989.
84. Stein L. A., Delegation is Inheritance, *Proc. OOPSLA-87*, SIGPLAN Notices, ACM Press, Vol. 22, No. 12, pp. 138-146, 1987.
85. Stefik, M.J. and Bobrow, D.B., Object-Oriented Programming: Themes and Variations , in Richer, M., *AI Tools and Techniques*, pp. 3-45, Ablex Publishing Corp., Norwood, NJ, 1989.
86. Steyaert, P., *Open Design of Object-Oriented Languages*, PhD Dissertation, Department of Computer Science, Vrije University of Brussels, 1994.
87. Steyaert, P., Codenie, W., D'Hondt, T., De Hondt, K., Lucas, C. and van Limberghen, M., Nested Mixins in Agora, *Proc. ECOOP '93*, pp. 197-219, Springer-Verlag, 1993.
88. Strachey, C., Towards a formal semantics, in Steele, T.B. ed., *Formal Language Description Languages*, North-Holland, Amsterdam, pp. 198-220, 1966.

89. Strachey, C., *The Varieties of Programming Languages*, Technical Monograph PRG-10, Programming Research Group, Oxford University, 1973.
90. Stroustrup, B., *The Design and Evolution of C++*, Addison-Wesley, Reading, MA, 1994.
91. Stroustrup, B., *The C++ Programming Language*, 2nd edition, Addison-Wesley, Reading, MA, 1991.
92. Stroustrup, B., *C++ Programming Language*, 1st edition, Addison-Wesley, Reading, MA, 1986.
93. Taivalsaari, A. and Freeman-Benson, B., *Towards Fine-grained Reusability with Self-sufficient Objects*, Extended abstract, August 23, 1992. Found on Web.
94. Taivalsaari, A., *Kevo—A Prototype-based Object-oriented Language based on Concatenation and Module Operations*, November 4, 1992. Found on Web.
95. Turner, D.A., Miranda—A Non-strict Functional Language with Polymorphic Types, *Proc. Conference on Functional Programming Languages and Computer Architecture*, Nancy, France, LNCS, Vol. 201, pp. 1-16, 1985.
96. Ungar, D. and Smith, R.B., Self: The Power of Simplicity, *Proc. OOPSLA-87*, SIGPLAN Notices, ACM Press, Vol. 22, No. 12, pp. 227-242, 1987.
97. Waterman, D.A. and Hayes-Roth, F.R., *Pattern-Directed Inference Systems*, Academic Press, New York, 1978.
98. Wegner, P., Tradeoffs between Reasoning and Modelling, in Agha, G., Wegner, P. and Yonezawa, A., eds., *Research Directions in Concurrent Object-Oriented Programming*, MIT Press, Cambridge, MA, pp. 22–41, 1993.
99. Wirth, N., *Modula-2*, Report No. 36, Institüt für Informatik, ETH, Zürich, Switzerland, 1980.
100. Yonezawa, A., Briot, J.-P. and Shibayama, E., Object-Oriented Concurrent Programming in ABCL/1, *Proc. OOPSLA-86*, SIGPLAN Notices, Vol. 21, No. 11, pp. 258-268, 1986.
101. Yonezawa, A., Shibayama, E., Takada, T. and Honda, Y., Modelling and Programming in an Object-Oriented Concurrent Language ABCL/1, in Yonezawa, A. and Tokoro, M., eds., *Object-Oriented Concurrent Programming*, pp. 55-89, MIT Press, Cambridge, MA, 1987.

Index